THROUGH THE EYES OF TIME
(Memories of a Soul)

By

Shawna A. Grey M.A.

Through The Eyes Of Time
Memories of a Soul
Copyright © 2020 by Shawna A. Grey M.A.

Library of Congress Control Number: 2020900941
ISBN-13: Paperback: 978-1-64749-041-6
ePub: 978-1-64749-042-3

Religion & Spirituality

All rights reserved.No part of this publication may be reproduced, distributed, or transmitted in any form or by any means, including photocopying, recording, or other electronic or mechanical methods, without the prior written permission of the publisher or author, except in the case of brief quotations embodied in critical reviews and certain other noncommercial uses permitted by copyright law.

Although every precaution has been taken to verify the accuracy of the information contained herein, the author and publisher assume no responsibility for any errors or omissions. No liability is assumed for damages that may result from the use of information contained within.

Printed in the United States of America

GoToPublish LLC
1-888-337-1724
www.gotopublish.com
info@gotopublish.com

DEDICATION

I want to dedicate this book to my son Sean, whose untimely death brought to me both grief and the evaluation of my life, and to my daughter who has encouraged me to write this book and has been a steady influence in its writing and development.

Thank you to all the people who have made this book possible with their suggestions and encouragement especially my good friend, Rev. Joyce A. DeFazio.

This is a record of my spirit's journey through time

On March 1, 2013, during my morning meditation, I heard someone calling my name. I sat at the computer and these words were dictated to me from Spirit.

"This is to show you that we are listening and watch your progress in the spiritual realm. We want you to continue with your work and not worry about the things of this world. How we help you is to guide you into making the right decisions and in the right choices in everything you do.

The world of Spirit is important to you because it is where you live most of the time. As you get older, it will be much more so until your last days.

Work is important too, but the work of the Spirit is more important. How can you help someone when you are not of their world? Being at the right place at the right time is a gift which we have given you. There is more to this process and you will learn as you go along.

Meditation for you is talking directly to Spirit. You don't have to visualize someplace to just be there. This is why your time in Spirit is so different from everyone else. How can you visualize the colors of the rainbow and just see it when you can be a part of its glory and feel the colors as well as see them? So much more is there for you if you just open your mind.

Relax and take a trip on the wings of Spirit and know that the ancient learning is here for you to tap into when you are ready. How you do it and when is up to you."

And so, it is.

Rev. Shawna A. Grey

FORWARD

Some people know their purpose in life as a child,
Others need a lifetime of experiences to find theirs.
Some never find it at all!

It is said that the eyes are the windows to the soul. We recognize people we have known from another life by looking into their eyes. Some recognition looks back at us and there is a connection. We continue with that feeling of knowing for a short time or sometimes longer.

Through the many centuries we have come to know people from all different backgrounds and in different circumstances. These same people play a part in our current life, sometimes we recognize them, but most of the time we do not. They are our parents, friends, siblings, and acquaintances. All of them have at some time played a part in our life in one role or another. The over bearing mother and the meek and mild father of this lifetime were once our brothers and sisters or they were our children. We have been both male and female with all the challenges of that gender.

I walked into church one Sunday in 2009. While waiting the service to start I had a vision of a very large room with a wooden table in the middle. Around this table sat men on one side of the table and women on the other side. They were listening very intently to a speaker out of my view. What happened next looked like the blur of a very fast shuffling of playing cards, with all the people in the room blending into only one man and woman standing in front of me. I then saw an arm, on my right, coming from someone wearing a brilliant while robe, extending an open hand to me. I was told that all the people in the room were me as I lived in different lives as a man or a woman. The man and woman remaining, standing before me, were my guides to help me in this lifetime.

We have faced every kind of situation with individuals playing their part in our life, bringing us the experience we need to learn the lesson for that lifetime. No one goes with a commanding part as each of us take turns being one or the other in the many lives of our family group. We meet and learn of our own failures and shortcomings in the way we interact with others, and their actions toward us.

If you had a difficult childhood, you were introduced to a life of struggle and eventually achievement. Your life story shows your interaction with people, when you sometimes react without thinking, bringing back to your conscious mind how this same scenario turned out in another lifetime. Unconscious reactions such as turning away from a hot fire have been learned in some way. When did you know that you were afraid of heights, and where did that come from? How do you know that certain fruits are good to eat and you dislike others? You have learned this from some time past when you tried to eat them and didn't like them. This all goes to prove that our reactions to people, places and things have a root cause if not in this lifetime then when?

PREFACE

The inspiration for this book came over a period of years when I either had a flash of a past life, or in a dream about some event in my distant past. It could be when I visited a new town, and I would experience the feeling of familiarity in a place I knew I had not visited before. These events came at different times in my life when I was actively engaged in being a mother with two growing children and a wife of an active duty military man. Sometimes I only got a glimpse of another life other time. If it was more than that, I would relive a situation from my past when I learned a certain lesson. Usually these events happened when I was questioning something in my present life or there was a message my subconscious was trying to bring to my conscious mind.

As I became more interested in the historical facts behind what I was seeing and questioned the reason why I needed to remember them, I realized that I was being shown something important to me, but finding the relevance to my current life took a lot more contemplation.

The path to self-actualization is filled with opportunities to learn about becoming nonjudgmental, to be able to forgive others as ourselves, and erase past guilt, remorse and anger from our aura which lower our light and our physical energies. We choose our path and our lessons to learn, sometimes difficult ones, but in the end the gain is so much more than the loss. Remember you are not alone on this journey. There are people around you to help you, but most importantly there is your inner Spirit, your "God Self" of inner guidance that is always with you. You just have to be open to listen and follow its directions. Each of us molds our lives with the choices we make each day. What we do today prepares us for the events of tomorrow.

As I have been writing my past lives, I have begun to see a theme through each different period of time, that of being a healer, and a person who was close to nature. Each lifetime taught me something new about myself. I faced both praise and ridicule, sometimes even death for my beliefs. Each experience brought another piece of truth to my collective self. So, if you like a good story, I offer this one. It is up to you to decide if what I have written resonates with you as truth.

INTRODUCTION

Faith sees the Invisible, the Incredible and Receives the Impossible

When I started planning this book, I had only the glimpse of my past lives to guide me in what areas I should address. I had the dream of Atlantis and the knowledge that I had some connection to Egypt, but that was all. Among my memories were bits and pieces of different lives and different circumstances. How all of this would come together I had no idea, yet as I started to work on this manuscript it seemed that I was being led into each lifetime with historical and personal information coming to me at just the time I needed it.

Over the years, I have had several sessions with psychic readers who told me over and over again, "you came into this life with the idea of finishing off your Karmic debt and clearing it all out of your subconscious. You took on a lot for one lifetime just to complete the job."

As you read my story you will see where it all began. Every negative word, deed and action I gave to others would be repaid by experiencing that same situation myself. It might be within the same lifetime or centuries later, but I did repay it all. That is the law of the universe. This was taught by one of the world's greatest teachers, Jesus: "Do unto others as ye would have them do unto you."

If we could stand on a mountain top and visualize our soul's path as a highway, reaching out in front of us, with all our past, present and future lives laid out before us, what would we see? There would be many sign posts along the way marking important events in our lives: the date and place when we graduated from high school, then college, or our first job, maybe the date and events leading up to our wedding. What would we see as personality traits? Would we see a series of challenges then achievements or a constant replay of rejection and failure? Would we see this pattern repeated over and over or would we see a point in time when we actually took stock of our life and changed our attitude and view of life for the better?

Changes in our life happen when we take an active part in making it happen. Each thought, word, deed and especially the intent behind them, pave the road ahead of us as well as control the situations in our present life. Our driving ambition to succeed, or our reluctance to step forward, has left a mark on our path. Both attitudes have a positive and negative outcome. A driving ambition can get you into the higher paying positions in a corporate company, but did you get there by using others as a stepping stone, disregarding their abilities and feelings? What was more important the satisfaction of a job well done or the knowledge that your actions were less than honorable? A person who is unsure of themselves and lacks the confidence to step out from the group is at a loss to achieve the personal satisfaction they so desire. Only you will know if you put your full attention and effort into a project, or let someone else do the work so you could take the credit. Do you really think what you did would not affect you?

People dream about a better tomorrow when all their problems will be solved and all their wishes fulfilled. They forget that the preparation for the land of enchantment begins with the world of reality here and now! The rewards come not with wishing for them but working towards them every day. Universal Law and temporal laws are not to be broken. You never "get away" with anything. We are accountable for what we do and say to others. The law of "Cause and Effect" operates whether you know it or not. Time is a man's invention so he could keep track of the seasons and know when to plant and the harvesting of crops, or the space of time the Earth goes around the sun. We live in a constant time frame with work days and leisure time doled out to us in hours or days. In the eternal, NOW time does not exist. What we might think of as years can be as the blink of an eye in God's time. Life is temporary and eternity is forever. What we do today we will be accountable for in the future, perhaps not right away, but nevertheless we will be called onto account for all of our thoughts, words and deeds sometime.

Do you really want to have a life that is joyous, beneficial, and fulfilling in every way? Start to look at the areas that you want to change. What challenges do you have and how do you plan to face them? What goals are you setting for your life? Are you willing to forgive that person who hurt you in some way or do you still cling to the memory of that hurtful experience?

The soul, or the breath of life, is a part of each of us which bears the records of all our thoughts and activities referred to in the Bible as the "Book of Life." This is sometimes referred to as the "Akashic Records." The soul is not something you have. It is something you are! It is a powerhouse full of probabilities, seeking to be expressed in the physical.

As you change your attitude towards yourself, others and your situation in life, you will see a change happening little by little in your life. Those dreams you thought were impossible will become a reality and you will be living the life you were destined to live, full of love, hope and looking forward to an even better future. Are you ready for this?

Automatic writing given to me July 2, 2012:

"I am the power of the universal being known to man as the giver of all things. I come to you with a gift of faith, love, and redemption, knowing that you understand my words as I speak to you often. My kingdom is of the heart. My joy is in seeing you live the life you were destined to live this time on the wheel of life. <u>Karma</u> is not just a word, but a part of life where all things are equalized. Spiritual things are in the NOW always, and cannot end or cease to exist.

Your part is to tell people about their God given gifts, especially that of contacting Spirit. Write what I tell you and it will be published. You will have the means to do it as we are helping you in that respect. Why do you keep doubting our help when you have seen it over and over again in many times and in many lives?

Our message is always the same for you and everyone: believe in yourself and in your Divine gifts. Help will come. You have only begun to complete your life's work. It is not enough to know the truth, but that we live by the truth we know.

Rev. Shawna A. Grey

Table of Contents

DEDICATION i

This is a record of my spirit's journey through time ii

FORWARD iii

PREFACE iv

INTRODUCTION v

CHAPTER ONE 1

    28,000 BCE Given as the date of destruction of Atlantis by Edgar Cayce 1

    ATLANTIS: FACT OR FICTION 3

    THE TEMPLE OF POSEIDON 5

    CRYSTALS AS POWER 7

    EXPERIMENTS 9

    THE TEMPLE BEAUTIFUL 10

    THE TEMPLE OF SACRIFICE 10

    CONFERENCE HELD IN ATLANTIS 11

    DESTRUCTION OF ATLANTIS 11

    THE FLOOD 13

    EXODUS FROM ATLANTIS 13

    PROPHECY FROM THE HOPI NATION 14

    THE DREAM AND ITS MEANING FOR ME 15

CHAPTER TWO 19

    THE LAW OF ONE 19

    EXODUS TO EGYPT 19

    PRE-HISTORY OF EGYPT 20

    THE CAT PEOPLE 22

    EGYPTIAN MYSTERY SCHOOL 23

    PREPARATION FOR INITIATION 24

    IMAGINATION-VISUALIZATION 26

    THE CENTERS OF POWER 27

    DEVICES USED IN THE TEMPLE 31

    HEALING OFFERED 31

- SELF HYPNOSIS ... 33
- MY EGYPTIAN EXPERIENCE ... 33
- KARMA TO REPAY ... 34

CHAPTER THREE ... 35
- 321 BCE Given as the rise of Mayan Empire ... 35
- A MAYAN NOBLEMAN ... 35
- TREE OF LIFE ... 37
- THE FABLE OF THE HERO TWINS ... 37
- MAYAN HUMAN SACRIFICE ... 37
- MAYAN CALENDAR ... 38
- CONFERENCE AT A.R.E. ... 39
- MAYAN MEDICINE ... 41
- MY MAYAN EXPERIENCE ... 41

CHAPTER FOUR ... 43
- TANG DYNASTY 618-906 AD ... 43
- THE MYSTERIOUS LAND CALLED CHINA ... 43
- LANGUAGE ... 44
- TANG DYNASTY ... 44
- THE SILK ROAD ... 44
- BUDDHISM IN CHINA ... 45
- POTTERY ... 46
- MY LOVE OF POTTERY ... 47
- ITALIAN POTTERY ... 48
- MAJOLICA ... 48
- POTTERY CLASSIFICATION ... 48
- MEMORY IN CLAY ... 49
- NATIVE AMERICAN POTTERY ... 50
- MY LIFE IN CHINA ... 51
- THE ZEN BUDDHIST CENTER IN NEW MEXICO ... 51

CHAPTER FIVE ... 55
- 800 BCE Rise of Etruscan 753 BCE Founding of Rome ... 55
- A LOST CIVILIZATION ... 55

- THE ETRUSCANS 56
- THE PEOPLE 56
- HOUSING 57
- TEMPLES 58
- CLOTHING 58
- TRADE 58
- THE CITY OF VEII 59
- ROME 60
- ROMAN CITIZEN 61
- SLAVES 63
- THE ROMAN SOLDIER 64
- THE FALL OF THE ROMAN EMPIRE 64
- MY LIFE IN THIS TIME 65

CHAPTER SIX 67
- First Crusade 1095-1100 Capture of Antioch 6/3/1098 67
- A Monk in the Middle Ages and a Knight in the First Crusade 67
- THE MONK 68
- CHRISTIANITY BECOMES LEGAL 69
- AUTOMATIC WRITING 70
- MONASTERY OF MONTE CASSINO 70
- MY LIFE AS A MONK 71
- PEACE AND THE TRUCE OF GOD 71
- AUGUSTINE OF HIPPO 72
- THE JUST WAR THEORY 73
- BASIC HISTORY OF KNIGHTHOOD 73
- THE REASONS BEHIND THE FIRST CRUSADE 74
- MY PART IN THE CRUSADES 78

CHAPTER SEVEN 79
- The Albigensian Crusade 1209 79
- The Cathars and Montsegur 79
- THE CATHARS 79
- CATHARS AND THEIR BELIEFS 80

- CONSOLAMENTUM 80
- THE "PERFECT" 81
- CATHOLIC CHURCH REACTS 82
- MONTSEGUR 82
- MEMORIES OF A CATHAR 83
- A PAST LIFE REVEALED 84
- MY LIFE AS A CATHAR 85

CHAPTER EIGHT 87
- 1934-1952 87
- FROM SOUTH TO NORTH 87
- MY WORLD IN BOOKS 88
- CATHOLIC BOARDING SCHOOL 88
- MORNING ROUTINE 89
- MENAGE 90
- SCHOOL FAIR 90
- CATHOLIC DAY SCHOOL 91
- SENIOR PROM 92
- SPIRIT WARNING 92
- ENTER WILLIAM 93
- MARRIED LIFE 94
- THE CHOICE 94
- CONTACT WITH SPIRIT 95
- DIVORCE 95

CHAPTER NINE 97
- 1972-1990 97
- THE ADVENTURE BEGINS 97
- NEW MEXICO 97
- TAOS PUEBLO 98
- MESA VERDI NATIONAL PARK 98
- THE TURQUOISE DEALERS 99
- COLORADO SPRINGS 100
- VISION OF THE FUTURE 101

THE PLANTATION 102

CHAPTER TEN 104

1980-1983 104

ANOTHER WORLD ANOTHER LIFE 104

A MILITARY MOVE 104

REMINI ITALY 105

LIVING THE ITALIAN LIFE 106

SHOPPING 108

ITALIAN POTTERY SCHOOL 109

VISITING THE ITALIAN COUNTRY 109

VENICE 110

THE BRIDGE OF SIGHS 111

FLORENCE 111

VINCENZA 111

THE PROFESSOR 112

REPUBLIC OF SAN MARINO 112

THE DUKE OF URBINO 113

THE TOURNAMENT 116

LEN'S MYSTERIOUS PAIN 116

FLIGHT FROM ITALY 117

CHAPTER ELEVEN 121

COUNTRY LIFE 121

PAST LIFE REGRESSION CLASS 123

MISSION OF TUMACACORI 124

MY LIFE UPSIDE DOWN 125

THE END OF A LOVE 127

MY SECOND LIFE DECISION 128

NATIVE AMERICAN CULTURE TOUR 129

THE HOPI NATION 131

THE NATIVE AMERICAN HISTORY GRANT 132

JUSTIFICATION FOR THE NATIVE AMERICAN GRANT 133

THE MUSEUM ON THE TOHONO O'ODHAM NATION 133

CHAPTER TWELVE 135
REINCARNATION 135
SOUL MATES 138
OUR CHOICE FOR LIFE OR DEATH 139
KARMA 140
CHURCH AND REINCARNATION 142
SOUL FAMILIES 143
FEARS FROM ANOTHER LIFE 144
THE CREATION STORY 145
The King James Bible and Reincarnation 147
BIBLIOGRAPHY 148

CHAPTER ONE

28,000 BCE Given as the date of destruction of Atlantis by Edgar Cayce
"You must remember"
"I have loved you through the ages as I love you now." Spirit Message given 5/2016

The sky was dark black with millions of small lights sprinkled all around. I don't know why I chose this place called Earth; all I knew was I didn't want to go there. I thought to myself "Can't I change my mind? Why did I decide to do everything in one lifetime?" Here I was plummeting to Earth into a life if an unwanted child, and all I could do was scream "I don't want to go!" Then, a sweet voice of my guardian angel whispered in my right ear, "But you must." At first, I resisted, then I calmed down continuing to fall until I found myself in a room with white walls and a harsh light from a bare light bulb hanging from the ceiling over me. There was an impersonal feeling to the place and I was all alone.

This dream is one I had when I was a small child. It set the stage for my life in a small southern town in the state of Virginia just before World War II. My mother had graduated from college in Virginia. She had fallen in love with her college chemistry teacher and then had come home for the wedding. It was a huge social event for the town with a church all decorated and my grandfather as the minister of the Baptist church performed the ceremony. The newspaper printed an account of the event on their social page and everyone in town was there to see the happy couple off for their new home in Colorado, the groom's home state.

In a little over a year later, my mother came back from Colorado with a few of her things in a suitcase and me on the way. I was told years later after my own wedding, that my mother had come home to file for a divorce from my father and to get an abortion. My grandmother put her foot down and told my mother she was having this child! My mother answered her saying "Well, then you raise her!" So, I have my grandmother to thank for my life. My mother did get a divorce which freed her, but put me into the dubious position of being a child without parents.

I was raised by my mother's family. My grandfather was a Southern Baptist minister who preached from the good book every Sunday. My grandmother taught kindergarten children in her classroom in the basement of the church. We lived in a small town in Virginia during the 1940s. My mother worked in a nearby town. I saw her about once a year or whenever she wanted something from my grandfather. My grandparents were both loving but distant from me. I never realized what a difficult situation my birth placed on my grandparents. In those years, it was unheard of that grandparents should raise grandchildren, but I was a responsibility they volunteered to take on for my mother. I knew I was loved, but still I felt the criticism of the community as to my being raised by grandparents not in a regular family comprised of a mom and dad. Of course, this was many years ago when grandparents did not raise their grandchildren, and it was an uncommon practice then, making me all the "stranger" to the other children of the community. Consequently, I lived more to myself without contact of other children, except when my time was spent in the school classroom.

When I was a child I use to go to bed at night and whisper into the darken room "tell me a story." Then as sleep overtook my young body, my mind opened to the pictures and stories of strange worlds and adventures. One such story has stayed with me all my life. I was six years old and as I did every night, I asked for a story. This memorable night started with flashing lights as if I was in a laser light show of today. Lights of red and blue flashed, then there was thunder of drums, the clashing of cymbals, and the beating of drums. All the lights and the noise stopped, and I was shown a room with the walls as well as the floor made out of large stones. There were large columns down the middle of the room reaching toward the ceiling so high I could not see the top of them. At each corner of the room was a large globe that lit that part of the room. In the middle of this room was a long wooden table with people sitting around it who seemed to be in animated discussion about something.

The women were dressed in long dresses with a low-cut front. Each dress seemed to be made of a red or blue heavy velvet material decorated with threads of gold. The ladies had their hair piled on top of their head and all of them had a jewel of one kind or another fastened in their hair. They also had gold chains and jewels decorated their necks. The men were dressed in long pants and a short coat made of the same color and material as their pants. They wore a white frilly shirt under their coat. On the left side of the jacket was a pocket with an emblem stitched in small beads on the front. I could not get a clear view of the emblem on their pocket; I just knew that there was one there.

I found myself perched on one of the columns close to the table. Across from my perch was an enormous pair of eyes hanging midair over the table. They had large dark eyebrows and long dark eyelashes that shaded two ice blue colored eyes. These eyes were concentrating on the speakers at the table and they would turn toward the speaker as each person spoke. I have seen only two people in my lifetime that had the same ice blue color eyes that I saw that night.

There was no noise from the group below me only an occasional creak of a chair as someone adjusted themselves in the seat, yet they were talking to each other. I watched a few seconds then asked my Spirit guide what I was seeing. I was told that they were planning the evacuation of the city. I then asked how they were communicating with each other, and I was told that they were talking telepathically. The people came from different areas and their languages were different, but they could all speak to each other by telepathy. I have regretted not having asked more about the eyes that hung over the table, but I guess the whole experience was way too much for me to think about asking more questions.

The next night I went to bed and asked for a story as I did each night. The lights starting flashing, lightening flashing, drum sounds, cymbals clashing, just as the night before. I said "I don't want to see this again. I saw it last night!" I was told by a woman's soft voice by my right shoulder, "But you must remember!" So, the dream played out as the night before. At the end I drifted into a deep relaxing sleep.

The third night the lights flashed and the drums starting beating. By this time, I knew I could not get out of the experience and I just wanted it to get over so I could sleep. There were three nights in a row that I had this dream, and I never had it again, but I remember it as if it was just last night.

I have read the saying that if the same things happen three times, within a short space of time, you should be very attentive to the message, the circumstances or something in the dream was bringing you an important message. All through my life I have tried to find out the meaning of this dream. Who were the people sitting around the table and why was their meeting so secretive? I have asked several psychic readers this question and they all have said the same thing, that I witnessed the planning for the evacuation of Atlantis before the mainland was destroyed.

ATLANTIS: FACT OR FICTION

When I was a freshman in college, one of the required subjects was American History. The professor that taught this subject held his class in an auditorium that held over a hundred students. We sat in seats that ringed three sides of the room while the professor stood at a table on a platform below us. This type of seating gave everyone a view of the teacher and the media board behind him. The room was a babble of noise until the professor walked on stage. He was a tall thin man with brown hair in his early twenties, when I knew him. He spoke with a soft voice and the room would get so quiet you could have heard a pin drop.

The hour flew by without you even realizing you were hearing history. The professor made a dull, boring subject come alive. As he taught it, you would be living it as if reading a novel with heroes and villains, plots within a plot and a purpose to the drama. The professor had a notebook in front of him which he referred to once in a while, but most of the time he just walked back and forth across the stage talking to us.

One day the class was being interrupted by several students talking a few rows behind me. The professor stopped what he was saying and turned in the direction of the disruptive students. He said, "I may be blind, but my hearing is quite good. Will the student in the tenth row, five seats from the left stand up?" We all turned to look and it was the one who was talking. Then the professor said "the student in tenth row, sixth seat stand up." These were the two causing the disruption. The professor continued, "Give me your names." He wrote them on a piece of paper in front of him then calling them by name he said, "I may be blind, but I know what is going on in my classroom. If you decide to stay in this class, you will have to be quiet during the lecture. If you decide to leave do it now so the rest of us can continue with today's work." He paused and the students answered him that they would stay. Then they sat down in their seats. The entire class erupted in applause and after we quieted down the professor continued with the class.

That is what history is: a continuous story of man's activities, thoughts and involvement with one another. With that definition of history, I will begin my story. Historical references may come in many ways, in books, or in stories handed down from generation to generation. References may be unconventional as information given in a channeling or in automatic writing. The reader must decide if he/she accepts the information as truth or not. I will do my best to share what Information I have on each subject. It is up to you to accept it as truth, or better yet, if you want more information, do some research on the subject yourself.

In 1923, Edgar Cayce, the sleeping prophet of Virginia Beach, gave a reading in which the first mention of Atlantis is made. He said that the Atlantean history extended from 200,000 BCE to the destruction of the last island in 9,500 BCE by the people's misuse of natural resources. He describes a continent that occupied a large part of what we now call the Atlantic

Ocean with the Gulf of Mexico on one hand and the Mediterranean upon the other. Evidence of this lost civilization can be found in the Pyrenees and Morocco on one side, the other British Honduras, Yucatan and America.[1] The people of Atlantis achieved great heights in scientific knowledge and a greater knowledge of spiritual laws than we have now. There are no records of this land or the people that lived there, but according to Edgar Cayce these records will be found in Egypt, among other places, in a chamber between the paws of the Sphinx. [2]

There are many books written on the legendary land called Atlantis a story first told by Plato 5th-4th century Greek philosopher, in his works entitled "Dialogue of Timaeus and Dialogue of Critias." He introduces us to a continent that time had forgotten. The land called Atlantis that became a powerful empire before being destroyed by a colossal natural disaster. The story of the lost continent was told to Socrates (469-399 BCE) by his grandfather, Caritas II, who had seen the story written on a temple column in Egypt. The column was inscribed in Egyptian hieroglyphics in a temple dedicated to the goddess Neith, in the ancient city of Sais, the present-day San el-Hager. The story is that Plato's father gave a dinner and invited the nobles of that era to his house for a feast. The guests at this dinner included Aristotle and other nobles of that era. That night, Plato, as a child, listened to the after-dinner talk of the group and heard the story of Atlantis. Plato (427-347 BCE) remembered the story and wrote about it in his later years. He wrote the story not as a carefully research historical document, but as an example of the vulnerability of a civilization and a warning against the dangers of arrogance and corruption.

Plato describes an island continent that became a powerful empire before being destroyed in a colossal national disaster. He placed Atlantis beyond the "Pillars of Hercules," now known as the Strait of Gibraltar, in the then uncharted and seemingly inaccessible Atlantic Ocean. In 300 BCE, a Greek lawyer by the name of Solon went to Egypt to determine if the story was true or not. He met a priest by the name of Sais who showed him the inscribed pillar in the temple; he also confirmed that more of the records from Atlantis did exist, but he did not know where they were located. The priest Sais told Solon that before the great deluge, Greeks had resisted an attempt of the Athenians to subjugate them and after that event the destruction happened. [3]

Many people down through the ages believed that Plato's story was just that: a story with Plato using a mythical situation to show what he thought was needed for an ideal civilization. Others thought that Plato was inspired to write a mythical story of Atlantis using the destruction of the Minoan civilization (c. 2700 – c. 1450 BCE) as a model, but M. Pierre Termier, Director of the Geological Chart of France, is one of a growing band of geologists who believe that the Atlantean continent did exist, believes that the reality of Atlantis is highly possible, with the only question of debate to be: on what precise geological area did this continent flourish? [4]

Two hundred million years ago, all the continents were one. They slowly broke apart along the lines of the tectonic plates which floated on hot thick liquid known as mantle. The cracks were filled in with molten lava and volcanic rock at the boundary line between the America plate and the European plate forming the Atlantic ridge. The Atlantic Ridge and the Azores Plateau (150,000 square miles) of flat land on the North-east side of the ridge comprised the mainland of Atlantis. [5]

The extreme northern portions of Atlantis experienced cold weather, but the rest of the country was of a tropical climate. The Andean, or the Pacific coast of South America, was then the western part of Lemuria. During this time, the Urals and the mountain regions were a tropical climate, and the Mongolian desert was a fertile plain. [6]

Shirley Andrews tells us in her book "*Atlantis*" that in 30,000 BCE to 10,000 BCE the ocean's water was lower than it is now and the continental shelf around the Atlantic Ocean extended out as far as two hundred miles from the present shorelines of America and Europe. Poseidon was a large island located on the Bahamian Banks completely above water. Extensive portions of the sea floor of the Gulf of Mexico and the Caribbean Sea were above surface. The lands were rich in red soil with rugged mountains ranges, whose tall peaks were covered in perpetual snow. Over time, plants and animals traveled over the land to the North American Continent, populating the land with common species on either side of the Atlantic. Today, Poseidon consists of seven hundred small islands extending fifty miles east of Palm Beach, Florida from approximately 676 miles north east in the direction of Haiti.[7]

The land had a tropical climate with lush vegetation of trees, plants and miles of rich farming lands, which was cultivated for gardens and for growing fruit and vegetables. The mountains furnished them all kinds of minerals. The most precious being a mineral known as orichalcum or mountain copper, which was considered more precious than gold. The island produced timber suitable for buildings. It also had numerous herds of animals, both domestic and wild, with large herds of elephants who found food in the marshes and river beads. The soil was rich for growing crops, grapes, fruit trees and all kinds of vegetables in season. [8]

Boats bringing visitors to the golden city of Atlantis would see the harbor filled with trading ships from many countries. The entrance to the city was by a waterway in which even large ships could navigate. A canal was the waterway into the city, shaped with alternating rings of land and water. If this area could be seen from air it would give the impression of a target with two circles of land followed by three rings of sea with one large island in the middle. On each ring were buildings and a temple for a different god, with areas for public exercise around them. Ships bringing visitors or trade goods to the city were able to unload their cargo within the wall city gates. The city was defended by bridges and towers with security gates, built over the canals.

THE TEMPLE OF POSEIDON

In the middle of the city was a large island on which was built a very ornate gold temple. Mr. Lewis Spence, in his book *The History of Atlantis*, describes the temple of Poseidon as having the exterior covered in silver, pinnacles glittering in gold, and the interior was roofed with ivory, gold, silver and the bronze of orichalcum. The most impressive of the statues, surrounding the main building, was a very large gold representation of Poseidon standing in his chariot holding the reins of the horses. There were also gold statues of former kings, placed all around the building. Near the central island there was a large amphitheater which was surrounded by the home of the high officials. Here the royal guards were lodged as well as those of the royal house. Outside the temple there were hot and cold springs bringing in water for the private homes in town as well as the various public baths. Extensive gardens provided shelter from the sun and gave the feeling of a large lush tropical garden to the entire area. The temple was surrounded by large grassy areas and many beautiful gardens with decorative fountains. Cayce tell us that there were large columns of onyx, topaz, and inlaid column of beryl, amethyst and stones that could catch the rays of the sun. These were built around the sacrificial altar in the temple. [9]

Atlantis was divided into ten states with each state having a king, who had complete control over the people. Twice a year the people gathered together to celebrate the harvested fruits of the land. There were several bulls allowed to roam free in the gardens. People would gather at the temple every fifth or sixth year for a special ceremony in the temple. One of the bulls would be chosen to be the sacrifice. They cut the bulls' throat letting the blood pour over a pillar in the temple, which had the laws of the land engraved on it. Prayers to Poseidon was offered while the bull was cut in pieces and burned on the altar fire. The kings sat outside the temple around a fire and ate some of the meat, while listening to the public on affairs of their state. They also passed judgment on each other and reviewed all state affairs since their last gathering. After hearing the evidence at hand, a judgement would be given. All decisions made that night were written on a golden plate and placed in the temple. Atlantis was governed with justice and a sincere concern for the welfare of the people. Peace among its kings and people was maintained this way for thousands of years. [10]

From Tom Moore's channeled information from his guide Theo, we find in his book on "*Atlantis and Lemuria, the Lost Continent Revealed*," a detailed description of the group that he founded, The Gentle Way, also the daily life of the people in Atlantis. Both women and men were respected for their achievements in many different areas of life. Occupations were as diverse in that civilization as it is in our modern-day lives. Most women did not work, but if they did they were found working as nurses, also in restaurants, temples, gardens and overseeing household staff. People were health conscious and ate more fruits and vegetables than meat. They enjoyed swimming, walking in the many gardens, and attending the amphitheater to watch popular plays. There were also boat and horse racing to be enjoyed. They had parades to celebrate the changing of the seasons, which they felt was more important than the celebration of the New Year. The people of Atlantis and their neighbors in Lemuria, the land in the Pacific, were family-oriented and cared for the elderly in their homes. Rich people had homes. The poor people lived in apartments with a green belt around it for gardens. The apartment buildings were two or three stories high. [11]

Houses were made of wood and some of varied colored stones. Large black volcanic stones, white and yellow stones were used in decoration. Some people had the mind power to change stone into a palpable substance which could then be reshaped into a useful item for the home. When the shaping was complete, the stone was then returned to its former hardness. There were stores for all household commodities. Some stores sold materials that were brought in by ship from the world outside the city gates. There were clothing stores with windows that displayed their goods for sale. Clothing that was worn were of a loose fit design, usually robes for women and children. Clothing for students in the temple was of a light color with each color showing the degree of enlightenment they had obtained. White was given to those in the highest rank. The men wore pants and shirts. The market had stores with fish from the ocean or vegetables from the extensive farm lands outside the city gates. All of this was paid with simple currency. There was some paper money and coins, and banks that extended loans for those who needed them. There was no poverty in Atlantis as everyone was able to provide whatever was needed for the family.

The children were educated from eight to ten years old. Only those with a scientific aptitude continued with their education, which included lessons on the use of crystals. Some of the young men joined the army. There were schools that taught languages, especially for those children who would work in international trade or would be a part of the exploration of unknown lands outside the vast lands controlled by Atlantis. There was a lot of home schooling in Atlantis, but the people of Lemuria felt that the children needed more contact with other children and set up schools outside the home. A limited knowledge of crystals and their use was given to students, unless they were studying in the temple. Crystals also were used to hold and to transfer knowledge to students. [12]

Most people married when they were young. Some believed that marriage was forever. Other groups believed that either party could end the marriage if they felt that it was not mutually beneficial to stay together. Birth control was practiced and abortions were rare, but the feeling was if it was better for the woman to terminate the pregnancy, then it was done. Men could have multiple wives. It was unusual for couples to stay together their entire lives. Families were usually small with one or two children. [13]

CRYSTALS AS POWER

Crystals of all sizes were mined in Atlantis and also in the area we know now as Arkansas, where today there are still a large number of quartz crystals that are found. Certain people in Atlantis were able to tell where the very large crystals were located undergrown and were able to extract them.

Crystals were used in many ways. They were the chief power source for individuals and for the nation. Crystals were able to hold a charge of energy and were developed to be used like a stun gun. The city and individual homes had light at night by glowing crystal balls placed strategically around the city. The larger the crystal the longer it could stay powered, especially if placed in a magnetic field the crystal could keep the power constant. Smaller crystals had to be powered more frequently. There was a booster station for the crystal energy every twenty miles around the city and in the distant off shore lands of the Atlantic. To obtain power, it was necessary for the crystals to be in a line-of-sight placement. The largest crystals were used by aircraft or ships on the ocean to boost power for long trips. There were some ground vehicles for both public and private transportation powered by crystals. [14]

Edgar Cayce tells us of the "Tuaoi" stone, which was a large, six-faceted crystal stone, which was the central power station for the city. It was found in a large building made of stone, with the walls of the building covered in a substance like asbestos. The building was oval-shaped with a roof that could be folded back to expose the crystal to both sunlight and starlight. It was used to carry power for all manner of things. Rays from this stone supplied the power for small airplanes, and undersea vehicles. Booster crystals were placed all over the Mediterranean for long distance travel. [15]

Another energy source was a V-shaped piece that looked like it was made of bronze. It was silvery and shone like glass, so small it was held in an individual's hand. For this device to work, it had to be held at a certain degree for the sun's rays to activate it. It could move things, light up things, and preserve food stuffs for use later on. Another one of the uses was to rejuvenate cells of the body to where an older person's cells could be renewed back to their younger years and they would look and have the same energy as when they were young. Only the priest knew how to operate the device. It was one of the things destroyed by the greed of the people in later years. People killed the priest and took the device. They did not know how to operate it, and mishandled it. The power of the device was disturbed, created a huge explosion eventually killing everyone in the area. [16]

They had all kinds of crystals that were used to focus energy. They had a certain type of crystal that could take sunlight and focus it into a stream of light that could be used as a laser. There were crystals that could filter out ultraviolet light and others that could use starlight to detect body heat, as our night vision glasses do now. [17]

There were two large temples. One was the Temple of Healing and the other was the Temple of Beauty. Both of these temples were important to the people. The people that worked in either temple wore special headgear and robes indicating the type of service they provided. The color of their clothing indicated at what level they had achieved in training, with the beginners or initiates wearing pale green and the more advanced wearing white. A head band of various metals would also indicate their specialized study.

Shirley Andrews writes in her book "*Lemuria and Atlantis, Studying the Past to Survive the Future,*" that the Temple of Sacrifice offered students opportunities to participate in a variety of activities intended to purify their body and mind. It was used as a hospital as we have now, a place for healing. In the Temple Beautiful, they spent long hours listening to music, surrounded with different scents of flowers and herbs, and hours surrounded by powerful crystals to help them heal and raise their vibratory rate to a higher level.

There were three groups with different philosophies in the land. The people who belonged to the group called "The Law of One" believed in kindness, love and the dignity of all living things. They believed in one Supreme Being and a small number of people believed in reincarnation. The concept of Heaven vs. Hell was held by some as this idea was more understandable rather than the concept of reincarnation and living multiple lives. There were people who had psychic gifts and were able to interpret dreams. These people were considered as oracles who advised the leaders and wealthy patrons at the temple. There were teachers who held classes on the many aspects of Spirituality, and there were healers who were available to anyone that required healing for their body, mind or spirit.

The second group consisted of the people who followed a leader named Belial. Their focus was on the materialistic and scientific pursuits. They developed crystals for use as weapons. They considered themselves better than the people that followed "The Law of One." This group called themselves "Sons of Belial." They wore clothing that distinguished themselves from the other groups, and their priests encouraged fighting for religious beliefs. They wanted to rule the homelands and all other lands that the name Atlantis covered. People who had left the mainland to form colonies in other areas of the world still considered themselves a part of Atlantis. The vision of the ruling priest was for his domination of all the people. They wanted the priests of Belial to have unquestioning control over the people, and the entire nation. [18]

There was a third group not as well-known as the other two, but one that influenced many people living in Atlantis as it brought to them an alternative social and religious solution, that of love for others and a peaceful community life that the two other main groups did not offer. The leader of this group called "The Gentle Way," taught the love between man and all creation. The group started small, but grew to be a large part of the population, not so many that the authorities considered them a threat since their existence was considered to be insignificant. As people became increasingly disturbed by what the members of the other two groups were doing, they began searching for an alternative and found a group of people who had found a gentler way of life. This group remained faithful to their beliefs through the years. They knew that a great disaster was coming, so as the years went by groups of people, sometimes several families at a time, left the area for other lands. [19]

All the people of Atlantis spoke the same language at one time, but as the years went by and the increased division of ideology became apparent, language changed separating the people as did their ideas. Both these groups were led by priests that were corrupt, controlling their people until eventually their greed and desire for power resulted in war, and brought about the final destruction of the land.

EXPERIMENTS

There were strange creatures that lived in Atlantis. They were a mixture of animal and human. These creatures lived in Atlantis for thousands of years on the land, before people arrived. As time went on, the Scientists who belonged to the Sons of Belial began to experiment with genetic codes. Some of these creatures were pleasing to look at and they could be purchased at the local market to be used as domestic servants. Some of these "things," as they were called by those living in Atlantis, were trained to work in the iron and copper mines, while others were trained as workers on the farms or in any other job requiring strenuous manual labor. They could not reproduce, so were just replaced with another when they died. They were captive in their body and mind as they were directed to their work by the mental control of their owners.

The Sons of Belial felt that it was their right to mistreat the "things," which they considered to be subhuman. They became subjects for the experiments of the scientist. The name "thing" was given because of the form they took, sometimes with hideous physical appearances. There were things with multiple arms, legs, or eyes, which were enslaved by the Atlanteans with mind control. They were used as slave labor, forcing them to pull a plow, or harnessed to a machine. The Sons of Belial used hypnosis and mental telepathy to control them. As the Scientists gained more knowledge, they were able to alter the genetic code and make them to look more human. [20]

There were great antagonistic feelings between those of the Law of One and those of the Sons of Belial. The people that belonged to the Sons of Belial looked down on the "things" as something that was without feelings and mistreated them horribly. They were bred like cattle for particular work. The Scientists conducted genetic experiments with human DNA and that of different animals, producing all kinds of strange combinations. People that followed the Law of One had compassion for the suffering captives and tried to help them by bringing them into the temple for healing. Deloris Cannon (1931-2014) was a hypnotherapist whose research can be found in the numerous books she wrote. In her series entitled "The Convoluted Universe," in

Book 1, Ms. Cannon tells us of her session with a lady that remembered a lifetime in Atlantis. She describes an event she is witnessing where several hundreds of these animal/humans are in a large arena, fighting each other to the death. It is like that of the "games" with gladiators the people in Rome enjoyed centuries later. Some of the "things" described are: horses with a human face, another with the face of a jaguar and the hind legs of a human, and another had the body of a bull, but it had human legs. People were sitting around the arena and watching the carnage without feeling any compassion for the participants on the stage below them. [21]

Stories found in the myths of many nations around the world, tell of horses with a magic horn in the middle of their forehead (unicorns), or women with fish tails instead of legs (mermaids), and horses that were half horse half man (centaur), are all stories from memory of these creatures that lived in Atlantis.

THE TEMPLE BEAUTIFUL

The students who entered the Temple of Sacrifice were taught how to expand their mind through meditation and concentration. The vibration of sound from their voice and from music was explored. Colors found in nature, their vibrational application, also scents of flowers, plants were studied. When students started their journey to priesthood, they wore different colored robes to indicate their level of education. Novices wore green, as they advanced in their studies they wore lighter colors until they were permitted to wear white, the sign that they had reached a high rank. [22] The classes were based on the realization of an individual's capacity to extend their awareness into another dimension. Of opening themselves to being a part of nature and the expansion of the universe. They were able to lower their breathing rate and enter into a state of trance, where they were able to explore the world of spirit. [23] The movement of dance, music and the expression of drama was studied and shared with the people in the temple to celebrate certain festivals.

This was a place of peace and joy where every day something magical was explored. Each student was given instructions in all subjects and if they showed an aptitude toward a certain phase of the work, they were allowed to pursue it as their contribution to the people and to the temple.

THE TEMPLE OF SACRIFICE

The students for the temple were chosen at an early age, by priests from the group called the "Law of One." If a child grew up showing tendency toward healing, then they were admitted to the formal training at the temple. They were taught the sacred sounds, how to make them and what resonated with each part of the body. They were taught the use of plants and herbs in healing; which plants were to be used and how to prepare and then administer them for different ailments. They learned the vibrations of colored stones and how to use them for healing. They could control the molecular shape of crystals and use them in many different ways. [24] A person could be treated with the use of sound, odor, light, and with the intensity of color which was determined for the treatment of certain parts of the body. Deloris Cannon tells us that they had crystals of different colors with each color corresponding to a person's chakra in their body. The students were taught how to open their minds to the internal workings of the body, and they were taught how to get in touch with their cells as well as those of another person to engage them in the healing process. The jewelry a priestess wore not only showed her position in the temple but it was also used as an instrument of healing. The jewel was placed so that a direct stream of sunlight could pass through it, with that light positioned on a specific place for healing to take place.[25] Meditation and prayer became the initiate's daily practice as they grew, their mind expanded to receive and understand the mysteries taught in the temple. The animal/people creations that had been made by the Scientists of the followers of Belial were offered medical assistance in the temple Here they were treated kindly with sedatives and surgery, removed the claws, tails, and other animal appendages. After their physical body was restored to wholeness, they were sent to the Temple Beautiful where they were taught with love and understanding to forgive those who had mistreated them.

CONFERENCE HELD IN ATLANTIS

There were dangerous animals and birds of the air that threatened the people, their crops and their children. These animals and carnivorous birds outnumbered the people and terrorized humans all over the planet. Hordes of gigantic elephants trampling the orchards and the crops in the fields, sometime destroying a year's production. There were large herds of mastodons, wild cats of several varieties and carnivorous birds that terrorized the planet. The people of Atlantis decided that something had to be done to protect their crops, and their families throughout the land.

They decided to send out men from Atlantis to all the countries of the world and request that a representative from that country be sent to Atlantis for a conference to study ways to combat the worldwide problem of the wild animals. In 52,000 BCE, representatives from many nations attended the conference.

The delegates came from the area we know now as Russia, the Near East, Sudan, upper W. Africa which became the Gobi Desert, and the remaining lands of Lemuria in the Pacific. The delegates from India and Peru joined the original group for a later conference. Since spears and swords were impenetrable to the hard skin of the wild animals, it was agreed that Atlantis would experiment with chemicals, expecting to extend their arsenal of weapons and defeat the dangerous animals. [26]

DESTRUCTION OF ATLANTIS

The records seem to indicate two definite periods of migration: one just before the second great upheaval 28,000 BCE when the continental area was broken into islands, and another in 10,000 BCE before the final destruction of Poseidia, the last large island. [23] As the year went by, the people enjoyed the effluent society they had created. Those who followed "The Law of One" prospered and increased their knowledge of the spiritual side of life. They used their mind powers for the good of the community and treated each other with justice in all of their dealings. The temple offered healing to those who required it as well as the returning soldiers from the many skirmishes outside the protective homeland. The temple was a place for the young people to study the wisdom that was found there, and to improve their mental capacity for greater service.

The Sons of Belial also had a temple where they practiced their chants and rituals. Theirs was not a temple of love, but of extreme mind control and the use of the black arts of evil by the priest. The negative feeling by the people and the hatred that was taught by the priest continued to encourage all disruption of the peaceful land.

Shirley Andrews tells us about the use of the Ankh that was said to have power over life and death. An ankh looks like a two-armed stick figure with a loop for the head. In Atlantis, the ankh could be powered with energy of thought and sound. It was held by the head to transmit the energy and to receive energy held by the arms. The priest could use this instrument to send out powerful sound waves of destruction. It could also create serious damage to the person using it, if they were not properly trained. [27]

The beginning of the end of Atlantis is described by Edgar Cayce. It all started with the explosives that were designed to kill the wild beasts. The uncontrolled powerful energy of the Tuaoi stone's frequency was turned too high when it was used to kill the wild beasts. Then the priest incited the followers of the Sons of Belial to launch an attack on those that followed the Law of One using the power of the amplified crystals, destroying millions of people at a time. Their land was turned into one of chaos and destruction, as it became increasingly unstable, caused by the destructive forces unleashed by the Sons of Belial. Their use of crystals to drill a hole in the core of the Earth created a fissure allowing molten magma to escape eventually causing earthquakes and the destruction of the land. The increased anxiety of the people allowed the priests of the temples to use their fear against them. With the instability of the land and with more and more earthquakes, the priest convinced the people that to appease the gods they must turn the altar fires, which formerly burned fruit and flowers, into instruments of human sacrifice. [28]

The remaining people of Atlantis became more and more disenchanted with their leaders. Their society had hit one of the highest technological levels for that age and those to come. The population had the opportunity for every comfort. There was medical care for anyone who needed it. If they became ill, their psychic abilities could tell them where the body was out of balance from the basic energy level of the universe. They had beautiful homes and temples in which to worship and gather as a people. Their children had the privilege of education and advancement in many different professions, yet, with all of these advantages, there was an undercurrent of fear and of dissatisfaction throughout the country. The reports of murder and theft grew each day. Where there had once been peace among neighbors, had now turned to fear. The feeling of depression and impending doom hung over the land. The priests in the temple of the Sons of Ballia kept increasing their experiments with crystal-powered ray guns until they could kill by destabilizing the molecular structure of whatever the beam hit. The destructive power of the atom used with the ray guns was found to be extremely lethal. With these weapons, they attacked the people that followed the philosophy of the Law of One. The ray guns turned out to be very effective killing everything in sight. It was a terrible conflict with millions of people incinerated at a time. This was a war fought for two weeks, with each side trying to completely destroy everybody and everything of the other group. The land was on fire, causing the destabilization of the land resulting in earthquakes and volcanic activity breaking up the land and eventually the ocean reclaimed the land. There was mass panic everywhere with people and animals trying to escape the fire and land instability under their feet. Even then some people were able to escape the carnage, but on the whole many people went down with the land.

Millions of people died. No other war in the history of the Explorer Race, including modern times, saw so many killed. They incinerated thousands at a time. [29]

As the fight with the wild animals on the mainland of Atlantis continued, there was accompanying shaking of the earth, and the eruption of noxious gas from the fissures in the earth created by the people with their explosives. The underlying volcanic base of the continent was being disturbed and the sleeping giant of molting lava, fire and hot ash erupted all throughout Atlantis, killing most of the dangerous animals and many of the people. The people that remained were caught in the upheaval of the land by volcanic eruptions, earthquakes and eventually the reclamation of the land by the ocean. The resulting rise of the ocean waters and the flooding of the land was felt around the world. It must have been a horrific event with large pieces of land breaking off and falling into the ocean, volcanic ash choking those still struggling for life, and then walls of water covering everything, washing buildings, humans, animals, trees and all vegetation out to sea. It is no wonder this event was recorded in the subconscious of the people that escaped and recorded in ancient records of many cultures of the earth.

THE FLOOD

At the height of the battle, the Atlantean Scientists turned the crystal guns too high and suddenly the slaughter of people turned into a run for survival for everyone. The rays stirred up the dormant earthquakes' underlying action of the land itself with the awakening of the volcanic action of the Atlantic ridge. As a result of the cataclysmic event, weather caused by volcanic ash, and the displacement of land into the ocean, forty million animals including wooly mammoths, saber-tooth cats, mastodons, wolves, giant cave bears, and herds of bison died on the North and South continents.

Edgar Cayce said this disaster was recorded in the Bible as the story of the flood with Noah who saved his family and animals in a large boat called an ark.[30] Most of us know the Biblical story of Noah and his family, along with his animals, escaping the flood in an ark. In Christian, Jewish and Islamic literature, the story of the deluge plays an important role. There are actually more than 200 great flood traditions scattered throughout the world. In the Epic of Gilgamesh, written over a thousand years before the Bible, they describe the flood over the entire Earth. Edgar Cayce's readings suggest that the flood occurred during the second destruction of Atlantis, causing the final migration of individuals from that land. The destruction of Poseidon's land mass affected all the lands that bordered it. Think of the reaction of a stone dropped into a lake with the ripples of water going out to the shore. All the land near the ocean was flooded with the high waves. It must have been like the tsunami reported in Live Science, October 15, 2015, which told of the earthquake in Japan and the following tsunami of 2011, where fifty-foot waves swallowed land and small islands.[31] People who lived far inland from the ocean beaches or near the top of mountains were not affected. The devastation was recorded in all the chronicles of the known world.

EXODUS FROM ATLANTIS

Early on, some of the people that followed the Law of One realized that the changing attitude of the people and the increased tension between the two groups was not getting better. Thousands of years before the final destruction of the land, small groups of people had moved away from their homeland. Colonies were formed by the refugees where they continued the culture they had in Atlantis. Now the people gathered together for protection and to plan how to peacefully leave Atlantis for other lands beyond the control of the priests. There were groups of families that took what they could and traveled by boat to the coastline of Africa where there was abundant wild game for food. Other groups settled in the mountains of the area between the countries we know now as France and Spain. The farmers of Atlantis found in the Amazon jungle rich land in which to build a new home. People went into the area of Yucatan, and along the coast of South America. Some groups going further inland to settle in the forests of North America or in the wide-open areas between the mountains. Wherever the people went, they took their culture, religious beliefs, and the story of a land rich in gold and silver, and the disaster that eventually destroyed their home continent.

PROPHECY FROM THE HOPI NATION

The Hopi are a nation of Native Americans that live in the Southwest part of the United States. They have a prophecy that describes the destructions of the world. The Hopi say that the world and the oceans turned over two or three times, which scientists call the shifting of the magnetic poles. The elders of the tribe know that we are at the end of the fourth world and the beginning of the fifth. The Hopi say that the world was destroyed first by fire, with the second destruction by ice, the third by flood, and we are now living in the fourth world.

On December 10, 1992, at a meeting at the United Nations building in New York City, Mr. Thomas Banyacya, and other Hopi leaders, spoke to the assembly. They explained that the creator made the first world in perfect balance when humans spoke only one language. Then the humans turned away from moral and spiritual principles, and misused their spiritual powers for selfish reasons. Eventually, the world was destroyed by the sinking of the land, and many died. A few of the peaceful people survived and went into the second world. After a period of time, they repeated the same mistake and the world was then frozen into the Ice Age.

A few survivors from the second world went into the third world which lasted a long time. The people spoke one language and they invented many technological properties that were helpful for man. They also had strong mental capacity which they could use for good or for evil. They gradually turned away from natural laws and perceived that of the material world more valuable. They succeeded in creating a world full of wondrous things, but again turned away from that of the spirit and their world was destroyed by volcanos and floods.

The third time a small portion of that population survived and started this fourth world where we now live. Our world is in terrible shape. We are in the final days of this prophecy. The sign of the end of the age is the Earth warming up, causing the oceans to rise. There will be reports of sinking land and islands that disappear from view. Scientists believe that the Earth is tipping southward because the melting ice is decreasing the weight at the North Pole. Chunks of ice weighing thousands of tons will break off and slide into the sea causing the level of water in the oceans to rise. For many years, there has been a danger for the start of a World War III. The Hopi believe that the Persian Gulf War was the beginning, but it was stopped and the weapons of destruction were not used. They believe that this is the time to weigh our choices for our future. We do have a choice. If the nations of the Earth cause another great war, the Hopi believe we humans will burn ourselves to death with ashes.

In 1975, Dan Evehema, Hopi elder, was asked if he could project an end date for the cycle of events in the world. He said, about 2050 AD. The Hopi elders usually do not give exact dates for each event. They speak in general terms about the closing of an age and the beginning of another. [32]

If you are aware of the conditions in the world now you see that these prophecies are starting to come true many in the twenty-first century. Food and water shortages in many parts of the world. Environmental groups are facing new challenges every year. People throughout the world are fearful for their lives. The unrest makes people prone to violence against each other. Families are torn apart by war and the terror of bombs. Every day we hear and see, on our television sets, the outcome of war devastation.

Our mission is to join those who are willing to look for a peaceful solution for the world's conflicts; to save our world before we destroy it, to awaken from our apathy and start looking for the actions that will save people and our world from another disaster caused by unscrupulous men in positions of power.

THE DREAM AND ITS MEANING FOR ME

This is the story of Atlantis, a civilization that lost itself in the tangle of personal greed, violence and dishonor. The dream I was given so many years ago was a reminder to me to remember who I am and what part I personally played in these events. As I said before, this dream has haunted me all my life, and now I have to search for information that would tell me just what significance it had for me.

The opening of the dream started with the sound of trumpets. In the days of kings and court etiquette, the blowing of a trumpet meant there was a person of importance coming into the area or there was an announcement of importance to be heard. The flashing of lights was an added attention getter for me. The building material of the room was large rock for both walls and the floor. It was apparently in a hidden area since there were no windows and the room had a feeling of being in a basement of a larger building. The ceiling was held up by four large columns with some kind of a ledge near the top of one where I was perched, and I was able to watch the action below me. Light for the room was provided by large round crystals placed at the corners of the room. You have read where this was the way of lighting that was common in the city of Atlantis. In the middle of the room was a large wooden table with people sitting around it discussing ways to evacuate the city.

Before the second destruction of Atlantis, the atmosphere was hostile towards anyone who was not a member of one of the two main groups in the land. By this time, both groups, the one that followed the Law of One and the Sons of Belial, were fighting each other and anyone else who challenged their authority. Their practices had degraded to the vilest of ways. Terror ruled the once peaceful streets and people feared for their lives and that of their children. The only solution was to leave the country quickly.

The meeting of my dream was held in secret because discovery of their plans would have brought death to them all. The people dressed in heavy clothing was a problem for me since everything I was reading said that the temperature in Atlantis was tropical, but there was a part of the land that was close to what is now Greenland and the weather could be very cold there. So, I think that these people were in the northern part of Atlantis planning their escape from that area.

The question of the pair of eyes watching intently over the table is solved if you remember that the people of Atlantis could use their psychic abilities to observe plays and sporting events from a distance just by projecting their minds to that event. Obviously, the majority of the people concerned with this group's success were at a distance from the meeting and this was a way to get the information to the others faster than waiting for the delegates to get home. The part I played in this was that of an observer. I do not think I was alive at this time, but my concerns and my thoughts were still with those trying to get out of the city. In my dream, I knew I was just a spirit watching as no one paid any attention to me, nor do I think they knew I was there.

The message for me was to remember the training I had received in the temple as a priestess. I was to remember the sacrifices that many people had made to get the faithful out of the country and away from harm. This feeling of concern for those I knew and had left behind when I passed into Spirit was so deeply imbedded into my subconscious that centuries later it revealed itself again to me in a dream. My life as a priestess, and a teacher in the temple, was rewarding and beneficial as I was able to heal with crystals, sound, light, color. One of my greatest accomplishments was to assist many of the "things" by sedating them and surgically removing their animal appendages. Their healing was not only of their body but also of their mind as well. After their bodies were cleared of the animal appendages, they were taken into the Temple Beautiful to learn how to live in their new body and especially how to forgive those that had abused them. It was in Atlantis that I learned compassion for those less fortunate. I saw how an idea of racial superiority could result in one person inflicting pain on another just because of that misconception.

Many of the people living today lived in Atlantis. They chose to return to Earth and live in this tumultuous time of Earth's history to make sure that mankind does not make the same mistakes again. We remember what happened when the power of the atom was released and how it destroys our world and everything in it. This horror is a distant memory we hold of Atlantis, deep in our subconscious. It is the driving force of people in places of political power now speaking out to encourage reason and moderation in our dealings with each other and with the other countries of the world. Men and women of integrity are responsible for the future of our planet and our civilization. Life patterns are repeated over and over again. We need to learn from the past so as not to repeat our mistakes again. Civilizations come and go leaving no trace except in the memory of those who live in those times. We must awaken to the memory of what the Atlantic experience taught us and turn away from the ways of self-destruction. The Prince of Peace came many years ago to show us the way to live with love and concern for each other. We need to start applying his teachings to our present world.

Death is not the end to our existence only the end to the physical body which sheltered our spirit while we were living on Earth. Before birth, we make a plan as to what we want to accomplish in our next life. We are free to decide what our next step will be. From our soul family, we select the people who will be our parents, those who can provide the opportunities we need for the challenges we have chosen. We agree together that a certain environment would be provided for our growth and development. We select the people who will be meaningful in our life, the physical challenges if any, our race, gender, and global location, economic position, education, siblings if any are to interact with our life's plan, and our talents are planned giving us everything we will need to accomplish the soul's plan. Even if in one life souls aren't particularly fond of each other, in the next life they will still tend to be drawn together by the force of their past interaction. Since we will have a specific goal to accomplish, we will be looking for people and situations that will help us fulfill that goal. To anyone who has asked you why you had certain challenges in your life, or you wondered why your relationships kept turning out the same every time, the answer just might be there was a lesson to be learned. Lessons are repeated over and over until we finally "get it right!"

The answer becomes available if you can tap into your subconscious where all your past lives are stored. We are the sum total of all of our experiences. We bring into our life at birth all the lessons we have learned in previous lives as well as all the fears we have suppressed. Life is but a continuous circle of beginnings and endings. It starts new and with each birth a step closer to perfection. How we deal with the circumstances of our life puts us ahead or behind depending on the actions we took. Eventually, you reach a stage of development where you become a teacher or spirit guide for someone else. This is sometimes referred to as "ascension."

You are at the level of understanding now that you have earned through many lives of experiencing. You have learned what is right or wrong and then adjusted your thinking to that new "truth." When you accept that people and situations are in your life for the purpose to help you advance in wisdom of your soul's path, then those things or people that affect you should be carefully looked at to determine what the lesson is for you in that situation. You are an eternal soul living from one life experience to the next, gaining higher wisdom as an individual, and as a collective of divine energy. The Ego or "I" versus "We" mentality will lead our world.

In my life in Atlantis, I was happy and blessed as I was able to study in the temple, to learn the diversified subjects offered there. I was known for my extensive knowledge, application and beneficial outcome in the preparation of healing herbs, the aroma of flowers, scented oils, and the specific uses of the colored crystals. I learned about the stars and the ceremonies used for special occasions. I learned the many methods of the healing arts, and I was respected by all people. I am sure as the years went by, I became more experienced in this work, and I became a teacher for the new students, a mentor to many of them. I was very clairvoyant in those days. I could look at someone and know what herbs would benefit them. As a counselor, healer, and priestess of the healing temple, I offered counseling on any level of their life, and I was respected for my wisdom, compassion toward everyone. I gained greatly in this life.

I know there are more past lives that I have lived, with different scenarios and involving different situations, but the ones that I have remembered now came to me because of a strong impression that happened during that time. Learning about your past lives is like being a great detective. Your soul gives you clues to time and events and, if you are interested, you have to find out the rest through prayer, meditation, dreams and active participation in past life regressions. My subconscious has given me clues to different lives so that I could trace more information about them and find out what happened in that life that I needed to know now. These clues have come in the form of dreams as with Atlantis, or a vision seeing myself in another time and space. Sometimes it is an impression on certain things or places. A dream this time helped me find my life in Atlantis. When I saw pictures of the" things" in a book on Atlantis, I felt such a deep compassion for their situation that I knew I had been one who worked with them in the Temple of Sacrifices. I have always been interested in beautiful stones and in all their different colors. In the several books I have read about Atlantis, I found that these stones and crystals were used in the temple for healing. When we lived in Tucson, Arizona, I went to the gem show every year, which is held in February, and I would try to find different stone samples for my collection. If you are interested in this subject, you can read about stones and their healing properties in other available books on the property of different gems and their applications for healing.

We carry certain traits from lifetime to lifetime as a core part of who we are. One of the traits that I carried from my life in Atlantis is the desire to work in the healing profession, to be able to help others in pain and in mental distress. In this life, this desire resulted in my receiving an AA degree and a certificate as a Licensed Vocational Nurse in California. In the years my husband was in the Air Force, I worked in the hospital and military clinics of the different bases where my husband was stationed. Each time he was assigned to another base, I was able to work in the base hospital and also find a class in alternative medicine in the local area. I took classes in Tai Chi, the Chinese art of meditation and exercise. I found classes in color and crystal vibratory therapy. One of the most detailed was classes in Jin Shin Jyutsu, which is the art of releasing tension in the body using the natural energy meridians. It is an ancient Japanese healing discipline rediscovered by Master Jiro Murai in the early part of the twentieth century, and brought to the United States by one of his students by the name of Mary Burmeister in the 1950s. More information on this way of healing, also contact information, may be found in the Reference sections of this book. This furthered my interest in healing.

At one time, I attended a school for laboratory technicians thinking that was the place where I would find self-fulfilling work, but after I failed the state test for a license by one point on three different attempts, I knew that was not where I was supposed to be working. As the years went by, I was introduced to different alternative methods of healing. I learned to use the vibrational healing powers of my hands to help others. I have been told by many people, that when I work with them, my hands get hot and soothing to their skin, but I never feel the heat myself. I found that I can sense where another person has pain or discomfort and I can soothe that area with the touch of my hand. These are the gifts I hold from my life in Atlantis. I gained much from that life as I dedicated my life to helping those in need of my assistance.

Each of our incarnations is an opportunity to evolve to a higher perspective as an individual and as a part of the collective. Each life has a blueprint that expands and enhances our soul evolution. We take a part of each race, white, black, brown and yellow; we learn the challenges of each sex as we live as a man in one life and a woman in another. It depends on the lesson for that life. We plan the circumstances of our birth and death. We also plan situations that will help us correct the negativity we brought to ourselves by our own actions in the last lifetime.

CHAPTER TWO
3100 BCE Egyptian First Dynasty

"My command is this: Love each other as I have loved you."
John 15:13 N.I.R.V. Holy Bible

THE LAW OF ONE

Edgar Cayce tells us about those that followed the Law of One. They believed in the oneness of all living creatures. This made everyone equal without signaling out one or another as being more privileged more than the other, despite their apparent weakness or strengths. Each person was considered equally valuable from those of leadership to those who worked in the kitchens. They taught that the tools for a spiritual life was found in prayer, meditation and the application of what was found to be true through their practice.

In Edgar Cayce's Association for Research and Enlightenment (ARE) blog, we find information about The Law of One in one of Edgar Cayce's readings #254-42. The Law of One is based on living the Fruits of the Spirit; not just understanding but showing their wisdom in words and deeds which was reflected in their relationship to their fellow man. In another reading, we see that the people were reminded that the law was ideal for those who were seeking the presence of God. They were told that their thoughts and actions reflected their inner spirit and that it was also evident in the way they treated each other. They believed that when the people lived the rule of Spirit in their life and the knowledge their inner-self gained with daily service and sacrifice, God was acknowledged as being within each person and his love and mercy was shown through the actions of the individual. [1]

In the reading #1336-1, it is written that the people who followed the Law of One were told "as ye would have another be, that be thy self." Do not ask another to do that which you would not do yourself. Make concessions to the weak, but also defy the strong if they are wrong. For God will not be mocked and whatsoever a person sowed, that he must also reap. Only in the fruits of the Spirit those of long suffering, patience, mercy, brotherly kindness, and gentleness may the true meaning of life experiences and the purpose of life and the association with others, be understood. The Law of One was manifested in the man Jesus and signified in the Christ Consciousness. [2]

The followers of the Law of One took these concepts with them as they moved into other parts of the world after the destruction of Atlantis. With their resettlement, the words of this philosophy are now found in many of the ancient religions of the world.

EXODUS TO EGYPT

In those days, the climate in Egypt then was less dry than it is today, and there were large areas of marsh land where waterfowl could be found in abundance. Wild game was plentiful and this is probably the time when they began to domesticate animals. Egypt was a land green and lush due to the yearly overflow of water from the Nile. [6] There weren't many people living there until the groups from Atlantis began to settle the land and construct their own villages. Groups of people who followed The Law of One had entered Egypt during the many years of unrest in Atlantis. About two hundred years before the final destruction of their land, the leader and followers of The Gentle Way joined their countrymen in Egypt. The total number in this group was close to twenty-five thousand people composed of men, women and children who settled in the area not far from the mouth of the Nile River. Over the years, families would send their children from Atlantis to Egypt to live with relatives in Egypt until they too could join them. Then at the last minute, just before the final destruction of the continent, a few hundred more people arrived from Atlantis composed of those that followed the Law of One and the Sons of Belial. Since the country was not heavily populated at the time, all of the refugees from Atlantis were able to find land and built their villages. [3]

Over time, there was a slow but steady stream of people into Egypt from Atlantis. The priest of the Gentle Way brought from Atlantis his healing crystals bowls which had true magical properties when elevated through verbal chant and mental concentration. The priests brought their written records from their homeland to be used in the temple, and to be stored there for safety. The leaders from Atlantis had many long talks with the leaders of the Egyptian people concerning their experience in Atlantis and the technology they were willing to share with the people of Egypt. Not everything was given to the Egyptians as those from Atlantis were afraid that the same corruption would develop there as it had in the homeland. At the time of the final destruction of the land, many people were arriving in Egypt with just the clothes on their back. [4] There was close communication from the people still in Atlantis to those who had settled elsewhere; they knew the challenges they would face. Their mode of transportation was varied, as some went by air and some went by ground. There was great sadness in having to leave the wonders of Atlantis, but with the social unrest, the constant earthquakes, and the irrational behavior of the priests, leaving the area was the only way of safety for everyone. [5]

PRE-HISTORY OF EGYPT

The history of ancient Egypt is the story of a series of stable kingdoms followed by periods of relatively unstable kingdoms until the unifying of the Upper and Lower Egypt under the first Pharaoh by the name of Menes in 3150 BCE. Egypt is divided into three distinct periods: The Old Kingdom of the Early Bronze Age, the Middle Kingdom of the Bronze Age, and the New Kingdom of the Late Bronze Age. Egypt reached the highest period of culture during the New Kingdom; after that, it entered a slow decline with invasions by a succession of foreign powers. [6]

The story of Ra-Ta starts many years before Egypt's kingdom unification. The story of this period of ancient Egypt comes to us from several books with one being the readings given by Edgar Cayce, the sleeping prophet of Virginia Beach. For those of you who read my other book, *The Shadow Child*, you will remember the story of Edgar Cayce and his ability to diagnose ailments and prescribe remedies while in a deep trance. Edgar Cayce asked about his own past lives and learned that in one of his lives he had been an Egyptian priest by the name of Ra-Ta.

Edgar Cayce tells the story that in the years before the people from Atlantis arrived in Egypt, the land was under the rule of a man named Raai. The king's son by the name of Arart, from a neighboring country, invaded the country of Egypt with nine hundred followers. The king of Egypt at that time was old and infirmed and did not resist the invaders. With the change in leadership, there was a major change in the government. Political power shifted to those followers of Arart. There was unrest among those of authority and the native nobility revolted, setting up another kingdom at the southern part of Egypt.

Arart realized that the situation would be corrected if he adopted a well-respected native sage by the name of Ra-Ta and placed his son and Ra-Ta as co-rulers of the land. Each of the officials of government had a place in the council with Ra-Ta acting as a chief advisor. This made assignments to the council according to the person's ability instead of their nationality. The priest Ra-Ta introduced the ways of the Law of One to the Egyptian people. He showed them the satisfaction of working together to build a nation of people dedicated to truth and love for each other, but there were those who were envious of his power over the people, and they devised a plan to get rid of him.

The son of Arart devised a plot to get rid of Ra-Ta and seize power. One of the new laws enacted by Ra-Ta stated that each man could have only one wife. The instigators of the plot convinced Ra-Ta that he was the most genetically perfect man alive and that he should ignore his first wife and family and mate with an equally perfect woman. Ra-Ta listened to their scam and mated with Isris a temple dancer, who gave birth to a child. With the evidence of the child's birth, those who plotted against Ra-Ta had proof that he violated his own laws, and brought him to court demanding the death penalty. The judge decided banishment was more fitting for the case and so Ra-Ta left the country surrounded by two hundred and thirty one followers, traveling through Libya, Abyssinia and Nubia in search of a place to settle. Finally, the princess of Nubia granted them asylum in her country. There was resistance to the new people at first, but the people finally accepted the new immigrants when they realized the benefit the council of Ra-Ta was giving to their princess was for the country. The praise of the people for their new counselor spread throughout the land.

The kingdom in Egypt was still in turmoil. During this time, even with the banishment of Ra-Ta and his followers, the people demanded that Ra-Ta be brought back to the palace and resume his work there. To add to this turmoil, there was a large influx of people from Atlantis who were there because of the war in their homeland. The stories of success and the increase of prosperity in Nubia, due to the efforts of Ra-Ta, were brought to Egypt resulting in Ra-Ta being recalled back to the palace. With all obstacles removed, Ra-Ta and his wife Isris were able to rule over a tranquil country that was again united in a spiritual purpose. [7]

There began great development in Egypt with small permanent villages where before there had been only a gathering of people in tents. People felt the calming of the tension in the land and there was a growing prosperity for everyone. Egypt became known for its achievements in scientific, cultural, as well as a spiritual center. The Atlanteans contributed much to the culture and scientific advancement, and they aided in the planning of the Great Pyramid.

The great teachers of the world were called into Egypt to learn the teachings of the Law of One. They unified all the teachings of the world with their study in Egypt, then they took this new understanding back to their home country. With the help of their students they spread their new message to the world, that of brotherly love and consideration for others. [8]

THE CAT PEOPLE

All through my life I have always loved cats and I seem to be able to talk to them not in words but in different tones of sound that they understand. I remember when we lived in Italy every house seemed to have a cat sitting in the yard or on the front steps. I would walk down the street and make cat sounds to each cat and they would always talk back to me. Cats are very psychic people. They choose to live with you or if they are uncomfortable there, they find their own home. One day my Italian landlady had a visit from a friend of hers who brought her young Siamese cat with her. I lived on the second floor of the building, and when I saw this small kitten in the hall, of course I had to pick it up and love it. A few weeks went by and one afternoon I heard a scratching on the door. When I opened the door, there was the Siamese kitten that had come to visit me. Her owner was not in sight! I had a grey cat of my own and the two cats seemed to be friends. The visitor had some food and curled up with my cat for a nap. Later that afternoon, he wanted to go out so I opened the door and saw him jump down the stairs to the front door. This went on for a few months until one day my land lady stopped me in the hall and started talking about the cat. Apparently, her friend lived several streets over from our building. In between our house and the friend's house were two streets that carried heavy traffic into the center of town. My land lady asked me what I had done to the cat to make him come to see me on his own. I said all I did was feed and love him a little. Maybe he came to see my cat. She said, that her friend had penned up the cat so he could not get out of the yard. She was afraid he would get killed crossing those two streets coming to see me. I had no idea he had such a long trip and across such dangerous streets. I never saw him again. I missed my visits with the Siamese, but I would rather he be safe at home.

Dolores Cannon tells an interesting story about the Cat people of Egypt in her second book of the series *Convoluted Universe*. This is the only story I have read on this subject and because it again strikes a distant memory in my mind, I want to share it with you, Dolores was a hypnotherapist who specialized in working with people who had a concern in their life, and the answer happened to be found in one of their past lives. The story goes that Delores was in Kansas City, Missouri, at a unity Church Convention in 2001. She had a client that asked for her help. After her hypnotic induction, the lady found herself looking at the pyramids in ancient Egypt.

The lady starting talking about a large gold statue of a cat. She said she works with Pharaoh in this special temple. She sees herself as a Priestess dressed in white flowing robes. She wears an elaborate gold band with gems that twists around one of her arms and extends down to her fingers. On her head is an elaborate headdress made out of gold with gems around the head, and the headdress extended to her shoulders. People come into the temple for healing. The gold she wore was not for adornment but for protection for the people she healed. The healing energy came from a powerful crystal that was brought to Egypt from Atlantis. The crystal was located in the back part of the temple where only the priestess could go. The power was transferred from the crystal to the priestess. The gold she wore protects whoever she was healing so that they could accept the light of healing, yet the gold shielded and filtered the power to a fraction of the full potential force of the power. The priestesses that worked in the temple were found as children to have the gift of healing. Their parents recognized the gift and brought them to the temple for training. They were taught the ways of handling the power and how to shield others from its potential death ray.

The temple was located on a hill in view of the pyramids. The Priestesses of the temple were called "cat people" because they had their temple cats and their golden ones. The golden cats were for people who were unable to come to the temple. The priestess would talk to the cat and tell them the person they were to go to see. If the cat was successful, the person would hold the cat and receive the healing energy sent to them by the priestess. When they returned to the temple, the cat would tell the priestess what they saw and what happened on the trip.

The people thought that it was the gold that the priestess wore that healed them. They started making little gold statues of cats and thought that the temple was unnecessary. The temple had to be destroyed because the people relied on the gold for healing, instead of the power the priestess projected. To honor the Cat People, the Sphinx was built in its place. It originally had a woman's face on a cat body, but was later changed.

When asked about a hidden room with records in the Sphinx, the lady said that some of the information about the temple, and the priestesses' healing techniques, was written and stored under the front right paw of the Sphinx in a special record room. [9]

EGYPTIAN MYSTERY SCHOOL

There were many Mystery Schools that taught the immortality of the human soul. Their work was the sacrifice of human regeneration. One of the greatest Mystery Schools was in Egypt at Giza. [10] They taught the mystery of the immortal soul and the science of human regeneration. The school was operated in accordance to both natural and universal laws. There were several schools known to exist in antiquity including those in Yucatan. The ancient Egyptians themselves believed that gods had walked with man in the early days of creation. Their priests were considered descendants of these people of the stars, and thus had powers beyond the normal man. The advanced mental powers of the priests from Atlantis only confirmed this assumption as their abilities were beyond what any Egyptian had ever experienced.

The initiates or the neophyte came into the school from all the surrounding countries. They learned the chants and ceremonies for each stage of their training. The mystic concept of life was that there were two ways of growing in knowledge: one was by slowly learning through cause and effect over hundreds of lifetimes, where in the living the world became the teacher of the truths in initiation. The second way was by passing through death by conscious intent and become purified, experiencing the entire cycle of life, death, and resurrection in the temple. This was not considered a shortcut, but the intensifying of the natural progression of human generation. [11]

The temple of Sacrifice and the Temple of Beauty were established in Egypt as they had been in Atlantis. Here they carried on the work of healing to the people who still carried in their bodies the animal contaminations. The training of those that chose to become priests and priestesses in the temple was strenuous. The candidates came from all over the country, but only a few were chosen, only those who were felt to have a real desire for knowledge of the spiritual. Students came from many different nations and they were prepared to take their knowledge back to their own countries to establish a temple there as well. Men and women were considered equals and both were considered for the temple as there was no preference for the male as it is now.

The first stage was in the Temple of Sacrifice where cleansing and purification was the focus. The altars were prepared with the acknowledged faults of the aspiring priest and priestess. The altar offerings were consumed by the fire of the Spirit and the commitment of the neophyte to follow the teaching of the temple to their best ability. These altars were never used to sacrifice animals or birds. This temple was built for those who looked for spiritual and physical healing. Within its walls could be found areas for surgery, rooms for massage, and rooms for healing with herbs, scented flowers and heated baths.

In the Temple Beautiful, each novice wore a long green robe reaching to the ground. The robe had long flowing sleeves with the robe held close in front with a gold clip. All other candidates for priesthood wore robes in pastel colors of many of different shades. Only the more advanced wore a white robe, setting them apart from the others. Those that wore white showed their degree of study with a band around their head of different type of metal with each metal designating their specialty. This temple was dedicated to those who searched for a higher meaning of life and wished to devote their life towards their soul development and service to humans and to God. These programs were open to everyone no matter where they worked; they were considered equally manifesting their ultimate potential. According to Edgar Cayce's reading for #294-149, the purpose of the temple was:

"That there might be a closer relationship of individuals to the Creator and a better relationship of individuals with one another" [12]

PREPARATION FOR INITIATION

Only those neophytes who were considered exceptional in their studies were considered for initiation. The training for the final initiation for all of the priests and priestesses of the temple was long and over many years. At each new phase of the course the student was tested as to their ability to perform the given assignment. Each phase having been more and more complex and required more concentration and perfection in execution than the last. Many of the neophytes did not make the final test. They were given the title of the last degree they attained and were not allowed to proceed any further. Usually these former initiates would set up their own school in other countries to prepare future qualified initiates. There were several of these schools known throughout the ancient world, which spread their influence to areas as far away as China, Tibet, and India. The study in the Mystery School was not from theory but from experience. They taught the methodology to access the infinite with direct experience with God himself.

The neophytes who passed their preparatory examinations received new, progressively more difficult tasks and assignments to train to **enhance their natural physical abilities.** The training was not only of the mind but of the body as well with daily exercises as a required part of the program. The first lesson was on how to control the breath. On inhalation, you are drawing yourself away from the body until the next breath. The interim between breaths causes you to experience something similar to death of the body when you withdraw yourself from it, and your body exhales for the last time. With the intake of air in your next breath, you bring into your body the gift of life which is the air around you. When you are able to control your breath, you will be able to center your mind and thoughts easily and maintain a more deeply, contemplative nature in your studies. A life of peace and unity with the universe starts with the control of self. First, the awareness of the physical body and how to consciously control it. Little by little the neophyte learns how to **identify all their internal organs**. They learned how to control their heart rate as well as their breathing. They learned that there is a point at the tip of the heart that controlled the electrical impulses to the heart, and by concentrating on this area the heart could be controlled to a slower beat. The neophyte learned how to not only control their heart beat but also to control the amount of air required in their lungs for life.

The training of the mind and soul started with work in **visualization** and of the **controlling of their emotional states,** both aspects of positive and negative. The neophyte was taught to experience both of these states and to experience them as if they were real instead of a lesson. The next step was to experience each emotion on command, starting at the lowest negative condition and moving up step by step to the highest possible condition. For example, to start with the emotion of dejection followed by indifference followed by joy and onto the extreme state of happiness. They practiced a fast change from one to the next. It took time to experience each emotion as if they were events in their lives. This exercise was completed when the neophyte was able to experience the shift from one emotion to another without hesitation.

There are many **levels of consciousness** from the basic level of the unconscious: the plant which looks for food and sunshine to grow and survive, the animals that seek food and exhibit feelings of emotion, and instinctual habits, to man who stands one degree above the animal. He has intellect, the ability to reason and make decisions at the same time as all the other degrees of consciousness as shown by the lower creations. The highest degree of man is one who has the ability to lift his consciousness out of the world of affect and into the causal world. He can see the larger picture of the situation and is able to express it in words to his fellow man. This man is conscious to a higher level. He is in touch with the plan of divine wisdom and universal love. The highest level and the last, most perfect manifestation of man is that of the God-man presence who experiences and radiates the divine creative force, and is awake in all other levels of vibrational manifestations.

The neophyte is told that they must learn to **control the twelve sets of opposites** as there are people in the world who are slaves of their bodies and they will try to use their influence over them. The twelve are as simple as keeping quiet or talking, obeying the rules or be a rule unto yourself vs. obeying set rules. The personal opposites of humility vs. self-conceit, or the ability to practice discernment, as to what is a true statement vs. accepting everything no matter what as truth. The opposite of peace to fight or to possess nothing vs. having everything at your command. A person who is loyal is valued over one who has no ties to anything and a person who is indifferent or holds contempt for death is considered a risk taker vs. the person who has a regard for life and has a loving nature towards others. All of these are the opposites we face in our lives. There are no bad characteristics, no bad forces only those wrongly used and wrongly applied forces. [13]

The practice of **telepathy** was another subject taught to the neophytes of the temple school. They were taught to first practice in front of the person they wanted to reach telepathically, and that person would try to receive their thoughts. With practice, one can activate the nerve centers of the brain. This is especially true during sleep as those nerve brain centers that are at rest during the day, are then activated to receive and conduct the vibrations of the Spirit. Then, as the neophyte continues to progress with the exercise the next step was to repeat the exercise at a distance, at an agreed time and place. After many different successful sessions, the third part of the exercise was to create a telepathic connection without the other person knowing when or where you would send it. Eventually, telepathic messages sent and received would become automatic without the thought about place or conditions of the transmission. Each degree of knowledge was taught to the neophyte by a teacher who had completed the mastery of the subject, and wore the white robe as benefited a person of knowledge. [14]

How to attain the state of **intense concentration** was taught, which is the transition between the projected world and themselves. There are three phases of concentration: intellectual, emotional, and spiritual. You identify the object of your concentration with your intellect. You use all your thinking and feelings to visualize the place, person or thing you are concentrating on. The third phase is when you can identify with that object of concentration. When you are able to lift yourself out of your body and out of your personal being to join the all-inclusive cosmic consciousness, you will have moved out of the world of cause and effect and into the realm of the eternal, out of the realm of death into that of life, and that is initiation.

IMAGINATION-VISUALIZATION

I will tell you a story from my childhood that will illustrate what I am saying about imagination, visualization, and concentration. My grandmother did not bake cakes or cookies for me at home. In fact, I got few sweet treats of any kind, which makes the story all the more interesting. My grandfather was the minister in one small town in Virginia and he also had another church about an hour's drive from our home. This church was in the middle of a large forest of pine trees and the people who came to it were farmers of the land surrounding the church. The ladies of the church decided that they would provide lunch for the minister and his family on the Sundays that he came to their church. So, once a month we would go to the church in the forest and have lunch after church with one of the families of the church. I will talk more about this later on, but for now I want to tell you about one of the farms we visited. It was a dairy farm run by a husband, his wife and the wife's brother. The farmer's wife had a special room off the kitchen that she used to store extra kitchen supplies. Somehow it was always cool in that room even in the hot summertime.

The attraction for me in this special pantry was what was stored inside it. When I got a glimpse inside of this wonderful closet, I saw that there were two or three different cakes displayed on one shelf. There was usually a chocolate three-layer cake with the heavy chocolate icing that a child could go crazy over, and there was a white or spice cake under heavy white icing. My mouth would water just looking at them. When we were served a piece of the chocolate cake for dessert, for me it was beyond wonderful!

During the following weeks after the dinner, I would wish I could have another piece of that cake. I started to imagine the pantry and saw myself opening the door to its forbidden delicacies. As time went on, I could visualize the door and handle. I could see myself opening the door and see the cakes. It took me a little longer to be able to not only see the chocolate cake on the shelf but see my finger touch the fudge frosting and put it in my mouth. I could actually taste the chocolate and enjoyed my bit of sweetness. This is a good example of visualization. To be able to be so involved in the subject you are experiencing, and it became real in your world.

Another lesson was the ability to **control emotions**. First, the neophyte had to learn how to recognize certain emotions and their opposites. They learned how to recognize these emotions in others and the possible reasons behind them. Those people who are self-seeking and materialistic will try to influence the seeker of truth with the idea that the only thing of value is that which can be seen. Therefore, the lesson of emotions and opposites was very important. Some of these emotions are easily recognized as a person who is receptive to new ideas as opposed to the person who is closed to any new information. The person who is seen as loyal to a certain cause and one who has no time to champion any cause, or someone who has contempt for life vs. a person who regards all life as precious. There are no bad characteristics only wrongly used characteristics and a wrongly applied focus!

The higher man learns to climb away from materialistic thoughts and desires, the closer he will bring peace to the world. Little by little, the passion for conquest and power will decline and instead of trying to fight each other, the people of the world will use their abilities to harness the forces of nature for the advantage and betterment of everyone. [15]

THE CENTERS OF POWER

After years of preparation, the time of initiation was offered to the neophyte. This was the final phase of their training for a priest or priestess. If the neophyte had mastered the necessary lessons that were required for initiation, they were prepared for the final test. In initiation, the candidate becomes conscious of every plane of consciousness, and they are able to consciously awaken each of the seven-energy centers of their body.

These seven energy centers are contained as part of the spinal nerve, which is incased within the spinal column. Along the spinal nerve is a series of special nerve centers with nerves going out to each part of the body. These centers are known by many names, but the name of **Chakra** as given by ancient people of India is used today. This name Chakra has come to the west to describe these spinning centers of energy. Each Chakra gives off a certain vibration or frequency as well as a color. The totality of all the vibrations blended to form one unique frequency designated to that person alone. The nerve centers are distributed throughout the body sending out electrical signals to every cell of the body. The base of the spine is where the first Chakra is found. It is visualized as the seat for the release or retention of energy and is found around the organs of elimination. For those who can see vibrational colors around other people, the color russet is perceived. When this area is activated, we receive the ability to let go thoughts, feelings, and beliefs that are no longer useful in life. Undeveloped ability of elimination is demonstrated by people who are hoarders. They hold onto everything, even useless or broken things. The opposite of this is someone who has an overdeveloped first Chakra, which can be seen in one who denies ideas and beliefs before they really understand it. It is important to clear the area of all misconceptions in order to be receptive towards new concepts.

The next area up the spinal column is reproduction which is life and carries the natural process of our being able to give energy to an idea or process. It is needed by all the other powers before they can be expressed in the individual. When this area is awakened spiritually, we awaken all other power centers including life itself. Those people that can see the energy vibrations of others see this area in the color red. Life is undeveloped in people who have little or no energy for daily life. These people have a disregard for their own wellbeing and find themselves experiencing one illness after another or a continuation of feeling "not well." Life is overdeveloped in people who are restless, nervous and apprehensive about everything in their life. They are constantly looking for a place where their energy can be used so that they can feel fulfilled. Without finding such an outlet for their abundance of energy, they experience "panic attacks," expressing their inability to control the situation. [16]

The Solar Plexus, or the navel area, is the place of order and self-identification. It is the area activated when we have a decision to make. If we go by the feelings of our gut when there is a situation in front of us that needs to be resolved, we will always make the right decision. Someone with a blocked third power area will show symptoms of chronic fatigue, digestive troubles, and hypertension. Order keeps us close to the harmony of our spiritual wholeness by alerting us if the action we are about to take is against our best interests. We use order to adjust and organize our thoughts, feeling and actions to remain in tune with to our true self objectives. The color here is seen as yellow.

The fourth power source is found around the heart. The primary difference between the third and fourth power center is self-awareness. When this area is free and open, we release love toward others and acceptance of them in whatever their situation might be. Forgiveness toward someone who we perceived has wronged us in some way is the challenge of every age. Forgiveness and prejudice are two barriers against the free expression of love. The discovery of the divine within every person is the expression of divine love within us. Another aspect of love is the ability to attract to ourselves something we desire, need, or feel we need, for complete happiness. Love's vibrations can be either positive or negative depending on the ability to see it before them and how it is applied. [17]

The primary difference between the third and fourth chakras is one of awareness. The throat is the fifth power center. From our mouth comes power in words and tones that can either harm someone else or heal that person. Words are so powerful when used, without any thought behind them, their power can be devastating to another person, especially a child or a person who is vulnerable and has not formed a strong self-concept for themselves. Sound was used to levitate huge stone blocks used to build the great pyramid. Sound was used in the Healing Temple. There were different tones or pitches that could render a person unconscious or even kill with the right combination of sounds. The color for the throat is bright blue. [18]

I have read where the ancient Siddhars of India were said to have many powers which included manipulating matter at the molecular level, just as the priests of Atlantic could do. They used the sound of their voice to create a vibrational conduit for the construction of desired objects out of the air around them.

The six-power area is found in the middle of the forehead. It is the seat of imagination that is the ability to visualize and mentally see a project completed. The person with an undeveloped imagination is unable to complete anything unless it is visibly before them. The other extreme is a person where they use their imagination to remove themselves from daily life, so that nothing is accomplished. My grandfather would say that a person could be so "heavenly minded that they were no Earthly good!"

We visualize what we want in our life with imagination locked with faith, wisdom and understanding. With our will we initiate our visualization to bring about that what we desire. The power of wisdom is used when we wisely choose that which will be a positive experience for us. This color can be seen as a dark blue or indigo.

Tom Moore, in his book "The Gentle Way," explains the gift of asking for a "Most Benevolent Outcome" from our guardian angels. This is a prayer for assistance from your guardian angel. It must be for something you want to happen. It will only work if what you ask is for the good of everyone concerned. You are asking for the most beneficial outcome for a situation in a positive way, and then be sure to say thank you after the request. I always ask for a "Most Beneficial Outcome" for my daughter when she goes to work, that she will travel in protection and safety and return home in safety and protection as well. Since her travel to and from her work area is by driving on a very busy freeway, and there are so many ways harm could come to her from mechanical problems with the car, to some interference from another driver. I always feel she is angelically protected with this prayer. [19]

The seventh and crown power source rests on the top of our head. When we reach this level, we have reached the level of enlightenment. This is the state of ultimate consciousness. We have achieved a state that is beyond reason, beyond senses, and beyond the limits of the world. The seventh power source relates to what we experience as mind. It relates to the higher part of our brain as an instrument of awareness where we receive and assimilate most of our knowledge.

The lower power sources relate to the physical world and the cycles of cause and effect. In the seventh, we touch cosmic consciousness by the union with our true self, that part of man that can reach far into the infinite source of all knowledge. With the uniting and opening of all the lower power sources we are freed from the cause and effect of the world and unite with the cosmic world of unlimited space and time. The color surrounding the head is seen as white. The painters of the Middle Ages in painting their portraits of saints indicated the presence of this higher awareness, with a white ring around the head of the saints they were painting.

When an initiate becomes conscious in one power area they are completely in tune with this area and it is their reality. After they pass the test of that level and move into a higher vibratory position, they realize that what they thought was true was only a dream on the level below. But if they identify with that level of power and if they are unable to pass the test and advance to the next level, then all the dreams of that lower reality become true for them. They must experience them in the world of time and space. That means that on the death of their body, they would have to return to the Karmic wheel and learn the lessons through countless reincarnations. If in initiation experience, you have passed all the tests for each level, and you have experienced each level in a dream and awaken on the next level of consciousness. In the cosmic consciousness of self, you have then been successful in raising yourself up to the seventh level; you become one with the highest and only reality of self. If you have reached this place of attainment and you are able to maintain that level, then you are worthy of being a high priestess in the temple. [20]

This is the meaning of initiation. It is the progression through each level of conscious awareness of the body and mind. To succeed is to be free of the law of action and reaction, but to fail is to create a new wheel for yourself and it will take many lifetimes' opportunities to return to the seventh level. A neophyte must be very sure that they want to enter this supreme test and must signify their understanding of the consequences also their willingness to continue by asking for initiation three times.

The day before the initiation, the candidate maintains a fast and only takes sips of water throughout the day. They clean their body and dress in a new robe for the ceremony. As the sun starts to dip below the horizon, the procession starts out from the palace to the great pyramid. There are several servants with torches and the high priest who leads the candidate for initiation into the long dark halls of the pyramid and down into the lowest area at the base of the pyramid. The room is barren except a sarcophagus in the middle of the room. The candidate is asked again for the last time if they still want initiation. With a positive answer, the candidate is helped into the sarcophagus and then they lie down. The stone cover is lifted over the top and total darkness is within the stone coffin. There is no sound only the beating of their heart.

This is the time when the years of practice in heart and lung control comes into use. The darkness is so intense that it is impossible to see your hand in front of your face, and the candidate feels the absolute confinement of their body within the sarcophagus. This is the time for reflection and practice of all the years of training that led up to this point in time. The initiate will remain in this confinement for three days when the fourth day will bring the release into the world of man again.

In initiation, the candidate becomes conscious of every plan of creation. The union of the unconscious and conscious mind takes place. With this union, the initiate must experience the seven power sources in the body. The first is found by descending to the lowest point of creation and experiencing a situation that typifies that level of awareness. By conquering the first level successfully, they move up to the next level of vibration and experience it to master that level. After the second power source, has been successfully conquered, the third through seventh are presented and the process continues. With the successful mastery of all levels, the initiate awakes on the seventh level of cosmic consciousness of self. At this point the initiate has completed the experience and reached the cosmic consciousness. This is no longer an awakening, but a personal resurrection! [21]

There are those initiates that cannot complete the seven steps and end their time in the sarcophagus with the unconquered level of one of the power sources. It is possible that the initiate had not experienced all the necessary Earthly situations before initiation for them to control the emotional content of that situation needed to pass that one area. One such situation would be that the initiate had not experienced the powerful urges of the basic power source: that which controls the sexual and life area of the body. In the initiate's dream, the presentation of a situation where the choice would be offered to take the pleasure of a sexual situation where the effects would be detrimental to the person was irresistible, where a more experienced person would have been able to turn away from the offer.

With the initiate unable to complete the complete initiation ceremony, they were released from their commitment to the high priest or priestess position and given the degree that they had obtained up to that time. The initiate would go back to the temple and be given some work that would capitalize on the abilities they had obtained while in training for their initiation. Their life would be one of service in many different ways and when the day came for them to cross over from the world of man to that of spirit, the realization would come to them that what they dreamed in the ceremony of initiation they would have to experience in many lives on the wheel of Karma. Their plan for the completion of their initiate would be stretched over time to the point when all had been completed, and they would be free to completely enjoy the fruits of their commitment and their efforts toward a unity with the infinite. [22]

DEVICES USED IN THE TEMPLE

The head priest of the temple had different energy devices. One was a tall staff made of a type of brass that sent out a high vibrational frequency of sound. It could be set at a high level where it would dematerialize anything it was directed towards. It could be set at a lower frequency where it could heal using the energy stream. The device could hold energy in its unchanged form for long periods of time. It was kept secret because if a person with a low vibrational nature would touch the staff, he would fall over dead—the same as struck by lightning. It was hidden behind a massive rock wall that provided insolation against its radiation.

In the time to come, the instruments for radiation, along with the last initiated Pharaoh and his deputies, will close the entrance of the great pyramid from the inside so that no one will be able to find it. They will dematerialize their own bodies leaving no trace of their existence. In this way, the power will be kept from the ignorant people who will search and destroy the pyramid. [23]

HEALING OFFERED

The healing temple of Egypt was open to everyone, given freely by the priestesses, and classes were offered to those who wished to join the priesthood. They used the rays of the sun through colored gems to promote healing. There were chants and special herbs used as well. In the book *Hidden Sacred Knowledge* by Dolores Cannon, she writes about a lady under hypnosis who describes healing by placing her hand on a device that would focus energy to a given spot. [10]

In 1978, Edgar Cayce's son Hugh Lynn Cayce brought a team of his associates from Virginia Beach to Colorado Springs where I was living at the time. There was a conference offered in a church camp hidden in the tall pine trees of a place called the "Black Forest." The theme for the conference was "Expectations for the Future."

The program started with a meditation each day, then a lesson followed by group discussion. We were to split into groups of twenty. There were approximately a hundred attendees at the conference. Each day we were given a different subject to talk about in our groups. On the last day of the conference, the meditation was to focus on our future and ourselves, what we would be doing. We were to report to our groups what if anything we saw.

I thought that it was an impossible task! The person who started the meditation told us to visualize ourselves in a quiet place and remain there in peace and relaxation. I visualized my grandfather's rose garden. His avocation was horticulture and he had silver cups from the American Rose Society for his prize-winning roses. I stood in the middle of his garden among the hundreds of rose bushes in the garden. The many colors and shades of those colors represented by the different rose bushes all around me. We were told, that when we were ready, to go into the future and see ourselves there,

One moment I was smelling the roses and the next minute I saw myself, not as I would have consciously chosen to be, but as a tall thin woman around twenty years old with black hair severely cut short straight by the ears. I was dressed in black pants and a white blouse with a long lab coat over it all. I seemed to be in charge of a room in a clinic.

My future self was standing in a small room that looked like a control center for some mechanical instrument. The wall to my right was filled with dials behind glass inserts in the white wall. In front of me was a large picture window where I could see a lady lying on a bed, on the other side of the window. The door to the room was on my left; directly in front of me was a desk extending across the bottom of the window. This desk had a raised box with a pad on top that looked to me like a baseball mitt. I would ask the lady questions and she would answer me. The lady did not seem to be in any discomfort and laughed ever so often at something I said to her. As the lady answered my questions, I moved my left hand on the mitt and then reached to my right towards the dials and changed one or the other to a different setting.

When I was finished, the lady got up and walked out of the room. I went out of the room as well going into a hallway where I saw many people all dressed as I was, walking up and down the hall or talking to another person. It seemed to be a very busy clinic.

I asked Spirit what I was looking at and what was I doing? The answer was that I was in a medical clinic, and I was a medical technician. In the room where I was working were tools for healing. When I put my left hand on the pad, I was psychically scanning the lady's body for any disease elements in any of her cells. If anything was detected, I used the dials on the right wall to direct an electronic charge to the specific cell and kill it. I was told that this technique was very common and that I was a highly skilled technician in the hospital.

When I reported this vision to my group later on and described what I had seen, one of the men in the group said he had seen a porotype of that machine in Virginia Beach. He told me that there was a doctor there working with light and sound treating autistic children, and that he had a high rate of success with the children. He gave me the doctor's name and I said I would be sure to look him up if I ever got to Virginia Beach.

A few months after the conference, I had a dream of walking through a house made of glass, and then it all broke into fragments around me. In time, my husband was given new orders from the Air Force for us to move from Colorado to Virginia. The dream made sense to me if you think of the phrase "breaking up housekeeping" when referring to moving, then the dream was a very graphic description of future events!

When we were settled in Virginia, I made it a point to go to Virginia Beach and look up the doctor I had heard about in Colorado, I found him and after explaining to him why I was interested in his invention, he invited me into his home and showed me his work. The instrument looked like a large light box with lights with a humming sound. The doctor said different children required different light frequencies and sound before they would respond; they needed many sessions with this instrument before there was any visible improvement, but once the improvement was seen, it was very dramatic!

The doctor was very excited that I had seen a machine like his in the future, but on a much larger scale. He told me that the American Medical Association (AMA) was trying to shut him down and take away his license. We corresponded for a few years, then I was sent a newspaper clipping showing that he had been censored by the AMA and could no longer practice under the direction of the association. I lost contact with him after that.

SELF HYPNOSIS

In March 2011, I attended a class on past life regressions at the church in Tucson. There were about twenty people in the class. The induction into trance was given. We were told that there was before us a hall with many doors on either side of the hall. We could choose which door to open. I opened the third door on my right, and found myself in a land that seemed to be nothing but miles of sand and hills. I saw myself as a young girl, nine or ten-years-old, and I was going to be a student learning the healing methods in the temple. I was walking with my mother to a large stone building where there was a small door in front of me. I knew that this was the temple of healing. I was a bit reluctant to enter, but at the door there was a lady with long dark hair dressed in a flowing robe who assured me that I would be all right, and to follow her. She showed me the way from the doorway down the stairs that ended in a lower room in the building. The light in the room was dim, but I could see that there were other people there working with something. I asked Spirit why was I shown this event and I was told by a familiar female voice by my right shoulder, "Remember who you are!"

In the class, there was a lady sitting across from me, who I had never seen before, but she looked very familiar. As students came out of trance, we were encouraged to talk about what we had seen. Suddenly, I knew she was the lady who I had just seen in Egypt, leading me into the temple. Her name was Denise in this lifetime. She said she had also seen me in her past life experience. She said that she had been a frontier woman in the western United States. Her home had been destroyed by fire from an Indian raid and her family killed. She had escaped the fire and had walked to the nearby town. She spoke to a lady at the general store asking her for a job. The lady had been gracious with her and not only gave her a job, in the store, but also a place to live in her home. Denise looked at me and said "You were that woman." I have no memory of that lifetime.

MY EGYPTIAN EXPERIENCE

Up until the year, 2016, I have not been able to look at anything or read anything about Egypt. Just looking at an Egyptian picture I would become fearful with nausea and headache. Something traumatic happened in my life in Egypt so severe that the fear and shame of it has stayed with me all these centuries. I knew I had lived in Atlantis because of the dream when I was a child. Recently, I came across pictures of the "things" from Atlantis and I felt a deep compassion for their situation, I know I worked with them in Egypt, helping to remove the horns, tails and other animal appendages from their body. Partially why I am writing this book is to help clear this situation from my subconscious, and to discover what it was I did and how I paid for the karma that I incurred then. After the story is told and understood, I can then release the painful memory once and for all.

In this lifetime, a long and complicated story was started, one I did not have a clue existed until I met my husband in this lifetime. When Len had his past life regression in Tucson, after we came home from Italy and he remembered he had been the Duke of Urbino, he also said that we had been in Egypt and in many other lifetimes together. I do not know just how we met or what influence we had on each other, but apparently it was strong enough to last for centuries, and since I have carried such an aversion to anything Egyptian, it only stands to reason this association at that time was not a good one.

Looking at my past lives as I have remembered bits and pieces of them, I can see where there were certain central themes in each one. As I understand the law of Karma, I can look back and see what I replayed and so deduce from that what were my attitudes and actions that might have caused the need for repayment.

KARMA TO REPAY

It is so easy to just deny any wrongdoing on my part for anything that happened in my time in Egypt, but that would not explain my feelings for the area or for the past feeling of dread of anything Egyptian. When dealing with the negative events of a past life, the first step is to recognize that we attract to us events that will set up a situation where we will have to face whatever it is we are running away from. Reviewing other lives through the ages I see where I have blamed others for my shortcomings. This type of denial could include repression of my true feelings, blaming someone else for the problem, anger for my situation and being constantly defensive when another person approached me, as being a threat to expose any negative situations hidden from my consciousness.

Another sign that there is a Karmic issue is when you see a certain scenario happen over and over again in your life. The pattern emerges with different people, different places, and year, but the basic situation is the same. I had a friend who seemed to be attracted to the same characteristics in a man each time she met someone new. The man was always wonderful to her in the beginning, treating her with respect and fulfilling all the attributes she considered in a man for a husband, but then as the time went by those same attributes started to annoy her and she eventually found out that his life was not what he had portrayed to her. She woke up to the fact that she was back into another abusive relationship.

How hard is it to look at our self and realize we have fallen into the same old trap or into the same old behavior? What makes us think that doing the same thing each time, the outcome the second time will be any different? How do we change and by changing grow in our understanding of ourselves and others we come in contact with each day? It takes introspection, understanding of ourselves, and especially the desire to change our ways.

CHAPTER THREE

321 BCE: Given as the rise of Mayan Empire

A MAYAN NOBLEMAN

**"Greater love has no one than this, that he lay down his life for his friends."
John 15:13 New International Version of Holy Bible**

Ever since 1590 when the theory that the early people came into the Americas over a land bridge from the western lands was presented by Jose de Acosta, it has been widely accepted by the experts as the true story of the settlement of the new lands. Over the last half century, archeologists have been finding artifacts that question this assumption. The proof of many different visitors to the Americas has been found in areas from the shores of the Great Lakes, to the middle lands of the Ohio River Valley, down the California coast and into the areas of Central and South America. Many archeological finds are physical proof that these lands were settled by more than just those peoples from the arctic region crossing a land bridge. [1]

Edgar Cayce tells us that many of the people from Atlantis traveled to North and South America after the destruction of the island of Poseidon, approximately 28,000 BCE. Their descendants were later known by the name Mayan, who settled in Mesoamerica, the area we know today as Guatemala and Ecuador. The Incas settled in the mountainous area of the Andes. [2]

The Mayan civilization inhabited a region of Southern Mexico which is now known as Guatemala, El Salvador, Belize and Western Honduras in the 3-10th century AD. By 1200 AD, their civilization had collapsed. We can only guess the reason why, leaving pyramids, temples and their plazas to be covered over and hidden by the jungle trees and vines.

In 1561, a Spanish Franciscan priest visiting Mexico was shown some of the buildings that had been found in the jungle that were decorated with pictures and hieroglyphs. In 1562, when there was found evidence of human sacrifice with a sacred Mayan statue, the priest in his ignorance and self-aggrandizement ordered the destruction of five thousand idols and as many of the written manuscripts that he could find. His justification for this was that they were all a part of devil worship and thus should be destroyed. He destroyed all but three of the sacred books and with this act he single-handedly eliminated the majority of Maya knowledge and history.

In 1880, one of the sacred Mayan books was found in the library of Dresden, Germany, by a scholar who worked there by the name of Ernst Forstemann, who was able to crack the code of the Mayan calendar. With his translation, the markings on the many temples and artifacts that had been saved from the Franciscan priest's destruction could be translated. He discovered that the Mayans had been able to calculate that the length of a year was 365.242 days. It was discovered that the Mayan calendar was more accurate than the Gregorian calendar we use today. [3]

The Hopi of North America and the Mayan people believe that their ancestors came to the land by boat after their homeland was destroyed. Both have a legend of a white brother leaving their land going to the East and promising to return one day to bring peace and harmony to the people. These immigrants from the East brought their knowledge of astronomy, and mathematics, which helped them to build towering buildings of stone. From these heights, they could plot the pathways of the stars and planets in their yearly progression across the sky. The Mayan priests were able to predict the movement of the stars, planets and their position in the Milky Way, and kept accurate records of these events each year. [4]

The Mayan civilization developed a structured society with a king over all, then the nobility, the priests and the common people with the last division of slaves. There were specialty classes for the stone carvers and polishers. The priests kept the records and the shamans cared for the physical ills of the people, and watched the heavens for messages from the gods. Food was plentiful as their agriculture was perfected with the use of an irrigation system using the fertile soil of the swamplands. [5]

The first pyramids built in Central America were built by people who migrated from Atlantis. They were built using the orientation of the stars in the night sky, especially those of Orion. They used the building methods of Atlantis raising the large stone blocks with the power of their mind along with sound. This sound was a special tone made by the people and by the blowing of horns. It was the same power that was used by the Atlanteans to construct their pyramids in Poseidon. As the centuries went by, there was a gradual loss of this ability, and building was done then in the conventional way using many slaves to place the stones in their desired order. [6]

Buildings were constructed around a large open plaza with the pyramid the focal point and other small buildings near it. Groups of small mud buildings surrounded the large open area of the square where people brought their goods to sell in the market. There was a large pyramid near the open plaza, with many steps that ascended to the heavens. Only the high priest was allowed to go to the top of this pyramid. There was a platform on top where the high priest conducted special ceremonies. There were calculations made by the priest for when the heavens were in the right position to celebrate the time of planting new crops in the field, and the time for harvesting as well as other special occasions. Buildings and cities were aligned to the unique energy being released from the celestial gods. The land was divided up into ten equal parts with each part having its own king. Each new king was consecrated at a specific time of the year when the alignment of stars would add to his power.

There was a special building where the top opened to the sky so that the priests could study the stars and the zodiac. All of the movement of the sky people was carefully calculated and the exact time for certain lights to appear in the sky was known. The movement of the celestial lights was recorded, from one cycle to the next, the time to predict their next appearance. Some of this information was written on the rocks of the pyramids, other information was written on bark that was bundled together and stored in a safe place. [7]

The people of the Mayan and Aztec world believed that the universe was alive with spiritual essence and an unseen power, which flowed through and connected all things in the universe. They believed that they could influence this force through their ceremonies and rituals.

Time was seen as a cycle of events where the shaman could predict the future by his knowledge of the positioning of the heavenly bodies.

TREE OF LIFE

The Mayans knew from their studies of the sky that the creation of their world happened on August 13, 3114 BCE on our calendar. This date appears over and over in inscriptions all over the Mayan world. The most sacred concept was that of the "Tree of Life," which was the conduit of communication between the supernatural and the human worlds, lifted from the primordial waters by a strike of lightening, and gave life to the world. It was believed that the "Tree of Life" stretched through the three worlds: heavens, Earth and the underworld in a straight-line ascending from the North Star and that it was spinning like a top. They believed if this spinning should stop it would bring about the end of the world, which rested on the back of a large turtle. Each time period was influenced by the "Bacabs," gods that held up the corners of the world in the four directions. Each direction representing a special spiritual inspiration, a different energy, and a certain color. **East** was seen as red with the red colors of the sky as the sun was reborn from the night each morning. The **West** was black as that was where the sun died each day. The **North** was given the color white as it was seen as the fullness of life and the brightness of a full day's sun. The **South** was seen as yellow with the struggle of the sun to be reborn. The center of the Earth was given the color green symbolizing the center of life or the Tree of Life. According to the Mayans, the World Tree is what creates and maintains the four directions of the world. After the Spanish conquest, the world tree reemerged as the catholic cross. [8]

THE FABLE OF THE HERO TWINS

The blood sport of the Mayan was told in their fables of the hero twins who were superior game players. This deadly sport involved passing a hard rubber ball to the next player using only the knees, hips and elbows. The ball was hit into a stone loop positioned high on the ball court wall. Players believed that they were challenged by the gods and by winning the game became gods ascending into heaven to be seen in the evening sky as Venus and in the daytime as the sun. The Mayans saw the disappearance of Venus as the evening star, descending into the underworld and its reemergence in the morning as the defeat of death. The hero story is represented in the ball court. It could be played with two people or a community team. It could also be played as a proxy to war with the losers being sacrificed. To die in the ball court was considered an honor. Mayan kings were sacrificed after losing a war and they were killed in the ball court so that they could join the lords of the underworld. [9]

MAYAN HUMAN SACRIFICE

The sacrifice of human life was the ultimate offering of blood to the gods. Only those of high stations taken as prisoners were sacrificed by cutting out their heart in view of the gods and in full view of the people assembled around the pyramid. Those captives viewed as of the lower social stations were not considered fit for sacrifice and so were used as slaves.

The central belief of the Mayans was that each person possessed a life force and that human blood was viewed as the source of nourishment for the Mayan deities. Ceremonies were held where volunteers would offer their blood to the gods. This was done by cutting a person's genitals, tongue or earlobes and let the blood spill out. The belief was that they were feeding the gods.

Historians believe that the Mayans were introduced to human sacrifice by the Toltecs, since that had long been a part of their religion. Mayans sacrificed animals, crocodiles, iguanas, dogs, jaguars, turkeys, and humans. This took place in an elaborate ceremony on top of the pyramid. Pictures of human sacrifice have been found on sculptures, murals and painted on pottery. Children made up the bulk of the sacrifices because they were believed to hold their innocence. Children were captured from other tribes for the sole purpose of sacrifice.

The sacrificial victim was taken to the top of the pyramid designated for sacrifice and laid over a stone altar. Four assistants, one for each extremity, took hold of his hands and feet causing the sacrificed victim to be bent back such that the torso was thrusted up toward the sky. The priest would use a sharp obsidian knife and swiftly cut open the victim's chest, pulling out his beating heart and hold it up to the people watching at the bottom of the pyramid. The beating heart was considered the greatest sacrifice to the gods. The victim's head was cut off and his body thrown down the pyramid steps. Other methods of sacrifice were drowning, beating and mutilation. In the arrow ceremony, the victim was tied to a stake while dancers took turns shooting arrows into him trying to hit his heart.

MAYAN CALENDAR

From the earlies centuries of human existence on Earth, the position of the sun, moon and stars in the sky were considered one of wonder and a spirit to be honored and worshipped. The cosmic order of the universe was a common belief among the Greeks, Hindus of ancient India, Egyptians, Chinese, and the Native Americans. Every civilization had some ritual and beliefs that they considered necessary for their survival. A usual amount of attention was paid to the study of Sirius and Orion during ancient times. Antiquity stories told them that visitors from the sky had their home in the Pleiades. The Peruvian legends considered the Pleiades to be the "Celestial Gates."

If the sun was clothed in clouds or the rain refused to water the parched Earth, man's entire life was at risk to be cut off from the substance of the Earth. Civilizations were built and areas deserted because of several factors, one was the lack of rain for the land. The knowledge of weather conditions, the effects of the celestial bodies on the affairs of man and the prediction of these events were the responsibility of the priests. Theirs was the duty to study the night sky and record the position of the different lights. Through years of observation and written records of the celestial events, the priests were able to predict the cyclic advancement through the twelve zodiac signs, the changing seasons, and when it was best to plant their crops of corn, squash, and later on the cultivation of cotton for clothing, were guided by the different phases of the moon.
[10]

Buildings of the cities were aligned for astronomical observation and the windows were aligned so that they benefited the occupants of the celestial energy from the night sky as well as the position of the sun. Windows were precisely placed to allow the sun to illuminate desired items at certain times of the day or the year.

Life of the Mayan was wrapped around the concept of time. Priests were consulted for the most auspicious date to settle civil disputes, or for the seasons to plant their crops and when to harvest them. The priest would consult the calendar for the best date to declare war on their enemies. Children were named for the date upon which they were born,

Time was considered cyclic and knowing what cycle was present gave power to the events of that day. The hours of the day were determined as well as the month and years plotted from the position of the lights in the night sky. Priests would determine the time for certain ceremonies. The cycle of time interacted with all levels of life: that of the Earth, the nine levels of the underworld, and the thirteen levels of the heavens above; using a numbering system and applied mathematics, they could calculate the length of a cycle as long as 26,000 years. All human activity was planned around celestial events. [11]

The life of the Maya revolved around the concept of time based on the sun's cycle throughout the year. They coded this information into the record books of the priest and carved it into the stones of their temples and cities. The number of stairs going to the top of a pyramid, the angles and segments of the building were all related to the Mayan solar year with specific dates and other information.

For thousands of years the observations by the priests of the night sky became a written record of the seasonal placement of the planets and stars. With this data, they could predict when the next eclipse would happen. This was the time of new beginnings for the people. The people had to prepare for the heavenly display. They believed that the fate of their world hung on the performance of their ceremonies during that time. Consider that the day of the event, in the Valley of Mexico, there were no fires anywhere as all must be extinguished before the great day when the sun would be challenged by its brother the moon. Pregnant women were locked up in a room of the temple less they turn into wild animals, children were pinched to keep them awake in the night, or they would turn into mice, and all pottery was broken in preparation for the end of the world. The people followed the priest up the hills to a place now known as "The Hill of the Stars," which is the top of an old extinct volcano. There they waited for the passing of Pleiades across the center of the heavens showing them that the gods had considered sparing the world for another fifty-two years. The entire Mayan valley was in darkness as the sun covered the moon. When the exact moment came, and the world returned to the light of the sun, a sacrificial victim was chosen and sacrificed there on the mountain. A new fire was started in the body cavity of the victim. Then the people took torches kindled by this fire, to all the houses and buildings throughout the valley. This was known as the New Fire Ceremony among the Mexica and the ceremony was known throughout the Mesoamericans. [12]

In the modern world, the astronomers predicted the eclipse of 1979 and the one of 2017, which went across the United States from Oregon to the Carolinas, was predicted as well as the future eclipse of 2024.

CONFERENCE AT A.R.E.

On July 23, 2009, I was privileged to hear Dr. Johan Calleman, Ph.D., speak at the ARE conference in Virginia Beach, Virginia, on the topic of the Mayan calendar. Dr. Calleman has studied the Mayan calendar since 1979 and was then touring throughout the world talking about his work.

The world was debating the reason for the Mayan calendar ending at the year 2012. Predictions were made that the world would be destroyed by some cataclysmic event. Other people thought that the world would just go on as usual, but with a higher awareness of spiritual values. Those of us that pondered these different alternatives concluded that the change would be coming toward spiritual awareness not destruction of the world. Why the Mayan priests could not predict a future beyond 2012, we did not know.

The Mayan codex, or holy books of records, detailed astronomical tables more accurate than the Gregorian calendar established in 1582 by Pope Gregory XIII. The reason the Julian calendar had to be replaced was that the Gregorian calendar used a more accurate way for calculating the cycle for leap year. To get the calendar in sync with the vernal equinox or the winter solstice, a number of days had to be dropped from the Julian calendar in use at that time. The written Mayan calendar was a series of dots and dashes with the drawing of a closed shell designated as zero. Zero was an advance concept in those days something that even the Romans were not aware of. The Maya were confident enough to use this symbol for an abstract idea of nothingness.

The Mayan priests obtained information from their three calendars. They could predict the solstices, the equinoxes and changes of the seasons, also the path of the planets of Venus and Mars. The **Tzolk'in** was the name given to the numbers that tracked the days of the week in a calendar month. It was used to predict the fortune of a certain day and helped the priest to plan for rituals and ceremonies. The second calendar is the agriculture calendar, and was based on the cycles of the moon. It was known as the **Haab** and consists of eighteen months with each month having twenty days, with the addition of five days each month named **Vague, or "bad luck,"** it completed the 365-day year. The reason for the calendar was to keep track of the days so that the seasons would fall on the same day of every year. [13]

With a fifty-two-year cycle, the Tzolk'in and the Haab would return to the same date. If the sun did not rise on the next day, the Maya knew the end of the world had come. The night before the new cycle all fires were put out, pregnant women were locked up in case they should turn into wild animals, children were pinched to keep them awake so they would not turn into mice, and all pottery was broken in preparation for the end of the world. A night time ceremony was held where all the people followed the priest to the top of the hills to watch for the passing of Pleiades, which would announce the continuation of the world for another fifty-two years. When the moment arrived, the priest grabbed a victim, slashed his chest removing his heart for sacrifice of the new cycle of life for the world. A new fire was started with torches carried to every village and temple to relight their fires. [14]

The third count for the Maya calendar, known as the "Long Count," was the calendar of global energy that started 8/11/3114 BCE the date of the Mayan creation story and it ended on the solstice 12/21/2012. This was a continuous record of days that started every 5000 years. As the world approached the year 2012 AD, many theories were advanced by the "experts" of the world. The general consensus was that something terrible was going to happen. As we all know sitting here in 2016, nothing world shattering happened and the world continued on as before.

MAYAN MEDICINE

The medicine practiced by Mayan healers was a combination of religion and science. Priests inherited their position from someone in their family who had been a healer. Their training was by observing and later practice under the direction of their teacher. As a child, they were introduced to the healing plants of the jungles surrounding their home village. A family member who knew how to gather herbs and how to prepare them for use in the future, taught the budding healer. Health was viewed as a balance between the disease and the individual's life habits. The person's age, gender, personality as well as the local environment with humidity and rain of the forest was considered in the cure.

The ancient people understood that the mind and the body were interactive, and they treated their patients with this in mind. The Maya took into consideration that not only physical ills of the body but the effects on the body reflected the individual's spiritual attitude toward life and its challenges. The healer was aware of the close communication between the plants they used for healing and themselves. They knew that each variety of plant had a song that would encourage the plant to share their secrets with the young apprentice, Songs were sought through visions, and spending a great amount of time with each variety of the plant to learn their song. At the completion of their studies, students were required to sing the song of each plant they used,

From the beginning of time, man has recognized his connection to the Earth, plants, animals and all growing things. They recognized that all creation had an interconnection to each other as well as towards the heavens. Because of the common birth of man and plants from the fabric of spirit, man is able to communicate with them. Before the preparation of any medicine, prayer was required to put the internal world of the patient into a receptive frame of mind. When the singing started, the healer was cautioned to place all their thoughts and intentions of healing into the music with the plants they were using. When the song and ceremony are completed, it is again necessary to pray to close the sacred space that has been created and return the patient and the healer back to the secular space and time. [15]

Anthropologists have discovered many healing practices of the ancient Mayan people. Maya could suture a wound using human hair. They could reduce a fracture and had material for a cast. They were skillful surgeons and made prosthesis from jade and turquoise, they were able to fill teeth with iron pyrite and they used obsidian blades for surgery, Modern science has discovered what ancient healers knew, that the obsidian blades were sharp and promoted a more rapid healing with less scar tissues. [16]

MY MAYAN EXPERIENCE

One night I had a dream. I saw myself as a young athletic man dressed in only a white loincloth, standing on a pyramid platform. The plaza below me was filled with people. The priest stood to my left. He had on a beautiful large headdress made with long blue and yellow feathers and the only clothing he had on was a white loincloth. In the priest's right hand was a long obsidian knife, which I knew was very sharp.

I could look over the edge of the platform and see the people below me. I knew I was to be sacrificed that day and I also knew that I was offering my life willingly, as an offering to the gods. My life's blood was to help the people with something that was a threat to them. I do not know exactly what it was; perhaps it was an unknown illness that was a plague to the people. All I do know is that the priest considered this a grave situation and only the blood from someone of the king's court could prevent this evil from happening. Since I was one of some authority, the people believed that the gods would hold my sacrifice higher than a servant or a slave. While viewing this life, I could not determine the reason for my sacrifice only that I knew that this unselfish act of mine would bring some great blessing to the people, and for that reason I was willing to do it.

From this life, I carried forward to other lives the fear of sharp knives, and the fear of heights. I overcame the belief that any human could set up a religion that would demand human blood sacrifice from a god as a payment for their benevolent blessings on anyone. I understood that religion was a way in which the priesthood could control the people and that it had nothing to do with the spirit of humanity, the expression of love for each other, or the connection to the great creator of the cosmos.

CHAPTER FOUR
TANG DYNASTY 618-906 AD

THE MYSTERIOUS LAND CALLED CHINA

As I have remembered each past life, I have tried to put each life into a historical order, with the clues Spirit has given me of my past lives. I have approximated the place on Earth where I lived, the person I was, and I have written a sense of the challenges of that life. This gives a setting that explains my impressions of that time and of my Karmic balance for that life. The next life that I was shown was in China.

I had a dream where I was running down a road in the middle of the night. I was in an area surrounded by mountains, and behind me sitting on a high hill was a large house enclosed by a high wall. The feelings I had were of fear, panic and the thoughts of escape, as I feared that my life was in danger. I could see myself as a small framed woman wearing a long robe. In one hand, I was carrying a bundle of my personal possessions. The impression was that this was in the land known as China and that I was running from a very threatening situation.

As a child, our class in geography never included the culture or the people of China; consequently, I did not know any Chinese history. In researching historical information for this book, I have had to read a lot of Chinese history to learn about the country. According to Scott Morton and Charlton Lewis in their book about China and Culture, they talk about the land and its people. Chinese scholars assign their history to the beginning of 2852 BCE. People have lived in the area since the Pleistocene Age some 500,000 years ago. It is said that China was ruled by three sovereigns followed by five rulers. China has been a land of mystery partly because of the geographical barriers of the land. China extends from the ice and snow of the Mongolian lands in the north to the gorges of the Burma border and the high plateau of Tibet. In the South and West are lands of arid and sparsely populated land of Central Asia. Contact with the other worlds outside of China has been through people who took to the sea for trade and exploration in the West and through Central Asia. [1]

China developed its own culture from the beginning without outside influences of the developing world countries. The vast expense of this land is almost the size of the United States with temperatures below zero in the north Manchurian Mountains, with a tropical belt in the south of the country offering balmy breezes. The nation is divided by the Qinling Mountain range giving the north dry, cold desert winds in winter while the south has a moist warmer climate of the summer monsoon season. The mountains not only divide the land but the culture and the society as well. China culture developed on its own in the many different areas of the country now known as provinces.

The crops grown on the land are different from the south and the north. Farmers in the north produced millet and wheat while those in the south grew rice, tea and the mulberry tree where silk worms feed to provide strands of material used for silk products. The people are also divided by their preference in food as in the southern part of the country a taste of sweet in the food is preferred, while people from the north would rather have something salty. Those people from the east preferred a vinegar taste in their food and the people of the west required a hot pungent flavor in their food.[2] The growing season in the north was four to six months while the south had several growing seasons with two or three crops possible in their nine-month growing period. The contact with the outside world came from the men of the south, who were the fishermen and traders, using their boats to travel outside the territorial waters for trade and exploration. Chinese society has always been predominately rural with the people living on small family farms, growing food for the family and a little more for trade at the local market. [3]

LANGUAGE

The spoken language of the people changed according to the province where the individual lived. Each area developed their language with their own dialect, where a person from one area could not be understood by a person from another province. The language spoken in the capital of Beijing was Mandarin and so it was eventually adopted as the national language in 1995. All commerce and business of the country is done using Mandarin today as the official language. [4]

TANG DYNASTY

According to an article introducing the Tang Dynasty, (618-906 AD) was considered as the "medieval" period of Chinese history and the height of Buddhist influence. This was the golden age of Chinese civilization and considered to be the most prosperous period with significant development in culture, art, poetry and technology. The country was united with borders as far as Korea, Vietnam and Southeast Asia. The rulers of the Tang dynasty welcomed a society that was liberal and largely tolerant of foreign views and ideas. Women could now attain a higher status at court and have a greater degree of freedom in society. [5]

THE SILK ROAD

Trade flourished and communication among the other nations of the world was possible. The Silk Road was the name given to a four thousand-mile-long network of trade routes that linked China and Central Asia. It began during the Han Dynasty (206 BC-220AD); one end was Rome with their gold, silver and precious jewels to trade, and China, at the other end of the road, offered silk, spices and ivory. It was a transcontinental network of trade routes that extended from China throughout India, Persia, Europe, and into Arabia. Silk was the most luxurious fabric of the ancient world. It attracted merchants who bought horses, cattle, furs, hides, and luxuries such as ivory and jade to trade in China. The precious goods traveling up and down the road was a temptation to the Tibetan bandits and prompted the building of a section of the "Great Wall."

Among the items traded were the translucent pieces of white porcelain. White is the color the Chinese believe to be the most beautiful and prestigious, so the porcelain pieces were considered most valuable. In 751, the Tang Empire lost control of the Silk Road, but the Muslim countries ruled Central Asia and became directly involved in extending the trade roads. [6]

In an article written by Holy Mountain Trading Company on Blanc de Chine includes the statement that: "Buddhism came to China from India in the sixth century AD. Its influence on the art of China was profound. Fujian Province was a stronghold of Buddhism where the first figures from Dehua were mainly of Buddhist deities. Dehua connection with Buddhism came at least partially through the Japanese, who had a strong influence on Fujian design and marks. The Japanese built the first Buddhist sanctuary on P'u Tuo Island three hundred miles from Dehua near the city of Ningbo. Communities of Japanese and Korean monks settled there. According to the ancient documents reported to be written around 1700, the white clay was mined in the hills behind the Cheng monastery."

The name "Blanc de Chine" or white China, was a name given by the French to a variety of ceramics manufactured primary in the southern provinces of China in the seventeenth and eighteenth centuries. It is produced in Dehua, Fujian Province, which is on the mainland located opposite the island of Taiwan. The clay found in Dehua is known by its white color which forms because of the absence of iron in the soil. The qualities of high percentage of quartz, kaolin sericite and feldspar combine to make a superior quality of clay especially good for the production of porcelain. Dehua ware and Blanc de Chine are interchangeable terms of the sublime porcelain produced there. [7]

The height of the importance of the Silk Road was in the Tang Dynasty (618-907) with the capital Changan as the starting point of the route. The 754 AD census showed that five thousand foreigners lived in the city: Turks, Iranians, Indians, Japanese, Koreans, and Malays from the east. All from the countries where the Silk Road passed through and brought new items for trade. There, rare plants, medicines, spices, and other goods from the west could be found in the bazaars of the city.

There were dangers along the trade route with troubles among the different tribes as well as the presence of the middleman taking a cut of the profits. There were also the dangers of bandits along the way and the taxes imposed on the caravan when passing through certain kingdom.

The first European arrived at Kubilai's court were Northern European traders who arrived in 1261. But the most well-known visitor was the Italian Marco Polo who wrote of his travels, the customs of the people and the wonders of the country. The constant threat of danger along the overland trade routes prompted the consideration of using ships for that purpose. At that time shipping goods by sea had become more reliable, and the travel by water would extend the potential trading area. This means of transporting trading goods also had its perils with unfavorable weather conditions, also pirates on the high seas. [8]

BUDDHISM IN CHINA

Buddhism was introduced to China probably by traders from the West, traveling over the Silk Road, about the first century. The Han Dynasty was deeply into Confucianism, which is a focus on ethics and maintaining social order. Buddhists emphasized the monastic life, offering a departure from the known religious practices of the people. A Buddhist monk by the name of Xuanzang traveled to India and brought back crates of books and materials that he spent years translating the works of the sutras, into Chines, which were written in Sanskrit.

Buddhism attracted interest because of its moral teachings and the promise of a better life for all people. One of the Bodhisattva (an enlightened being), Guan Yin the goddess of Mercy, was introduced to the people through stories of her life. By the ninth century, a statue of Guan

Yin (Quan Yin or Kwan Yin) was found in every Buddhist monastery. She is said to have lived in northern China healing and saving sailors from shipwrecks. She is shown in many forms frequently as a young woman with flowing robes with a white lotus in her left hand, a symbol of purity of an ideal woman. There are also statues of her as a provider of children, often depicted with a child near her feet, and another with multiple heads, eyes and arms. In this last one, she is the omnipresent Divine Mother sensing the problems of humanity. She is reaching out to console all beings with her boundless expression of compassion and mercy. It was thought if a woman wished to conceive a male child, her prayers to Guan Yin would assure that wish. [9]

The people turned to Buddhism as a way to escape the suffering from all the problems of the country. This was a religion that allowed all the people to participate. In the past, only the families of the gentry were allowed to have ceremonies to the ancestors. The common man was drawn to Buddhism. By the Tang Dynasty (618-906 AD), the Emperor Taizong encouraged the devotion and gave money to establish monasteries and build statues across all of China. The Empress Wu (690-705 AD), the only woman to reach a position of leadership invited scholars to come to China and spread the Buddhist teachings. Monasteries became the place for travelers to rest, where they could receive medical attention as needed. It was a place for merchants to store their money and goods for safe-keeping, Wealthy people donated money and land to the monasteries, increasing their influence among the people and in the country. [10]

With trade now open to the West, the benefit of a secure storage of trade goods by the monasteries and the open encouragement of the merchants by the emperor to advance trade beyond the borders of China, the economy of the age was at the highest point in history. The request of religious items for the monasteries and home altars increased. The emperor Xuande (1426-C1435) instructed that the pottery used in the monasteries should be made in white porcelain. It has not been explained by scholars why the preference of ritual vessels formerly made of wood must now be made of white porcelain, which was more expensive to produce. It is assumed that the color white must have been chosen for a particular reason. It is possible that the color white chosen for religious items may express a ritual purity, a belief that extends until today. [13]

POTTERY

The word "Ceramics" is the term used to reference items made of clay, and fired in a very hot, specially-made oven called a kiln, needed to make the clay object solid and hold its form permanently. There are different types of clay used for different purposes, and for the temperatures needed in their firing. The clay used to make a tile for the garden is different from the clay used to make dishes for your table.

In the beginning, the pottery was being made by several families using their own small kiln, and their own secret techniques. But as the demands for porcelain increased, larger manufacturing areas were needed. It took many people to complete each piece of pottery as each person in the assembly line was an expert in that one part of production. The large orders from the Imperial court for porcelain led to the expansion of the production at Jingdezhen maybe as early as 557CE. [13] Historians have claimed that there were different times in China when the production of porcelain was raised to a new artistic excellence. The times are given with the ruling families and their dynasties. First is the Han Dynasty (100-200 AD). The second is the

Three Kingdoms (200-380 AD), followed by the Six Dynasties (220-589 AD), and the one that fits my time line, the Tang Dynasty (618-906 AD).

In the time of Marco Polo who traveled from his home in Venice, Italy to China, one of the cities he visited was Quanzhou which was then known as Zayton. Marco Polo wrote of this city as one of the richest cities on the Earth. This was the gateway to the west where ships sailed out to the Middle East and ports in Europe, taking wares from Chine such as lacquer and stone wear, and silks, later to add tea to trade. [12]

In the article entitled *Major Chinese Pottery and its History,* the following information is found: "Pottery was first made as early as Neolithic Age, which was in colors of grey, red, black and white. Porcelain was first made in the Eastern Han Dynasty and production techniques reached its peak in the Song Dynasty (420-479). The production techniques became more advanced in the Tang Dynasty (618-907). In China, the violet sand Earthenware of Yixing in the Jiangsu Province, Nixing pottery of Qinzhou in the Guangxi Province, water pottery of Jianshui in the Yunnan Province and Rongchang pottery of the Sichuan Province are the four most famous Chinese potteries." The pottery of the Tang Dynasty is typically shown painted in three colors of glaze of yellow, green, and white or green and blue. The boldness of the tri-colored pieces and the unique style show the high artistic standards of the Tang Dynasty. The area along the Fujian coast was one of the export centers. Over one hundred and eighty kiln sites have been found in this area dating from the Song Dynasty to today.

From the Ming Dynasty, porcelain objects were constructed with a glass outer coat. The clay in the area of Dehua in Fujian Province has a very small amount of iron in it which brings out a warm white or pail ivory color to the clay after glazing. The colors of these pieces set them apart from those pieces that were constructed and fired in the imperial kilns of Jingdezhen. [14]

With the interest in the Buddhist goddess, the porcelain replica of the form of Quan yin is still one of the most prized devotional items in individual homes and in the monasteries. When Buddhism came to China from India in the sixth century, home altars included the statue of Quan yin along with other religious items. The white of purity of the statue, and the artistic curves of the artist's touch made the devotion to Quan yin more powerful for the people. Because of the profound trust in Quan yin's healing power many believed that even the simple recitation of her name would bring her instantly to their side. [15]

MY LOVE OF POTTERY

I was reintroduced to the joy of pottery and working in clay in my college freshman year, when I took a summer class working with a pottery wheel, at American River College in Sacramento, California. It was in this class that I knew I loved working with clay. As I learned to make all kinds of items, small plates, cups, and jars with their own tops, my fascination increased. In the years my husband was in the military, I was able to work with clay using the potter's wheel in craft shops located on military bases. I also was able to take pottery classes from local teachers where we were living at the time. I had classes with students from the University of Washington in Tacoma, Washington, and classes with a group in a cooperative pottery shop in Colorado Springs, Colorado.

ITALIAN POTTERY

Another part of my pottery training came when my husband was stationed in Italy; there I was able to attend an Italian pottery school. On our arrival in Italy, we were housed in a local hotel until our furniture arrived from the states, and we could move into our own apartment. I found out that one of the maids working in the hotel had a son, Daniel, who understood English. I sent a note home to him asking him to translate some things for me. One day I heard that there was a pottery school in the center of town. I asked Daniel if he would go with me and translate for me at the school. When we arrived, I asked the school secretary what the qualifications were to go to the school. She said, it depended on the professor that taught the pottery classes, if he would accept me as a student or not.

I will never forget the day I stood in front of the professor, and with Daniel translating for me, he said, "I don't speak English and you don't speak Italian, but one day you will speak Italian! You will not be able to take the written classes, but you can do the practical work in the workshop with the students." That is how I got into an Italian pottery school. I was able to learn the technique of their pottery making and use some of the traditional patterns of thirteenth and fourteenth century Italian pottery. The students in this school were from all over the city. These young people were considered "slow learners," and they were not able to attend regular school. The pottery that the students made was offered for sale to the public each spring, with the proceeds going to the school for its expenses. The students accepted me without question and went out of their way to teach me the language as well as how they made their pottery. I had two years of instruction in Italian classical design and in working with majolica pottery.

MAJOLICA

This is the beautiful ware of Italy, prepared by tin-glazing earthenware and firing a second time. The techniques used in producing pieces in the majolica process originated in the Middle East in the 9th century. By the 13th century, majolica ware was being imported into Italy. The Italian craftsmen were fascinated with this new process and soon started to copy it and making it their own by adding their own creativity and traditions. The peak of the Italian majolica popularity was in the late 15th century and early 16th century. The patterns we used in the Italian pottery school were from broken pottery with patterns from this time. [11]

POTTERY CLASSIFICATION

There is a science behind the production of pottery that most people do not know:

EARTHENWARE is usually a reddish or white clay. This was the earliest material used in Chinese pottery. The clay we worked within Italy was a reddish color and needed a glaze (liquid glass) over the fired piece and then re-fired to harden the glaze. I have several plates and bowls that I made while I was in the pottery school in Italy. The underglaze colors are many and varied for achieving different results. The nonleaded colors are used for stoneware on items that would come in contact with food of any kind, while decorative gold, copper or silver, when applied, can be used for other items. The glazed stoneware, after the final firing, is impervious to water. It is usually used in pottery that will be used as a decoration.

STONEWARE is a heavier clay mixture which is fired at a higher temperature. It is hard enough to resist scratching of a steel point and is usually brownish grey or dark brown. I saw a small pot in Italy that was shaped as a pig and used for baking in the kitchen. It was big enough for an entire small chicken and vegetables to cook at the same time. The pig was unglazed and held the heat of the kitchen oven. In the **Italian** school, the technique called **Majolica was used.** The clay used could be made into a decorated plate or bowl. First the item was made on the potter's wheel, by several men in the school, dried to remove all the water from the "clay body," and then fired to a very hard form called "bisque." I tried to convince the professor that I could make pieces on the wheel, but he said that was man's work.

We were given a piece of a broken pottery and told to decide what form the pattern would look good on. After choosing the item we were to reproduce the pattern on our chosen project, but before we painted on any color, the item was sprayed with a white glaze and fired a second time. After the pottery cooled, we decorated with underglaze colors. The colors used in Italy are in powdered form and they were easily rubbed off while painting on top of it. The trick, I learned after many disastrous attempts, was to paint from the inside of a plate to the outside rim. The underglaze colors made in the states are in a liquid form, and much easier to handle. I also found out by many frustrating starts that the powered color's intensity could be changed by how much water was used. As an example, to get a very light blue, a small amount of powder and water was used. A darker color needed more powder, less water. The same went for all the colors. The challenge was not to accidentally wipe off the sprayed on powdered glaze as I was trying to paint on top of it.

After the pottery item was painted, it was sprayed again – this time with a very light liquid clear glaze – and fired the third time. After the appropriate amount of time, the kiln was opened and the pieces brought out and placed on the table. It was just like Christmas looking at our products, some to the delight of every one and others with words from the professor, "Well, you will do better next time."

PORCELAIN is made of a very special clay containing a mineral of kaolinite and is fired at an extremely high temperature. It is not usually offered to ordinary students as the process is considered to be only for the very talented and gifted people. The fired piece of porcelain is impermeable even before glazing and is white translucent and resonant. The porcelain clay I have worked within the states felt smooth and silky in my hands, a totally different feeling from the stoneware material of that clay used in Earthenware. A final firing of 1,690 degrees Fahrenheit made the glaze interact with the metal oxides used in the decorations and created a deep brilliant translucent color specific to majolica.

MEMORY IN CLAY

When I decided to write this book on my past lives, it was important for me to find what the circumstances were when I worked with clay. Perhaps my frustration in my pottery construction came from my excellence in a past memory from another time and another place. With this in mind, I started to research the making of pottery in China. When you buy clay already processed from a store, it is ready to be shaped into your desired item. I never knew all the work behind the preparation of clay before I had to do it myself!

When I lived in Tucson, I took a class in Southwest archology. Part of that class was learning to make pottery using the Native Americans technique, by first gathering our own clay. My son and I went out with the group one Sunday. There were several cars filled with the class students, who followed the teacher's car to a special place on private property, where he had permission to dig up clay. Everyone in the class brought buckets of clay home with them. We filled two buckets with heavy chunks of clay and brought it home. That was the beginning of the process. First the clay is broken into many small pieces and placed in a bucket of water to soften it, and where twigs or grass can be flushed off. Next the clay soup is poured through a fine mesh to get all the small stones out of the clay. Then this mixture is poured on something like a bed sheet and allowed to dry completely in the sun. A day or two later, the clay is dry enough to peel off the sheets and crumbled into a powder. Clay in this form is pure and would not hold a form of any kind, so additives are now mixed into the clay. The exact amount of water to reconstitute the clay body is crucial as too much will result in a soupy mix, and with too little water the clay will be too hard to form into anything. The Native Americans would add amounts of powdered old pottery to give the new clay strength. We used commercial powered feldspar to get the consistency we wanted.

The blending of clay, water and body elements is a technique very critical for the final production. The potter puts this mixture on a table and starts to work with the clay ball. If you are a baker and make pastry for pies, you know that over working the pastry makes a very hard crust when you want a flaky crust and yet be able to hold the filling in the pan. Now, take that same kneading action with clay, only the objective to the kneading is to get all the air pockets out of the clay. The clay ball is rolled over and over on itself until the potter feels they have gotten all the air out. One quick check is cutting into the ball and seeing a smooth surface not a hole where an air bubble had been. If all air bubbles have **not** been taken out of the clay with this first step, there could be an explosion in the kiln when it is fired. If you are lucky, there will not be any damage to yours or anyone else's pottery in the kiln.

From here on, it is a matter of forming the object you want. According to an article about Chinese porcelain and the history of ceramics in China, the potter's wheel was used to create items with clay. By that time the production of pottery was in such a large scale that it was done in production form, with many people having a part in the construction, painting and firing of the pottery item.

NATIVE AMERICAN POTTERY

I took classes in the hand building techniques of the Southwestern Native American. It always felt like I had done this work before. I felt that I had been an expert in the construction of many different items. Unfortunately, my fingers did not share this conviction of my memory, and my pottery pieces usually did not meet the high standards I had set for myself. I became a decent potter, but never reached the degree of excellence that I felt I should be able to. Memories of past skills and my love of pottery came back to me as I worked in the clay, but the ability to construct perfect pieces brought me only frustration. I was deeply upset when I had to sell my kiln and pottery wheel when we moved from Tucson to the smaller house close to my daughter's work in Phoenix.

MY LIFE IN CHINA

As I have been writing this chapter, I have been asking myself when was the time and place where I fit into this story? The dream I had showed me that I was running from an area that had mountains and a large house or walled city on a hill. With my readings of Chinese history, I have learned that the Northern part of China is hilly and that the Southern area climate was not as harsh as the North. I also have found that the women of the Tang Dynasty were treated a little better than those of other times. The culture was rich in artistic art expression, and the experience of seeing new things being brought into the country from trading with distant lands was exciting. The monasteries were open to students, teachers, healers, and people who were willing to help others in the surrounding communities. The people were healthy with growing crops in the fields and plenty to eat, and the culture of that moment in time was united with nature in peace and tranquility.

I feel that I found my way south into one of the monasteries where I was healed, over time, from the trauma I had experienced while living in the North. My thoughts of this are that I was forced to leave children in the household of the man I worked for. Children were considered to belong to the war lord and did not belong to the mother/concubine. I was sent away from the home I had known, for some offense against the war lord. The exact reason I do not know, but I do know that I arrived at the monastery at night and in fear for my life. This is why I was so positive about not leaving my children in this lifetime, when I was offered the chance to leave this world in California. That part of my story you will read in a later chapter.

My love of art and the ability of my hands to do delicate carvings brought me to the attention of one of the monks. Even though the major pottery works were for men, I was encouraged to work with the potters, first carving molds out of wood then later shaping clay into statues of Quan Yin. My devotion to the work and the image I carved showed an excellence that brought me recognition in the pottery world.

THE ZEN BUDDHIST CENTER IN NEW MEXICO

In 2012, I had a strange dream. I was on a very congested interstate highway with two or three bridges crossing the interchange carrying traffic in all directions. I knew I was lost and pulled off the freeway, and I parked the car under one of the bridges to take a look at my map. I was there a short time when another car pulled up behind me and a man got out of the car. He walked up to me and asked me where I was going. I answered "I don't know." He said, you need to go down this freeway about four hundred miles and you will find it. I showed him a book I had been using for directions and he said," We have a new book now. Get rid of that book, as the new one is much better." Then he said, over and over "remember four hundred miles east." I woke up with the directions in my head with no idea where that would lead me.

The next Sunday in church I asked one of the ladies what the dream could mean. What was four hundred miles from Tucson going due east? She told me that there was a Zen Center in New Mexico where a retreat was held every year by the followers of the teachings of an Indian Guru by the name of Sathya Sai Baba, and that was approximately four hundred miles East from us.

I learned all I could about Sathya Sai Baba (11/23/1926-4/24/2011), as apparently, I was being called to go to the retreat in New Mexico on the next Labor Day weekend in September.

Sai Baba was an Indian guru, teacher and philanthropist. He lived in Puttaparthi, India with his family. The story is told that in March 1941 he was stung by a scorpion and lost consciousness for several hours. Upon awakening, he was able to sing songs in Sanskrit, which is the ancient language of India. He could heal people and his wisdom was acknowledged by the elders of the area. In October of that year, Sathya revealed that he was the reincarnation of Sai Baba of Shirdi, a revered Indian saint who became known in the late 19th century. [16]

The first year I attended the retreat I found that the mileage was just as I had been told in my dream. I traveled East from Tucson into New Mexico, just over four hundred miles one way, and up into the Jemez Mountains between Santa Fe and Albuquerque. There I found the Zen monastery in a valley. There were tall pine trees all around it and a wonderful hot spring pool in the back of the buildings that could be used by any one attending the retreat.

Each year when I went to the retreat, I met many people from all over the western states who had visited India and had been to the ashram and spoken to Sai Baba. He had answered their questions and gave them presents, which he manifested out of thin air right before their eyes. I was able to hold in my hand several of these items; one a ring with three large diamonds, and another a necklace made of gold. The speakers that came to the different retreats were people, from his organization, who had spent time with Baba in India. They told stories of how his words and counseling had affected their lives, and what projects they were working on in their home town.

In 2013, I made my last trip to the retreat. For many years I had driven my car to New Mexico, but this year I had a car pick me up at my house and take me to the airport in Phoenix where I got a short flight to Albuquerque, New Mexico. I joined a group being picked up at the airport. The van from the airport was filled with people from all across the United States going to the retreat. There was even a lady from Hawaii. The driver was pleasant and the conversation among the passengers stimulating.

Each year the retreat is offered by the Sai Baba group in Santa Fe, which is a part of the worldwide Sai organization formed by Sathya Sai Baba. Members were encouraged to work in their own communities in social service projects. Prayer and service to others was the message of Sai Baba. His organization built several hospitals in India where all services were free to the patients. Each year there was a different speaker for the retreat. When the construction of a large, very modern hospital was going on, one of the volunteer surgeons came to speak to us at the retreat that year. He was from one of the major hospitals in Los Angeles, California, and he had volunteered his time and his expenses to travel to India to work in the hospital for one year. Volunteers from all over the world staffed the Sathya Sai Baba hospitals in India.

The Zen monastery complex is composed of several buildings that form a large square. As you come into the compound, the prayer building is on the left, then the kitchen and dining building. Across from those are the dormitory buildings that house Zen students during most of the year. The area is rented out for small groups like ours for weekends, and in the summer. After the dormitory buildings are another group of buildings with meeting rooms and more dormitories with bathrooms and the end of the building. The dormitory building was furnished with bunk beds that could accommodate four people in each room. There were shower rooms at the end of the building. Blankets and sheets were provided. Even at the end of summer, the mountain air could be quite cool when the sun went down behind the mountains. There is a long porch that runs across the dormitory buildings. Here you could sit and watch the hummingbirds that gathered at the several tubes of nectar that hung on the porch. I saw as many as five hummingbirds at one time and got a few pictures of these beautiful birds.

The number of people at the retreat varied from year to year. There were some people that attending the day services only. We all volunteered to work on our times away from lectures or special meetings. I usually chose the kitchen as I enjoyed working with the group there. The menu for each meal was vegetarian. I got to learn to appreciate many new foods that way. The last year I was there we counted 80 people for the meals.

There were usually three or four of us in the kitchen helping the cook by preparing the vegetables or cutting up lettuce and tomatoes for salads. One year the cook showed us a recipe for Mexican corn bread that I helped make. It is now one of my treasured recipes. It has pieces of corn, onions, and green chili in it, and baked to a golden perfection. The time spent at the retreat started very early in the morning with the wakeup call of the flute player. The retreat participants would walk all around the compound following the flute player singing songs of praise and thanksgiving. My favorite song had the phrase "May all the beings of all the worlds find peace and be happy."

The last hours I spent at the monastery are those that made a lasting impression on me. I don't remember who the speakers were that year, nor did I make some new friends that I saw again after the retreat. The most memorable was the last day of my stay. My flight out of Albuquerque was for 8:45 that morning. With all the security at the airports now, I had to leave the center by 6:00 A.M.

The abbess at the monastery and I had become friends over the many years I had been at the retreat. She found a friend of hers who was willing to drive another person and myself to the airport that morning. The people in the van, who I had arrived with the first morning, were going back on a later flight, so I was very glad to have a way to get to the airport that morning. In the early morning hours, I went over to the dining room hoping that there was someone there so I could get some tea to drink. One of the ladies I had worked within the kitchen was there and she boiled an egg for me as a quick breakfast.

While I was eating Hosen, the abbess came in and saw me. She asked if I would like to go with her and see the morning prayers with the Buddhist nuns, in the large prayer house next to the kitchen. I said I would love to go. After I had finished eating, we went across the grass to the building. The sun had not as yet come up and it was very dark with only a little moonlight to guide us. When we entered the prayer building, there were two other Buddhist nuns there who I recognized as being part of the school.

There was one large room with a huge gong and a drum at one end and a platform at the other end of the room with a large statue of Buddha on it. There were benches around the wall and straw mats that covered the floor with corners of a highly polished floor showing at the ends.

You had to take off your shoes and put on socks to walk on the floor. I sat by the wall and watched the service. Hosen gave me a card with the English translation of the words they would be chanting. The room was quiet except for the chanting of the four nuns, and an occasional beat of the drum, which sounded dull and muffled to me. It was so peaceful in there that I must have drifted off because the next thing I remember was that I was in a sunlit room. To my left was a large staircase constructed of stone with steps going up both sides of the landing. There was a black iron railing on one side of the stairs. I started to climb the first set of stairs and saw that there was a second landing ahead of me. This second landing was more like a large raised stage, larger than the first landing. There on the stage was a very large white statue of a lady. Behind the statue was an area that opened like a clam shell and a window with glass that split the sunlight into tiny slivers of shimmering light that played all over the beautiful white statue before me. The statue was so large that I was dwarfed by comparison to it. It glowed with the reflective sunlight from the window and I heard the word "Quan yin."

    The chant was over and I got my shoes and went outside into the predawn morning of the mountains. Since I still could not see the path, Hosen took my hand and led me down the path back to the dining room where I had been before. I told her about the vision and asked her who Quan yin was. I told her that I had seen myself in orange robes lighting candles in a monastery, and that the sound of the Tibetan bells sounded so familiar. She said that the monks of Japan and Tibet wore orange robes and that Quan yin was a goddess of the Asian people known for her love and compassion.

    When we got to the dining area, I had some more tea and the driver of the car that would take me to the airport, also the other passenger, arrived. We left after I thanked Hosen for her kindness to me, [17]

    If you put all the facts together, they make a compelling story of a past life that I dimly remember, except for the impression made on me of the goddess Quan yin and the work I did in the creation of her statue in clay. I also took away from this life the determination of not deserting my children again and the desire to return to working with clay. The details of this life are not important only the lesson given and learned in the years I spent in China centuries ago.

CHAPTER FIVE

800 BCE Rise of Etruscan 753 BCE Founding of Rome

A LOST CIVILIZATION

Meditation March 1, 2013: "Civilizations are formed and then pass away from history. Many centuries of mankind have existed now without a trace. Your present civilization will pass away soon, without leaving a trace except in the minds of the people who lived it. How much more valuable is the word of Spirit that lives forever than the word of man?"

The souls look for a time, place, community where the lesson they have chosen to learn next can be experienced. From our lofty position in the etheric we are able to look through time and see the world as a large checker board with places, circumstances of birth and challenges indicated. The choice is ours. What is the next lesson we are willing to experience? How much are we willing to invest in energy, strength, and perseverance to accomplish the new challenge?

In our thousands of life experiences, do you think we thought of ourselves as being under a cloud of misfortune or of fortunate circumstance? Do you think we questioned the reason for our life or were we just too caught up in every day affairs that these thoughts never entered our head? There are many people living today who have not reached the point of questioning or searching for their purpose in life. For those who have dared to look into higher motivations for their life, there is a moment when the clouds part and the way becomes a little clearer. Where are you on your path to self-actualization? What have you learned about your fears, hopes, and plans for a more fulfilling future? Do you think only of yourself or can you see that you are a part of the whole called humanity? All questions for the enlightened mind.

When we arrived in Italy in 1980, I had no idea how my life would be changed. My husband was to be stationed in a small town on the Adriatic called Rimini. You have read in the first chapter my experience in Italy and the Duke of Urbino. Writing this chapter now brings back my memories of that time and the impression I have of the country and the people. I felt at home there, and now I understand why. Italy was another place where my soul descended into a life in centuries past to learn more about my life's purpose and how to have compassion for others. This was a time to finish up the many lifetimes my husband and I had spent together. I realized in years later, after our Italian experience, that was the case. The book was closed between us and the chances of meeting again in another life are small.

During my lifetime, several people have looked at me and said they saw a man dressed as a roman soldier superimposed over my face and body. I have seen myself dressed in a piece of course material, ragged at the end, thrown over one shoulder and hanging to my knees. I felt that I was a young male soldier, in an unknown time and place, guarding a doorway with a long stick that was pointed on the end. The feeling was of dejection and sadness.

THE ETRUSCANS

I imagine it all started by wanderers coming into the Po Valley of Italy. This was the area that divided the land between the mountains and the sea. Rolling hills that could be used for growing crops of grain, flax, and where olive trees would flourish along with the grapevine. In the hills, there was ample iron ore to supply their needs for centuries. Here the explorers saw rich farmland, and decided to stay. [1] With the passing of time, more people came to settle there. The small group of mud huts expanded and over time it became larger and expanded out into the countryside. New arrivals increased the groups of homes, eventually forming large city-states, which were independent of each other, but still linked together by common language and religion. [3]

Between the 6th century and the 3rd century, there was the "Villanovan" culture (1000-700 BCE) in the land now called Italy and in what is known as the Iron Age of the developing world. Historians now realize that this was the beginning of the people on the Italian peninsula, known later as Etruscan. There is a discussion among historians as to whether the Romans were in the land first. Some say that the Italic tribes arrived in this land first, and those that called themselves Etruscans came later, but this theory has been proven wrong as the Etruscan cities have been dated to be much older than those constructed by Rome. Etruscan cities were built on the top of mountains for the easier defense of the people there. These cities were self-governing, united by their common language and culture. By 650 BCE, the Etruscans dominated the land.

The land was fertile with open areas for orchards and an abundance of lakes and wetlands for food and trade.[2] They had tamed the horse by then, and they were using it to help in working around the farm. All that we know about these people is from the things they left in their graves and the pictures they painted on pottery and other funeral offerings. There has not been found any written information as of this date. This is probably why the civilization of the Etruscan people is not well known or taught in schools as part of the world history class.

THE PEOPLE

The Etruscan lands were bordered on the North by the warlike tribes of the Celts, and the equally menacing Latin speaking people of the east. They needed to defend their people by setting up armies and providing them equipment to use. The low mountains near the shoreline of the Mediterranean provided much needed tin, which when used with copper made bronze. The Etruscan cities were independently linked together by a trade network that connected them to each other and to the tribes in the north, also other nations such as the Phoenicians and the Carthaginians. Among the traded goods were slaves and Greek pottery. There were many seaports along the coast that profited from the semi-independent trade that was found along the Tyrrhenian coast. Etruscan city-states joined Carthage to defend their trade interests against the Greeks in the Battle of Alalia, sometime between 540 BCE and 535 BCE. This was a naval battle off the coast of Corsica, between the Greeks and the Etruscans with their allies from Africa, the Carthaginians. The Etruscans emerged as the dominant control of the sea until the 8th century, which was contested by the Greeks in the western Mediterranean in 750 BCE. [4] But there was a great threat to their cities and their culture rising in the growing area dominated by the Latin speaking tribes. By the late fourth century, Rome was beginning to be a contender for the land with the final hold out, the city of Cerveteri conquered by Rome in 273 BCE. The Roman

Empire was taking shape. As the Etruscan cities were conquered, the people were often butchered or sold into slavery. The conquered areas were then repopulated with veteran Roman soldiers and their families. The Etruscan culture and language was lost deferring to the use of Latin and Latin ways. It would be centuries before the discovery of Etruscan tombs that revealed artifacts and vibrantly painted walls, pottery and other burial items that told the story of this lost civilization. [5]

Through the artifacts from these tombs, we learn that their society was arranged into several layers of acceptability with the royals inheriting their right to the throne, aristocrats, architects, and merchants at the very top. Farm managers and servants were considered below this as a servant was considered to be a part of their master's household. House slaves formed a close association with the family whom they served. Below this group of people were the laborers, farmers, and soldiers. Within the bottom of the social scale were slaves who were composed of people captured from the surrounding lands as part of the spoils of war.

The painting in the Etruscan tombs show women had more freedom than their counterparts in other areas. They are three women pictured as watching a chariot race, something that would be unheard of in Greek society. Pictures show women as property owners and the right to drink wine, additionally proven by graffiti on a pottery vessel, which a woman owned. There are references to women where they are referred to using both their first name as well as their family name. There were discovered tombs constructed just for a female occupant. [10]

HOUSING

The first houses were of a circular shape, partially sunk in the ground, made of mud and sticks with a thatch roof. There was a fireplace in the middle of the hut for warmth and cooking. Several of these huts were grouped together, and had a wall of the same building materials built around them for protection. Archeological findings show that these huts were eventually replaced with rectangular houses scattered throughout the region and found predominately on the six hills of the area. Groups of homes with their entrance turned inward, and their back-stone walls used as part of the town's surrounding defenses. The aristocrats lived in large, single-story houses with a gabled roof that was covered in terracotta tiles. Their houses were built in a rectangular shape with an area called an atrium in the center of the house. This area was open to the sky, with an open area in the roof to gather rain water. The atrium was surrounded with individual sleeping rooms. There might also be found a tree or flowering bushes, possibly plants growing in pots surrounding the tile floor of the atrium. The entrance door for the house faced the street. [6]

This architecture was copied by the Romans years later, and can be seen now in the houses restored in the ancient town of Pompeii. The Roman houses of the rich increased the interior designs with elaborate house floors covered in mosaic pictures made with tiny pieces of colored tile. The walls were decorated with pictures of people in different activities, with a large border of red color around each picture. This paint remained bright through the centuries in its intensity, even after having being buried for centuries in ash as in the restored houses of Pompeii. As the Latin speaking peoples in the land began to establish their own villages, their huts of mud and tree branches gave way to the style of the stone houses as built by the Etruscans. Huts on the west side of the town, later to be known as Rome, were cleared off and the Earth packed down to serve as a city gathering place known as the Roman Forum. [7]

TEMPLES

The religion of the Etruscans was polytheistic with gods who controlled everyday life. There was a god of the sun, one for the growing crops, war, death, and the underworld. Some of these gods were adopted from the Greeks, probably introduced with the active trade between the two countries. The two main features of their religion were the reading of omens from birds and lighting strikes, and the information obtained from the examination of the entrails of sacrificed animals. There were also ceremonies and rituals that could reverse the meaning of a sign and omen. The sacrifices and ceremonies were held outside of the temple. Votive gifts from the faithful ranged from food stuffs to pottery and bronze statuettes. Archeologists have found both precious and everyday items in Etruscan tombs, which indicate that the Etruscans believed in a life after death. The wall paintings tell the story of an afterlife filled with endless banquets followed by games, dancing and music. [8]

CLOTHING

Most clothing was made of cotton or wool in colors that went from yellow to bright red, and pink with a tinge of orange. The clothing for an Etruscan man ranged from just a loincloth, which were worn by slaves, to the ankle-length, Greek style tunics worn by the aristocrats. The tunic might be decorated with a geometric design on the edge or just plain without any design. Men of high rank wore colored scarves around their neck. In the sixth century, a man wore a tunic with a semicircular cape draped over his left shoulder and going under the right arm. Shoes were worn only by the rich, as they were a valued item. When they were not worn, they were placed on a special bench for storage. In the sixth century, a cape was included which would be draped over their left shoulder and tucked under their right arm. Capes had borders of blue fabric on the edges. This was later used as the identifying dress for a Roman senator. The middle and lower classes wore knee-length tunics without any decorations.

Women wore the long or short tunic with gold ornaments in their hair if they were from of an aristocrat household. They painted their eyebrows and used a red pigment for their lips. A woman of this social rank kept herself fit with time in exercise and waxing unwanted hair from her body. Apparently, cosmetic dentistry was known to the elite with gold crowns, bridges found in skulls in the graves of the early people. There is also an account of finding gold fillings and the replacement of missing teeth using animal teeth to fill in the space. [9]

TRADE

Etruscan cities spread across the valley and in the northwest Etruscan cities controlled the copper, iron and silver mines in the mountains. The Etruscans used the Greek letters for their writing, but in their own language to describe their trade goods. Inscriptions have been found on tombs and on goods found in them. This unknown language has yet to be translated. [11]

The people lived by agricultural means and as the time went by, they began to trade with the surrounding countries. The iron mined in the hills was of interest to the Greeks. In return, the

Etruscans received ivory from Egypt, amber from the Baltic, and pottery from Greece and Ionia. Coastal cities acted as a point of trade. In the Etruscan tombs, archeologists have found evidence of trade with other countries around the Mediterranean. Items found were ostrich eggs, ivory goods, glass paste jewelry, and metal items such as glass bottles for perfumes, oil lamps, and pottery. [12]

In the eight century, the Etruscans became a local power uniting with the Phoenicians to become trading partners exchanging goods and participating in raids together. All of this changed with the arrival of Greeks in the western Mediterranean in 750 BCE. As time went by, the Greeks colonized along the coast of southern Italy and in most of Sicily, attempting to interfere with the sea lanes' trade traffic. There was an inevitable clash coming between the two countries. The Greeks carried on their political and commercial enterprises just as they had done on the Greek mainland, taking more and more of the sea trade. This area of Southern Italy and Sicily became known as Magna Graecia. [13]

To protect their trade routes, the Etruscans and the Carthaginians joined forces and fought the Greeks in a naval battle off the coast of Corsica. This was known as the Battle of Alalia and took place between 540 BCE and 535 BCE. The Greeks losing almost two-thirds of their fleet decided to retreat. According to a legend, the Etruscans stoned their prisoners while the Carthaginians sold their prisoners into slavery. [14]

THE CITY OF VEII

Veii was an important ancient Etruscan city with over 300 years of history that included stories of battles with the Roman Kingdom and later the Roman Republic. It continued to be occupied, even after the its capture in 396 BCE by the Romans. The site is now protected as part of the Parco di Veio established in 1997. Veii was built on a hill and had an additional advantage in that it had a river that ran close by the city. The archeological evidence shows that this city was occupied in the tenth century, the late Bronze age. By the seventh century, the area had taken on the looks of a modern city with buildings in block arrangement around a square containing a water cistern. In the eighth century, both the potter's wheel and writing were introduced from Greece.

The prosperity of the city of Veii came from its location as it was built at the mouth of the Tiber River, giving it a direct trade route to other areas of the Mediterranean where they could sell their greatest wealth: salt. Sitting at the mouth of the river, they could also control the river traffic. By the sixth century, the town was well established as an important place with large buildings featuring terracotta decorations. The streets of the town were wide with a regulated spacing for side streets and a city water supply of canals and tunnels. Outside the town there was a large temple built of volcanic block to honor Minerva. The building was square with columns creating a large porch at the front of the building. The roof was decorated with terracotta figures of river gods. On the tiles of the roof in the middle of the building was a life-size standing figure of Apollo dated to 510 BCE and can be seen today at the National Etruscan Museum of Villa Giulia in Rome. [15]

The declining influence of the city was seen when the control of the local trade route fell into the hands of Syracuse in Sicily, and the attention of the city's southern neighbors, the

Romans, started to interfere with trading of the city. In preparation for possible trouble from this area, they fortified the walls around the city, with gates to roads that connected to other Etruscan cities.

In 406 BCE, Rome declared war against the capital of Etruria, the city of Veii. The ten-year war cost Rome dearly with soldiers and siege equipment, as the city was well fortified with defensive and offensive equipment. It also had all the provisions to withstand a long siege. In 396 BCE, a Roman commander by the name of Camillus proceeded to dig in the soft rock under the city walls and then he sent men to infiltrate the city through the city's drainage system. The intent was not to bring the city to surrender, but to completely annihilate the city and its people. The Romans slaughtered the entire male population and made slaves of the women and children. They plundered the city, taking anything of value to Rome. The city never recovered its former glory and was eventually abandoned by Rome, forgotten until the seventeenth century when it was rediscovered. [16]

ROME

In the Po valley, there was the home of several different tribes while the Etruscan villages grew into large complexes of buildings and eventually formed into individual city-states. In the same valley, there were Latin speaking tribes that also grew into a formidable force. This is the story of the mighty Rome.

The land was ruled by an Etruscan king representing the majority of the people, but there were other tribes in the country who, according to a Roman historian, were called Etruscans, Sabines, and Latina, with the people divided into six levels of society. These divisions were not based on ancestry but their wealth. The richest man was expected to defend the country and provide his own equipment of swords, bronze helmet, shield, and spear. The poor man brought his sling and stones that he used to defend his sheep from prowling wolves, in the hills. [17]

Since the sea victory at Alalia in 535, the Etruscans had a hard time remaining in power throughout the land. City by city, the Etruscans lost control of the people and the land to the Romans. If that was not enough there were the Celts of Gaul that came into the area looking for land to add to their holdings. These were wild people who lived for the hunt in war and in the acquiring of the wild animals for food and clothing. Their invasion began around 505 BCE extending as far over as the western coast of Europe, and maybe to the island of Britain where the large ring of standing stone at Stonehenge is a testimony to their presence. When the last king was removed from power in 509 BCE, the Roman Republic was established.

The Roman Republic responded to this invasion of the Gauls by appointing a dictator for the first time. This was for only six months appointed by the ruling council with full powers to impose death on citizens outside the walls of the city, but inside the city the criminals were judged by a popular vote in what type of punishment they should receive. The dictator's voice was that to be obeyed with no possibility of appeal. This is the first time Rome suspended the rights of its population, but would not be the last.[18] Established in 390 BCE, the city of Rome was attacked by the barbarian tribe called Gaul, who destroyed what might have been the history of the founding of the city.

Rome took what the Etruscans had built and claimed it for their own. They copied the engineering accomplishments of building waterways and aqueducts for the distribution of water to the agriculture lands. They also took the planning of the city with its well-placed main streets and cross streets as a standard for all Romans. The style of architecture considered now as "Roman" was copied from the Etruscan buildings. Even the large private homes of the Roman rich were patterned after the designs that first appeared in an Etruscan town. They had the open court yard in the middle of the house and colorful mosaic patterns decorated their floors. The Etruscans built public works using arches and vaults and laid out bridges and roads. Houses were made with wide porches and garden areas, as well as a sewer system below the house, not in the street as it was commonly used then. [19]

ROMAN CITIZEN

When Rome was a republic it had a long history of democratic rule. After the Etruscans were taken out of the government, the city-states were ruled by a Senate and an assembly with elected magistrate, counsels, and tribunals with offices that had limitations. After conquering the Roman peninsula, Rome gained considerable land from surrounding conquered lands. The size of the republic placed a strain on the ones in leadership positions, resulting in certain men taking a command of the situation in their area. The change started by the senate giving Julius Caesar the title "dictator for life," and his subsequent murder by the senators, left the three generals in the field in the position of having to contend for that of the supreme commander.

The political and military life of Rome changed with the three leaders of that time, Octavian, who later was known as Augustus, Mark Antony and Lepidus, all generals in the empire. The battle between Mark Antony and Lepidus eliminated Lepidus as a contender for the most powerful position in Rome. Octavian then assumed the leadership of the Republic. [20]

The republic was once again transformed by one man's will into a shadow of its former glory. The senate remained in name only without power to stop the constant drain on the treasury or the appointment of undeserving men to powerful positions. All was being controlled by Octavian. He remembered the fate of Caesar and organized a guard for his personal protection, which came to be known as The Praetorian Guard.

With his new power, conferred on him by the Senate, he now commanded the army's twenty-six legions, and had the control over the provincial governors that ruled the conquered lands of Rome. He now had authority to call an assembly of the people to enact laws, which he could also veto any action he pleased in the future. No one could run for office unless he was approved by Octavian, or Augustus as he was later called. He effectively controlled all future legislation. [21]

With the control of the army and the ruling class in the senate, the last area of influence was religion. The Roman people believed in the importance of the family and the value of religion. They believed that citizenship defined what it was to be truly civilized. The many wars and the influx of other cultures and gods had a profound effect on the Roman culture. Citizenship for the Roman territories would be debated in the future, but in the beginning citizens were of Rome alone.

The influx of the Greek influence affected the Roman culture and religion. In Rome, an individual's personal belief was unimportant as long as they strictly adhered to the rules and ceremonies dictated by the prevailing gods and avoided any show of religious fervor. Temples honoring the foreign gods were built throughout the empire. [22]

The division of the classes could be seen throughout the empire, but especially in the city of Rome was it amplified. Rome was filled with refugees who came in from surrounding towns and farms seeking elusive jobs, leaving them in the street as beggars. Any possible jobs were taken by the many slaves obtained from the endless wars with surrounding nations.

The name "plebeian" was given to the common people who found the only shelter for them was in one of the second story apartments, usually constructed over a shop on the ground floor. Mr. Cowell, in his book *"Life in Ancient Rome,"* gives a very descriptive picture of the hazard in living there. There was always the chance of fire, or the building collapsing because of faulty construction. The chance of epidemics and disease was high throughout the city, but probably more so in the tenements as they had no water, circulating air or sanitation. The byproducts of digestion, as well as that from cooking, were thrown out onto the street to run into a drainage area. The evidence from Roman tombs show that the dirt, flies, unhygienic foods and drink brought the average citizen to their grave on or before the age of forty.[23] The very rich had their houses outside the city where gardens were in abundance. There were fruit-bearing plants, flowers and fountains. In the yard, there might be found birds, doves, pheasants, ducks, and partridge either walking in the yard or in aviaries. During the Empire, the growth of the city population increased, and with the demand of land for the building of tenement housing, many private homes and their gardens were obliterated. [24]

The great baths were available to everyone, but soap was unknown. This item was made out of goat's fat and ashes and very expensive to buy. Cleansing was done by rubbing oil over the skin, followed by the individual going into a sweet room, followed by a cooling bath afterwards. Sanitation was not considered a problem for the city as everything was washed out of the city and into the Tiber River. The smell in the summer must have been horrible. Perhaps that is where the practice started, of everyone in Italy taking a vacation in the month of August just to get out of the stench of the city.

The risk of infections was high from polluted water and contaminated food spread by flies and mosquitoes. There was the human illness that was brought on by accidents and the normal day-to-day living of harsh labor for the poor and the overindulgences of the rich. The suffering of the sick and injured people could have been alleviated with simple hygiene practices and the use of herbal medicines, but that was not to come until centuries later. The beautiful buildings and the elegance of the dress of the rich hid the underlying purification of the popular practices. [25]

In the early days of the republic, all clothing was homemade of wool or flax cloth. Each home had a hand loom that was used to weave the woolen threads into a piece of cloth that was a simple square, with a hole for the head. Everyone wore the same style clothing with a little color on the edge for those men of the senate. This process required more people than the usual Roman household had: therefore, clothing to be cleaned went to a group of people, called "Fullers" who were responsible for that work.

In F.R. Cowell's book *Life in Ancient Rome*, he describes the way this cleaning was done.

"This job was done by the fullers, who used carbonate of soda, potash or the special kind of alkaline clay known today as Fuller's earth. Soap was not used for cleaning. In a wall painting found in Pompeii, fullers were depicted at work in large vats, treading the cloth with their feet. Finer woolens made for the rich were bleached by being placed over a wicker frame and placed over a pot of burning Sulphur. The fuller's trade was hazardous to their health as breathing Sulphur fumes, plus treading cloth in vats of chemicals day after day, was liable to produce skin diseases. The occupation was dangerous with the additional of the use of urine from the public lavatories, and when their knowledge of chemicals was limited. The final operation was for the fuller to fill his mouth with water and spray it over the cloth." [26]

Years later, the use of flax was made into a linen cloth, with a guild of linen weavers for that. As Rome became a great empire, the call for this material increased as it was used in the sails for ships. The better linen product was produced in Egypt. Clothing was expensive and only the rich had more than one toga and cloak to wear.

Food for the common people was a simple gruel of wheat boiled in water with perhaps a drop of honey for flavor. If possible, vegetables, herbs, fish, mushrooms were added, and a little meat if it could be found. It was only the rich that could add anything to their daily gruel. The addition of meat was offered only on very special occasions, such as a religious feast or some type of civic honor, or a wedding at which time animals were sacrificed and the meat was shared with the guests. At this time, honey sweet cakes and fruit were served. Wine mixed with water was served, usually warmed in the winter. In the summer, it was cooled by preserved ice and snow from the winter months.

SLAVES

With the expansion of the Roman territories and the conquering of foreign lands, Rome was filled with foreign slaves from Spain, Greece, Macedonia, Asia Minor, and from Britain, especially in the second and first century. Naked men, women and children were paraded in front of prospective buyers and sold to the highest bidder. Their only dress was a placard hung around their neck that advertised their qualities and defects. The children of slaves became slaves, property of their owner. Some were taken into the mines in the mountains where tin and other minerals were dug from the earth. Others were taught the tasks of farming, or the grinding of grain. The fortunate few boys and girls were chosen for work in the house of some rich man, or because of their beauty for sexual pleasures of the household. There was no limit to how many slaves a person could own or nor were there laws covering what their eventual fate would be. The life of a slave just as the life of a person who was poor had no value. Only those in power, the rich magistrate, the senator or the rich governor were considered of usefulness to the community and therefore valued. Any slave that tried to pass himself off as a free citizen might be put to death. Slaves could not join the army, but they were made to do the heavy labor associated with the army, such as all kinds of heavy manual labor. Any hint of disobeying an order was quickly put to rest, with the threat of crucifixion in which any slave could be condemned. In spite of the brutality, some masters treated their slaves humanely and protected them in times of persecution through affection and gratitude for their services. [27]

THE ROMAN SOLDIER

The Roman soldier was composed of men from the poorest of the population. According to the constitution, every free-born citizen was a soldier and bound to serve. The higher positions of command were given to the men from Roman's privileged few. The Roman soldier served in legions of four thousand men, and divided into horse soldiers and foot soldiers. The legions were then divided into small units, each with their own leader. Roman soldiers were either of the well-to-do families of Rome who served as a necessary but an unpleasant duty, and who brought a slave to provide for his personal needs, or of the poorest of the population. Each man was required to carry his own baggage and prepare his own food. The standard enlistment time was for twenty-five years. A stela, which is a marker stone, was found with the information about a Roman soldier's life. It said that they enlisted at eighteen and usually died by age thirty. The cause was not listed unless killed in battle, but many soldiers never saw combat as their fate was to die from possibly blood-poisoning contracted from an infected wound, or other infections. There was disease that took many soldiers, caused from unsanitary living conditions and other events, that could have been prevented if a knowledge of sanitation and the sterile treatment of wounds as we have now. [28]

In the early republic, soldiers were not paid as they served only occasionally and left their farms when duty called. The soldiers of this time were the farmers who took up farming instruments to defend their land, and went home when the danger was concluded. By the fourth century, soldiers received a small daily cash payment with which they were required to buy their own clothing and food. The main staple was a whole wheat biscuit, sometimes with honey, bacon, cheese, and sour wine. If the camp was in place for several days there might be a more varied diet with some beef, poultry, fish and fruits. It all depended on what was available around the area where they we camped. [29]

The Roman soldier was taught his destiny was to die in battle, as a death in battle was considered not only his duty but would also bring him glory. Both religion and duty bound them in war. Roman discipline was harsh. Punishment was given for cowardice, disobedience or treachery, and could range from whippings to the most severe, a sentence of death by his centurion.

The centuries rolled on and the Roman Empire continued to control the known ancient world with their laws and with the continued oppression of the conquered peoples, but not those of Roman birthright or those that were of the rich ruling class. By 285 CE, the Roman Empire was so vast it was no longer able to control all the conquered countries from the central location of Rome. The Emperor Diocletian divided the empire into halves with the western portion known as the Holy Roman Empire and the eastern known as Eastern Empire governed from Byzantium later known as Constantinople. [30]

THE FALL OF THE ROMAN EMPIRE

In my research for information for this part of the book, I found something relevant to our society today in the twenty-first century. In a book written by George Burton Adams called *"Medieval and Modern History,"* published in 1900 on page 27, there is a paragraph that stands out as being prophetic:

"It is not possible to explain briefly this decay of the Roman strength. Its cause was mainly economic. The universal use of slaves, making free labor degrading; the heavy taxes which were collected that the burden resting with killing weight, on the middle class; the debased currency, giving an unsteady standard of value; a practice, begun in the last days of the Republic , of feeding a part of the city population at the expense of the entire state, making an idle and dangerous mob and constantly tempting the middle class to give to hopeless struggle with taxes ,slaves competition, uncertain prices, and declining population, and take life easy at the public expense; official corruption, which, in spite of all the efforts of the emperors and of temporary reforms, continued to look on public wealth as source of private wealth; a general decay of the Roman manhood and moral strength which weakened the army and the resistance of the whole empire"[31]

History has been proven to repeat itself. Here we have a mighty empire falling because of the greed of its officials, the lack of determination and work ethic of the middle class and the continued posture of the elite, rich population to control the misery of those of the lower classes. The most damaging is the loss of pride and self-confidence in personal achievements that seem to be looked on now as worthless efforts on the part of anyone who tries to rise above their lot in life.

MY LIFE IN THIS TIME

It has been hard for me to write the story of the city of Veii, as it has been relived in me as if I was still there experiencing the siege of the city with the dead and dying people all around me. The cry of children and the screams of the women being dragged out of their homes by a Roman soldier pulling them by their hair. The event burned into my subconscious until today when I relived it again. I was part of this time and I have held this pain until I could release it now as I write this story. The lessons learned from this are many. Among these is compassion for the injured and dying, respect for the hard work of others and their achievements in many areas of life. I think that I must have questioned then in my own mind the justice in the killing of defenseless people, and the savagery in which it was done. As I write about this city and their people many centuries ago, I feel I was a part of this time in history. Now I understand why I had a complete aversion to learning Latin in the Catholic boarding school in my 8th grade, first and second year of high school. Latin was one of the required classes and we were taught to read and translate it into English. Of course, this gave a great basic for the French that I was required to learn at that time, and the Italian I chose to learn in later years.

When we returned home from living in Italy two years, I brought back to the states two reproductions of Etruscan pottery. One was a funeral urn painted with black figures on a red base. The other piece of pottery was a tall thin vase with a pictorial design. Both of these pieces of pottery were placed on a high book shelf in my home in Arizona. One morning I came down to breakfast and found the funeral urn had been moved to the bottom shelf of the book case. It was not broken, just placed in a new area. My family all said they had not touched the urn, so I just put it back on the top of the book case and did not think anything about it. Several days later the same thing happened again. This time the top of the urn was off and placed beside it. This continued for several days. A month later, I read that the library was having a sale of some of its books and I thought the Etruscan pottery would be a great gift to the library. I understood they were able to raise some money for the library with the sale of that pottery.

My time in Italy, in this lifetime, was filled with the rediscovery of the beauty of the land and the friendly people. It was also a time of remembering a lifetime gone by and the events that happened. With my life in the city of Veii, I do not know if I was part of the population that was slaughtered or if I was one of the soldiers that did the killing. All I do know is that the destruction of the city and the fate of its citizens affected me deeply even now. The second part of my Italian connection was when I visited Urbino with my husband and felt the discomfort in the duchess's bedroom as I will described later .

CHAPTER SIX

First Crusade 1095-1100 Capture of Antioch 6/3/1098

A Monk in the Middle Ages and a Knight in the First Crusade

Time is irrelevant when it comes to reliving past lives. Spirit does not exist in any specific time line, but in the eternal now. Glimpse of past events is given to us when we need it, with the message necessary for us to remember and understand. Maybe the message is hard to understand and it takes us a while of thoughtful contemplation before the meaning is revealed. The message is the same even though centuries may have passed between the two events. The connection may be so evident it hits us between the eyes with the impact of a fist! Such was the time of my next story.

One day in 2009, I was shopping in our local pharmacy store and one minute I was looking at some beautiful birthday cards and the next moment I could not see out of my right eye. It was as if someone had pulled down a shade over the top half of my vision in that eye. Seconds later, the dark area dissolved and my vision was clear. During this event I was thinking "Now isn't that interesting?" The emotional side of me started screaming "What has happened to my eye?"

When I got home, I called my ophthalmologist and got an appointment right way. After a complete eye exam, my doctor told me that she did not see any cause for vision loss, but she did recommend I get an appointment with a cardiologist. Perhaps I had a clogged artery that was throwing plaque and somehow blocking the optic nerve. I called my primary care doctor to arrange further testing. The person making appointments did not understand that I felt this was an urgent situation and after several attempts to get an early appointment, I finally succeeded. When I saw the doctor, I was given a referral to a cardiologist in a few weeks. The cardiologist decided that a special test was needed and I was scheduled at the hospital outpatient clinic.

The day of the test I was in a hospital exam room. The nurse had started an intravenous injection of fluids, so that when the doctor got there, he could administer the sedative and he could do the procedure. I arrived early for the appointment as requested and waited for the doctor for over an hour before he finally appeared in the room. He did not say a word to me, no apology for being late or anything, just told the nurse to administer the sedative.

Conscious sedation is not what it sounds like. You are given medicine by IV that makes you not care what is being done to your body, but raises havoc when you become fully conscious and they are not finished with the procedure! This is what happened. The doctor had put a long black rubber tube with a small camera down my throat looking at my heart from inside my body. When the sedative started wearing off, and he still had the tube in my throat. I came out of the sedation gagging and struggling to breathe. The doctor pulled the tube out of my throat. He spoke to me for the first time in that hour and gruffly told me to go home and they would call me with the results. He stormed out the room without another word.

This is when I got really, really angry! How dare he treat me as if I was some lab rat! Not only did my throat hurt, but my sensitivity as a former nurse was injured. The nurse that had been with me was sympatric to my concerns, and I did write a letter of complaint to the hospital, against this doctor and his lack of profession manners. Apparently, mine was not the first letter they had received against him.

My anger came from the fact that I worked as a nurse for twenty years in military hospitals and clinics. I made sure that my patients were cared for and comfortable in their different situations. I explained procedures and comforted those who were fearful or apprehensive. Here, in my time of need, this same caring process was denied to me! I was furious at the lack of personal regard and concern for the patient from this doctor.

The next visit I had with my ophthalmologist was within a week of the fateful test. She told me the test had been negative and she was glad that I had followed her instructions. She said that the condition I had experienced with my eye was temporary and might never happen again. The next thing she said really stuck with me: if the blindness had lasted longer than it did, I could have lost permanent vision in that eye. She would check me in another six months. Here, ten years later, I have never had another event.

THE MONK

My first Life in the Middle Ages, Time to Forgive

In December 2009, I went to a meeting held in Tucson, AZ. It was a group of about fifty men and women gathered for meditation, prayer and discussion on some spiritual topic. The night I attended the topic was on healing. There was a lady playing a harp and another person had several of the beautiful crystal bowls that have a tone when they are rubbed around the rim. The room was quiet except for the music and the lady's voice, who was conducting the mediation, bringing a calming feeling into the room.

I was comfortable in my chair, enjoying the music, when all of a sudden I saw myself as a man standing on a hill overlooking a burnt-out building in the valley below me. I was leaning against a tree and looking in the distance for several minutes, then I proceeded to walk down to the building below. As I started to approach, I realized it was a church. The next events were like looking at a movie with the pictures running backwards. Where the burnt walls stood, there were clean, new logs and where the roof had caved in, the former sturdy roof held again. The building was whole once more!

I walked up to the massive wooden doors and pushed one open. The building was filled with men talking in small groups. The room was lit by torches at one end of the room and the feeling of the room was of gaiety and comradery. I saw that I was a tall thin man wearing a brown monk's tunic, with a rope as a belt in the middle. Everyone seems to know me by name and welcomed me into their group.

The next thing I knew, a group of men carrying pitch forks and sticks came bursting into the building. They were yelling and screaming as they grabbed me by the arms and someone put a rope around my neck, then the entire group started dragging me out of the building. I knew I was heading for torture and death. I asked Spirit to take me above this event, as I did not actually want to feel the following torture again. I found myself floating above the church feeling at peace, yet looking down at my body being brutally beaten.

I asked Spirit why I was being shown this and I heard a low sweet voice whisper in my right ear "Forgive them." I came back to the room seeing that nothing had changed, all was as it was before my vision. The music still playing and the lady, who was conducting the meditation, was closing with her words of comfort and relaxation as people began to open their eyes.

A few days later, I was talking to my friend who is a Spiritualist minister in Boston, Massachusetts. She listened to my story of the difficulty of getting an early doctor's appointment, and my frustration and anger of the way I was treated by the doctor when doing the procedure. I also told her of the vision I had of being a monk and being killed. As I talked, I began to realize that the same feeling I had experienced were in both situations. I felt anger that my position was not recognized as a monk, and in this life as a former nurse. I resented the way I was treated by the doctor during the entire event. My friend kept saying to me "Listen to what you are saying. Is that not the same feeling you had in the vision? What were you told then?" I repeated, "Forgive them." She said. "So, what have you learned?" I thought a few minutes and it was all clear to me. Forgiveness and compassion break down the firewalls between myself and my soul. I needed to stop and forgive them all.

CHRISTIANITY BECOMES LEGAL

As the known Roman world began to disintegrate and reorganize into regions of land and groups of people of the same language, the only organized formal system that remained in place was that of the church. The pagan rituals were forbidden and their temples destroyed, yet there were still groups of people that held onto the old ways.

After the fall of the Western Roman Empire, the church was the only organized form of law throughout the land. As the everyday world transitioned from a conquered Roman province into lands held by a king with people composed of individual farmers, shopkeepers, and free men. The church became the controlling constant for law and order in the land. The bishop took up his residence in the capital of the regional area. The archbishop took his residence in the largest province of the area, and the priests had their groups of villages in which to administer to the people. They worked with the people sometimes using their position as pastor of the church to settle secular disputes and they also acted as a reference to the bishop in the larger town. In this way, the network of the Roman Catholic Church spread all across Europe. Everything was organized under the controlling head of the Pope of Rome. This powerful position in Rome was a prestigious one, which was contested by many different people over the years.

The name of Charlemagne is known in history as the king who turned the pagan world toward Christianity. He was known as Charles the Great, born in the country now called Belgium, around 742 AD. He was the brother of Pepin the Short who became King of the Franks. Charlemagne waged war against the pagan tribes and was reported to have said that anyone who did not get baptized or follow Christian traditions were to be put to death. To reinforce the relationship of the church with Charlemagne, Pope Leo III crowned him Emperor of the Romans on December 26,800 at St Peter's Basilica in Rome.[1] In return, Charlemagne brought the church under royal protection.

The culture changed drastically as before Christians were considered an outlawed cult. They often worshiped in hiding in order to avoid both physical and social oppression from various pagan and Jewish groups. After Charlemagne's imperial endorsement, the Christians relaxed only to realize that with the new freedom prestige and power came corruption and even acts of arrogance from some in leadership positions.

There were the spiritually pure individuals that wanted only to be able to worship God as they desired and carry on their life away from all social unrest. This was the beginning of the Christian monastic lifestyle. Individuals, both men and women, sequestered themselves in caves and on mountain tops to commune with God and nature alone away from the distraction of the life in the valley below them. There were also individuals that devoted their lives to spiritual work as prayer, social service, teaching and spreading the Christian faith. [2]

AUTOMATIC WRITING

September 14, 2012, I received this message by automatic writing:

"As I told you we will be working together bringing back the old thought and knowledge of the ancient world you so love. How is it that you feel so much more at home in the ancient past than in the world of today?

Is it because the basic blocks of learning and education were laid there and mankind is just rediscovering it again? How can the ancient voice of reason reach the mind of today's people if you do not speak out?

You were a scribe in ancient Egypt in the temple where everything observed was written down. You learned much and kept that knowledge buried in yourself until now. It is not because anyone told you of this. It is because now is the time the world is waking after a long sleep where the information was buried or burned by the ignorant.

These are your days, as those who have become enlightened are willing to listen to the voice of reason and will follow its lead. There are those who will be open to whatever you write. How hard it has been to reach you. You have put up defenses against opening your mind, but now you are ready to start. We are with you always."

MONASTERY OF MONTE CASSINO

For you that are reading this, you might remember it from an American history class as one of the battles of WWII. In 1944, the Monastery at Monte Cassino in Italy was the key point for the German defensive line blocking the allies' advancement to Rome. The monastery was destroyed many times over the centuries, but then rebuilt. The latest destruction in modern times was in World War II as the Germans were using the monastery as a part of their defense line for Rome. It was considered a key observation point for those troops fighting in the field. On February 15, 1944, the abbey was almost completely destroyed by the allied armies. The abbey was rebuilt after the war by Pope Paul VI and consecrated in 1996. [3]

The town of Cassinum was first settled in the fifth century by the Volsci people. They built a citadel on the summit of Mount Cassino, which sits three miles higher than the valley.

The Romans conquered the area in 312 BCE and renamed the settlement Casinum. They built a temple to Apollo. Modern archology searches have not found any indication of it, but they have found the ruins of an amphitheater and a mausoleum from Roman times. According to Gregory the Great's biography of "Life of St. Benedict of Nursia," a monastery in 529 was constructed on the crown of the hill. Benedict's first act was to destroy the temple and smash the idols placed there by the Romans. He then built a chapel dedicated to St Martin of Tours, and another for St. John the Baptist placed where the altar for Apollo once stood.

Once the monastery was established, Benedict never left it. Here he wrote the rules for monastic life, which would be the guidance for other monasteries as it eventually spread across the western world. The abbey continued to flourish until 580 when it was pillaged and burned by the Lombards, only to rise again in 718 under the direction of Abbot Petronax, who built a new church over the tomb of now St. Benedict. In 1058 until 1087, Abbot Desiderius was the leader. He would later be elected Pope under the title of Victor III. [3] The monastery became a hospital for the local people and for travelers in the area. The monks began to buy and collect medical and other books by Greek, Roman, Islamic, Egyptian, European, Jewish and Asian authors resulting in their library becoming one of the richest depositories of knowledge of that time, holding the knowledge of many civilizations. Monks copying the medical texts learned a lot about the human anatomy, and methods of treatment. These they used in the hospital. By the 10-11th century, Monte Cassino had become the most famous cultural, educational and medical center of Europe. The first medical school was opened in nearby Salerno. [4] Under Abbott Petronax's direction, the monastery housed over two hundred monks and the school of copyists and miniature painters became famous throughout the West. The rules of Benedict required monastic vows of stability: a lifelong commitment and a promise of poverty, with all personal wealth given to the community, also obedience to superiors. His order placed high emphasis on the spiritual benefits of labor, prayer and a consistent schedule. Those men and women who joined the monastic groups sincerely hoped to find freedom and victory over the things of the world, and they were willing to give up all their worldly goods and concerns to achieve it. [5]

MY LIFE AS A MONK

I believe I was a monk at this time, because of the vison, and also because of my strong love of books, and what they contain. I also feel that I was one of those monks who copied the ancient parchments for the monastery library. The second part of the focus of this life was in the practice of medicine and learning from all the cultures of the known world. This was also a part of my life in this present period of time. I continue to this day being interested in the medical field and active in the healing processes.

PEACE AND THE TRUCE OF GOD

The bishop of Rome was known as the Pope. In the early days of Christianity, this was a title given to all bishops. In later years, it was reserved for the Bishop of Rome. He was thought to be the successor of St. Peter of the Bible and conducted the Roman Church affairs from Rome. In the Middle Ages, the Pope played a role of secular importance in Western Europe often acting as a mediator between Christian monarchs. At that time, the Pope was given temporal as well as religious power among the many nations of the world. In this way, the church controlled the millions of people under their influence and those that governed them. [6]

Constantine I called for all the bishops of the Roman Catholic Church to convene in a conference at a city called Nicaea, which is now in the country of Turkey. There had been many different opinions among the clergy on articles of faith. This convention in 325AD was called for the purpose of setting certain standards of belief for the members of the Roman Catholic Church. It took days of debate and discussion with a vote from the participants of the convention to set the doctrines that are held to this day by the Catholic Church. The doctrine of the Trinity, the divinity of the Holy Spirit, and the belief that Jesus was God, were some of the topics to be decided that day. The Council of Nicaea determined the articles of faith that all Christians were to obey. [7]

Constantine furthered the Christian cause by donating property for a basilica to be built for the Bishop of Rome, and he gave the Christian clergy privileges and legal immunity from taxes. He ordered the demolition of pagan temples and the new construction of churches over the site of Christ's nativity in Bethlehem, the site of His crucifixion in Jerusalem, and the tomb where He rose from the dead. [8]

He did not feel that Rome was in the main stream of the current affairs of his kingdom as he preferred a place that was strategically placed near Europe, Asia, the Black Sea and the Mediterranean. Constantine renamed the city Constantinople and began building a number of large churches. The Hippodrome, first begun under Severus, was enlarged; an imperial palace, public baths, and streets paved and decorated with statues from surrounding areas adorned the new city. All pagan temples were destroyed and the sacrifice to pagan gods was forbidden. Constantinople, or nearby towns, became the site for many of the church council that were held in future years. [9]

There were constant disputes over land boundaries and right of control or passage through the disputed land. Large parcels of land were controlled by a King, or another person of nobility. Each maintained fighting men for the protection of their kingdom. In an attempt by the church to promote peace throughout the land, and to get the individual land holders to agree to stop fighting among themselves, the church instigated within its members a law called "The Peace and Truce of God." This law had no legal standing among the people and could not be enforced, but it was hoped that the hold the church had over the people would reinforce this desire of the Pope.

AUGUSTINE OF HIPPO

In 354 AD, there was a boy, Augustine, born in present day Algeria, who would become the philosopher to bring clarity to several points of doctrine to the Christian church. Augustine traveled to Italy and became friends with Ambrose, the Archbishop of Milan. In 387, Augustine was baptized by Ambrose and then he returned to his home in North Africa, where he became a priest, and eventually he was made bishop of Hippo. With his study of the Neoplatonist beliefs, he accepted their theory that the soul is separate from the body, and he began to read the Bible as an allegorical story of past world history. For Augustine, evil occurred on the Earth because man focused on things of the Earth instead of those of the spirit. He saw time in a linear fashion with the progression from creation to the final judgement of man as a map all plotted on a designed course. He saw the soul as greater than the body since it allows man to understand things beyond the everyday time and conditions of the world. Augustine maintained that man had free will, but that by his choices he chooses either good or evil actions.

As a Christian, Augustine believed in pacifism although he does acknowledge that there could be an occasion when a defensive war with the goal of establishing peace could be waged. The "Just War" theory was taken up again in the thirteenth century by Thomas Aquinas. [10]

THE JUST WAR THEORY

The historical aspects of the Just War Theory deals with the rules or agreements that have applied in various wars across the ages. The first recorded document on this subject is found in the ancient Hindu epic "Mahabharata." This is a document in which is written the discussion of five ruling brothers on the causes of war and the restrictions that should be obeyed by all parties. The discussion includes such information as the use of chariots, which are not to be used for attacking the horses of the cavalry, but only other chariots, and the prohibition of the uses of poison arrows. Egypt held the Just War Theory long before Christianity, and ancient Rome might have used the "Just Cause" to repel an invasion of another tribe, or the breach of a treaty by another party. In the Middle Ages, the theory was based upon the writings of Augustine to protect the peace and punish wickedness when forced to do so. He states that the defense of one's self could be necessary, especially when authorized by a legitimate authority.

Nine hundred years later, Thomas Aquinas (1225-1274) gave the three points when a war could be considered justified. First, it must be instituted by a recognized authority to bring about peace. Second, it must have been done for a just purpose not for self-gain or the exercise of power, but to restore something lost or the purpose of punishing an evil perpetrated by a government or even a civilian population. The third reason, there must be a central motive that soldiers who are fighting can claim as their intention as well. Once war has begun, there remains a moral limit to any action as to the protection of all hostages. [11]

BASIC HISTORY OF KNIGHTHOOD

Knights were not part of a full-time army. They were soldiers, but had other duties as well. They were aristocratic lords with large tracks of land, and huge manor houses or castles in which to house their treasures and their household. The land was farmed by families who pledged their support to the lord or king of the land, as their welfare and security depended on his good graces. The common people of the land were known as serfs, and if and when the lord went to war over some slight of his neighbor or some infringement of a neighboring lord, then the serfs were called up to make up the bulk of the fighting men led by the knights of the castle. Each part of this community depended on each other and they were self-sufficient within their villages and in their legal lands. The knights themselves might be expected to be engaged in some skirmish several months of the year. They fought in areas around and close to their own lands.

In 1095, the knightly class of men was still in its infancy of development. What made the knight stand out from all other warriors was his ability to fight from the saddle of a horse. The cost of outfitting a knight was staggering as, for one, the cost of a war horse could be equated to a mortgage for a house in the twenty-first century. There was not only the war horse, but a second horse was required for everyday use. The battle equipment for a knight was another large expense. Chain metal covered the knight over a flowing white tunic. For those who went to the crusades, a large red cross was made on the front and the back of the tunic. The head peace was of metal that would protect the knight's head and face, and he carried a shield with his house emblem on it. A large double-edged sword completed the outfit.

Not only the expense of the chain metal coverings, sword, and shield, but there was the additional expense of a saddle, and maintaining the horse with shoes and food, also paying for the equipment and food for any other person accompanying them. These expenses made it difficult for men of lesser monetary means to enter into the knightly world and so it remained for only the society of the aristocracy to be a part of the knight's world. It was for the vessels of the land to support the knights and to carry out their duties of service even when the knight was in battle. All equipment that any vessel needed was provided by the lord, since the serf was part of the lord's servants on his land. [12]

To become a knight there was a ritual and a vow required to be repeated before the altar of the church before the title Knight could be given to any nobleman. This was a solemn church ritual with fasting the night before the event, prayers in the church and a sword presented to the knight at this ceremony. The rite of "dubbing" was first found in a poem "Song of Roland" written between 1140-1170. It describes seventeen principles that make up the Knight Code of Chivalry:

1. To fear God and maintain His church.
2. To serve the liege lord in velour and faith.
3. To protect the weak and defenseless
4. To give succor to widows and orphans
5. To refrain from the wanton giving of offence
6. To live by honor and for glory
7. To despise pecuniary rewards
8. To fight for the welfare of all
9. To obey those placed in authority
10. To guard the honor of fellow knights
11. To eschew unfairness, meanness and deceit
12. To keep faith
13. At all times speak the truth
14. To persevere to the end of any enterprise begun
15. To respect the honor of women
16. Never to refuge a challenge from an equal
17. Never to turn the back upon a foe.

Of the seventeen entries in the **Knights Code of Chivalry**, according to the Song of Roland, at least 12 relate to acts of chivalry as opposed to combat.

THE REASONS BEHIND THE FIRST CRUSADE

Pope Gregory (1015-1085) believed that the Pope should have unlimited power over the faithful, and that his power took precedent over kings and princes of the land. He felt that the

Pope should maintain an army under the control of St. Peter. The popular belief that monks were soldiers of God, as they prayed and meditated constantly for the salvation of souls, and as such they were obliged to defend the Latin Church in actual warfare. Gregory justified his claim with the rationale that since God was the ruler of the Kingdom of Heaven, the people of the church were his vassals, and under the direction of the Pope. This rationale was used in later years by Urban II in his sermon to start the crusade.

Gregory tried to recruit support for an army in France and Germany to help the Christians in areas then controlled by the Byzantine Empire. He alleged that the Christians were being persecuted by the Muslims of Asia Minor. Gregory used the reasoning that if the Roman Christians freed the Christians in the land controlled by the Muslims, it would be an act of charity bringing them merit in the eyes of God. [14]

The next Pope, called Urban II (1035-1099), came from the nobility of France, and he understood the layers of responsibilities from the land owner right down to the vassals who farmed the land. He started his religious life as a monk and then was moved up the ranks from abbot to archbishop then voted in as Pope. In 1095, Pope Urban II had just completed a tour through the land of France, speaking to the nobles about a possible crusade and gaining their support.

An ecclesial council in Clermont, France, had been called in the fall of 1095 to discuss several ideas that Urban had for reform in the church. He had received a message from Constantinople in March 1095 concerning the difficulties the church was having with the Muslims in that area. With the war between the Byzantine army and the Fatimids of Egypt coming close to the gates of Constantinople, the call went out to the west for help. Urban may have thought that his army would go to Constantinople and the Byzantine emperor would take over adding his military might to the expedition, but that is not what happened. Before the conference Urban took the opportunity to visit several of the monasteries in the area and to speak to predominant knights of the area that he knew, about the formation of a military crusade. He developed the ideal of an army to aid the Christians in and around the city of Jerusalem. He reasoned that this would bring the expansion of his sphere of influence as a pope to the now Byzantine-controlled area, as well as increase his power within the Roman western world. [15]

Urban knew the strain on the conscience of the knights as he proposed this crusade. The knights had taken an oath, before the altar of the church, to maintain peace. All Christians had been taught the dangers of sin, and to kill was one of the seven deadly sins. A pilgrimage to some holy site had always been considered an act of devotion, but in the eleventh century a pilgrimage to the Holy sites in Jerusalem was occasionally prescribed, sometimes by a parish priest, as a penance for sins. Somehow Urban had to resolve this dilemma of consciousness for the knights, so that they would agree with him in fighting a Just War." He had to convince them that the war was to defend Christendom, not only a **just act, but a holy act.**

Before the church conference at Clermont, Urban visited numerous churches in the country. He contributed monies for the building of new buildings throughout the area. This attention to the local area produced a super charged atmosphere that many people found impossible to ignore. Urban should not have been surprised at the speed in which the people took up the cause, especially when he was promising that all their sins would be forgiven if they should participate in this adventure. [16] Urban emphasized that only those with the highest motives should undertake the trip. To add substance to the knights' commitment of going on the crusade, the knight who vowed to go on the crusade was given a cloth cross to be sewn onto their tunic at the shoulder showing their commitment. It also showed that the crusader was entitled to certain legal privileges, that of being exempt from his taxes and a moratorium on his debts. The knight who refused to go after his pledge to do so would be excommunicated from the church. The crusader who did go to the crusade left his family and possessions under the protection of the church while he was gone. Those who sought to take the cross began to sell or mortgage all their possessions in order to buy provisions for the long trip. Most of the land went to the church, who obtained vast tracks of land for a fraction of what it was valued at.

Urban's sermon at Clermont was so compelling that not only the knights responded, for whom he intended the message, but also the common people. With the crusade fever growing by the day, the word went out from the local bishops that forbad monks and clergy from going on the crusade without express permission from their superior. The bishops did what they could to prevent men from deserting their family to go on the crusade. The fear of torments in Hell after life pushed the elderly and the sick to join the groups of people on their journey. The lure of adventure and the promise of spiritual rewards were irresistible to everyone. The bishops tried to deter the old and the sick from going, but some went anyway. [17]

Peter the Hermit was a charismatic itinerant preacher, who took up the call across Germany and Hungary, persuading people to make the crusade. His words attracted several bands of less organized knights and peasants to the cause. They came together under the direction of this popular preacher. This group was called the "People's Crusade" as it was composed of serfs, the poor and the common people. He went throughout the countryside preaching the call to the crusade. As the group increased into the thousands, they moved through Germany and Hungary heading toward Asia Minor. They were unable to distinguish between the Muslim and Jewish communities they passed. Consequently, many of the Jewish people were massacred, men women and children. The plundering of churches and homes of the Jews provided the funds that were needed for their journey.

When this group reached Constantinople, they were advised to wait for the main body of crusaders. A camp was set up for them outside the city. A small group of Germans in the group became restless with the waiting and ventured out from their safe environment to attack the Turks in an area near Nicaea. When they were trapped there, the main body went to rescue them. As a result, they were all killed by the Turks October 21, 1096. This was the end of the People's Crusade. [18]

Two months after the action of the undisciplined mob, the first contingent of the army arrived at Nicaea with Count Hugh of Vermandois, a cousin of the king of France, who brought a small group of knights. In December, a larger force arrived led by Godfrey of Bouillon, and Baldwin of Boulogne, also a cousin Baldwin of Le Bourg. The group included knights that spoke either French or German. Next came a contingency of Normans led by Bohemond of Taranto. Another group of powerful nobles from northern Europe, each group bringing their knights, servants, and their pack animals. The Turks thought that this group was an easy pushover like the group before them, but the Turkish garrison in the city was no match for the heavy armored knights and they were defeated. [19]

The next objective was the city of Antioch. The crusaders were not used to the heat of the summer and the shortage of water became a problem. The Turks had scorched the Earth, so there were no grains for food to be found. Before they could get very far, they were attacked by the Turks. The recue came from Godfrey of Bouillon, his knights and those of Count Raymond of Toulouse with Adhemar of Le Puy who sent the Turks running. The crusades got their first chance at booty.

The army continued to march across Anatolian plateau, which is the western protrusion of Asia making up the majority of modern-day Turkey, fighting not only the Turks but hunger and thirst as well. Two more battles faced them before they were able to rest and refresh themselves at the Armenian capital of Marash. On October 1097, they reached the city of Antioch. This had been a major metropolis of the Roman Empire, and was still a strategic point for all of northern Syria. It had a large Christian population, but garrisoned by the Turks, who had captured it from the Byzantines twelve years before.

The crusaders could not decide whether to attack the city or wait for reinforcements. The Turks took advantage of this hesitation and made sorties out of the city to strike at the crusaders, especially when they were looking for food. It seems that the crusaders had some hidden help by the way of a spy in the city, who was in the employment of Bohemond of Taranto. Under cover of darkness, the city gates were opened to the crusaders and the knights rushed in. After the battle, the crusading army decided to remain in the area through the summer and continue to Jerusalem in the fall.

Time went by with the crusaders wet, hungry and becoming discouraged. A large amount of horses were lost on the march across Anatolia, requiring the proud knights to join the foot soldiers of the army. Their situation further deteriorated with the outbreak of typhoid, with the unsanitary conditions of the camp and the lack of adequate medical treatment for the injured. Letters dictated by crusaders to priests, who wrote them and sent them to their home church, describe the affairs of the crusaders at this time. There were no horses for the knights, hunger, exhaustion and the death and dying of comrades all around them was taking a toll on morale. With the heavy casualties sustained in Asia Minor and in Antioch, there was a steady stream of deserters. In July, the crusaders were afflicted by typhoid. To escape the sickness many of the crusaders left Antioch. [20]

On January 13, 1099, they set out of Antioch toward Jerusalem and arrived on June 7, 1099 to set up their tents in front of the city walls.

"Only one-third of those who had departed from western Europe two years before remained alive discounting non-combatants, pilgrims, among them women and children, meant a fighting force of around twelve thousand foot soldiers, and twelve or thirteen hundred knights." [21]

There are nine letters written during the crusades that tell the story of the fighting, victories and the conditions of the battlefield. The first letter dates after Nicaea had fallen. Five letters were written during the siege of Antioch and one after the battle. These are eye witness accounts of the battle and of the leaders of those battles. [22]

MY PART IN THE CRUSADES

On July 5, 2010, I had a dream where I was a knight in the crusades. We were in heavy hand-to-hand battle. The fighting was furious. I heard someone refer to me as Sir Knight. I did not have a horse, but was fighting on the ground with my squire fighting to my right. His swing of the broad sword was as effective as mine. I recognized my friend Mary in this life, who lives in Tucson, as the squire.

We were fighting in a large meadow-like area with bodies of dying and dead fallen men all around us. I could see a walled city in the distance. I could see men running toward us out of the city gates. My white tunic had a large red cross down the front, now spattered with blood. When I woke that morning, I called Mary and told her about our being together in the crusades and I described the cross on my tunic. She said that each crusade had a different cross and the one I saw was used in the first crusade. From the historical accounts I had read about the crusades, all the knights rode horses, but I did not see a horse in the entire field. This made me doubt that it was the crusades I was seeing, then I started read the different accounts of their battles.

Later that year, I attended a healing group in Sierra Vista, Arizona. I was told that there was a place in the middle of my back where I had been killed with a sword in a past life. The angle of the sword's penetration was in an upward thrust. I do have a place in the middle of my back now, where the muscles that hold the vertebrae in place, is weak.

From the research I have done on the story of the crusade, I feel my death came at the battle of Antioch. There was a feeling of being shamed because as a proud knight, my horse had either been killed in battle or used as food for my men. The disgust in the lack of leadership of the powerful lords, and the general feeling of horror at the atrocities committed in the name of Christianity, also the deep aversion to the mass slaughter of men, and the disillusionment of papal authority to direct such carriage, tortured my soul.

From this experience, I have brought into my soul the distrust of so-called infallible doctrine from anyone, the aversion to war and its cruelty done in the name of country The realization that to follow a standard that agrees with your inner Spirit of right, is more important than to go along with what is the popular action.

It is also interesting that the land fought over centuries ago, bathed in blood of dedicated men to a cause, are now in the twenty-first century battlegrounds again. How many of our soldiers are coming home with post traumatic shock syndrome after seeing the brutality of war up front and very personal?

CHAPTER SEVEN

The Albigensian Crusade 1209

The Cathars and Montsegur

The siege of Antioch lasted until June 3, 1098. Within days of their occupation of the city, they were under siege by the Muslim relief army. The situation was very serious, and rumors of visions of the saints appearing to visionaries, also the discovery of a lance, under the floor boards of the church, gave rise to the theory that it was the same lance that pierced the side of Christ while he was on the cross. On June 28, 1098, they went out of the city and put the Muslims to flight. This became the climax of the crusade. The crusaders decided to rest until November when they would resume their march to Jerusalem.

Those crusaders that return home from the long march across Asia Minor were changed men. They remembered what it was to feel starvation, the fear of death and the smell of blood in their nose. Returning home, or what was left of it, became a battle of another kind, that of survival. The nobility had sold their land or mortgaged it for the money to buy provisions for themselves and those who went with them to the Crusades. Most of the land had been sold to the church. With these large tracks of land that once belonged to the local nobility, the church's power increased, and the serfs who worked the land found their taxes increased, resulting in general unrest among the people. [1]

During the middle ages the church had become a state within a state. They had their own laws and courts. The church claimed jurisdiction over such matters as wills, marriages, as well as their decision on sorcery, and blasphemy, with the Pope as the supreme lawgiver of Christendom. The church levied taxes and established the power of "dispensation." If so persuaded, the Pope could set aside a law for a specific person or a situation, where the church would profit from that decision. The first crusade had been the time of blind faith where the people did whatever the Pope requested. Later, after the first crusade, it took a lot more intellectual persuading to get people to participate once again.

THE CATHARS

For the crusaders that survived the battle of Antioch and the following battle of Jerusalem, they brought back from the Holy Lands many things, some tangible like gold and precious jewels, others things not so tangible as a different philosophy and purpose of that life. In Constantinople, they heard about a group called Bogomils who had a way of looking at life differently than that taught by the Catholic Church. During the 11th and 12th century, this belief spread westward. By the early 13th century, this new form of religion had spread to Europe with other groups of dissenters: two in the east, the Bogomils and another called Paulicians. The Cathars in the west formed a network stretching from the Black sea to the Atlantic. There was a wide spread anti-clerical reaction to all priests and the church as a whole. The priest was described as a man who kept a mistress, ate and lived well, gave lip service to the church doctrine, yet still exercised power over the congregation. There was a growing literacy of the people in the urban areas and this opened the way for information to be obtained independently of the church representatives. People were starting to think for themselves and what they saw in the Catholic Church and its representatives in the villages was the life of the self-satisfying priest, which turned many people from the church of their forefathers to a new open religion called Catharism. [2]

The people who followed the Cathar form of religion were found in Western Europe, in the Rhineland cities. In the twelfth century, they were found in the southern part of France particularly in the area called Languedoc. They were also in the northern cities of Italy up to 1325. The cultural region of Languedoc encompassed the southern Mediterranean lowlands of France that extended from the Pyrenees in the southwest eastward some 125 miles to the right bank of the Rhone River. The country came to be known as the feudal county of Toulouse. It was one of the largest fiefs of France.

The Cathars were supported and protected by the nobles of Languedoc as well as the people of the area. Another name given to the Cathars was Albigenses because they had a large group of Cathars around the town of Albi. Cathars were branded by the Catholic Church as heretics with Pope Innocent III preaching a crusade against them, and bringing the French northern army into the area in 1209. This war lasted until the mid-thirteenth century, ending the political independence of the people in the area. [3]

CATHARS AND THEIR BELIEFS

The community formed by the Cathar believers was peaceful and loving people, who abstained from eating meat, and practiced unconditional love to every living being, rock, plant and animal. They would not swear an oath to anyone as they belonged to no one. This went against the feudal society of the Middle Ages, which was built on a society where serfs swore allegiance to their Lord of the land, and in turn, the lords swore fidelity to the king of the area. This oath taken and given was considered a binding contract between principals. When a knight was accepted into service of a king, he was required to give his oath of fidelity as described in the last chapter.

The Cathars believed in a creator who they called the Source, the giver of all good things, the point of absolute goodness and a condition of pure Spirit, while the ruler of the world was evil and called Satan. They believed that the soul was doomed to continue to reincarnate into the world to work through a self-imposed purification of actions and thoughts they had during their life on Earth. Each life would balance the scales of truth until they could rejoin the realm of the Creator as a pure spirit. They believed that all body functions were natural including that of sex, and that they did not need a church's permission to dictate their life style. Cathars believed that their Spirit was trapped within their physical body, a creation of an evil god, and it was only the rebirth through the Consolamentum given by the Perfect that they could be released to the state of perfection. Spirit was considered sexless; therefore, they considered women equal to men and equality capable as spiritual leaders.

CONSOLAMENTUM

The Cathars had only one sacrament unlike the Catholic Church. The ceremony took place in the forest or in one of the many caves of the Pyrenees Mountains. This was called the consolamentum which was a rite performed by the "Perfect" for an individual who was close to death. According to Cathar beliefs, when a person dies their soul is pursued by the powers of the air and the soul would seek safety by entering into the first form whether it be human or animal. The soul would then be condemned to cycles of death and birth trapped in that physical body to be reincarnated many times until the soul committed itself to self-denial of the material world. The "Perfect" conducted the Consolamentum which was a laying of his/her hands on the individual with special prayers to release them from the negative aspects of life and bringing their Soul into the state of perfection. It was only by receiving the Consolamentum that the soul would be freed from reincarnation. The Cathars believed that by leading a good enough life, at death they could return to the immaterial world of light and the rhema of the "Good God," and that they were a spark of Divinity imprisoned in a body of flesh. They believed that the world was controlled by the "Bad God" where they could be tortured with disease and famine, including man's inhumanity towards each other. To avoid the Bad God, it was necessary to abstain from all Earthly temptations and to fortify themselves with prayer and meditation. The idea that flesh was inherently evil was taught to the Christian mainstream and was later formalized in the Doctrine of Original Sin by the Catholic Church. [4]

THE "PERFECT"

The Cathar society was divided into two: the "Believers" and the "Credentes" or "Perfects." The Cathar's leaders came from the inner circle, who took long periods of training before they would lead a severe ascetic life. They were the Cathar's elect or as later called Bonhomme, good men or "Perfect." The "Perfect" was chosen from the community to be the spiritual leader. He or she had to abide by set rules for their life beyond that of celebrity and a vegetarian diet as required for all other members of the community. Cathar beliefs varied from community to community as Catharism was taught by ascetic leaders who had few set guidelines. Cathars went against all that the Catholic Church taught. They refused the baptism of water as performed by the Catholic Church. Their reasoning was that water was in the material world and as such was corruptible and could not sanctify the Spirit. They rejected the sacraments of the Catholics especially the belief of the Catholic Church, that of the Eucharist being the bread used in the mass was said to be transformed into the body of Christ. The cross that was venerated by the Catholics was considered by the Cathars to be a symbol of torture, and they would not worship it. The Cathars refused to take an oath which went against everything that was required for the legal affairs of their society, as a serf was bound to the Lord or owner of the land where they lived, with an oath of service.

The Catholic Church was furious that these Cathars did not acknowledge them as their religious ruler, and they had their own "Perfect" who was their spiritual leader instead of the Catholic priest or bishop, nor did they pay church taxes, fees or tithes. Cathars sought an individual connection to the Divine through transcendental mystical experience. They believed in a path to divinity by using the method of inner silence through meditation and prayer. They offered a personal challenge to an individual to throw off the yoke of any other judgment except that which came at one's life end. They believe that each person's soul knew the errors that were made and they were ready for atonement for these errors of consciousness. [5]

In a world where war between kingly domains were fought for control and in the pursuit of obtaining more land from surrounding lords, the communities of Cathars stood out as they refused to fight. Killing was abhorrent to them. Catharism grew at an incredible rate among both the low and the high born of society. Many powerful nobles in Northern Italy became supporters of the Cathars. They saw the spirit as more important than the body, and it as being immaterial and sexless. The beliefs of the Cathars became predominate especially among the female aristocracy as they permitted females to be equal among the men, and women were considered capable of being spiritual leaders which undermined the very concept of the Catholic Church. Cathars were against marriage since arrangements of marriage at that time was like the bartering of goods, described as the same as bartering for a cow. [6]

CATHOLIC CHURCH REACTS

The Catholic Church saw the growing interest in the Cathar religion and its effect on the people. The church was not only losing their control over the people, but they were also losing income from the former faithful. Pope Alexander III sent a monk named Diego de Osma, later to be known as St. Dominic, to hold debates between the Catholics and the Cathar leaders. When Dominic failed to convert them back to the Catholic Church, the pope took his revenge on the nobles protecting the Cathar communities. He removed them from the church or excommunicated them: Count of Toulouse, the Viscount of Beziers, the Count of Foix, and other Occitan nobles living in the southern lands where the Cathars were the strongest. He then talked to the nobles of the northern province of France and offered them riches and forgiveness of their sins if they would initiate a crusade against the Cathars. The northern nobles were more than willing to enter the crusade as it would bring more land under the control of the Frank king, and hopefully unify the country. In 1208, when one of the pope's legates to the north was killed, the beginning of the crusade was triggered.

MONTSEGUR

With the assassination of the papal legate, Pierre de Castelnau, the stage was set for Pope Innocent III to preach the Albigensian Crusade in 1206. An army of 300,000 men composed of mercenaries, nobles, knights, and their servants descended from the north onto the southern cities. The first city to fall was Beziers in 1209 with 20,000 people killed and the city burned. It is during the siege that the question was asked of Abbot Arnaud Amaury by the commander of the northern army. The question was how to recognize the heretics from the Catholics. The answer has gone down in history as the battle cry of this crusade. The abbot answered "Kill them all! God will recognize His own!"

In 1229, the city of Toulouse was destroyed. The people of Toulouse were not Cathars, but they did sympathize with them. It was decided that this area and its people were too powerful to be left out of the battle forcing Raymond Count of Toulouse to sign a treaty recognizing the French King ruler over Toulouse and chasing the Cathars out of the territory.

Today, the ruins of Montsegur are perched at 3,900 ft., on a rocky plateau in southern France. It is located in the heart of the Languedoc-Occitan region, an area inhabited from the stone age to modern times. The fortress that is visited today by tourists is not the same building as that of the Cathars. The entire fortress was pulled down with its capture by the northern French army in 1244. The current fortress was rebuilt in the seventeenth century. [7]

Recent archeological digs have discovered that the plateau was frequented by prehistoric people and that the Cathar village was within a very small part of the land. The castle was in the middle of the land, built with an open-air courtyard. Around the courtyard was built a three stories collection of shops, arms room, and storage rooms. Upon the third floor, there was a walk way that commanded the view of the castle and the valley below. In the lower levels, there were places for the mules and horses for the men of the garrison. The arms room had a supply of spears, javelins, knives, slingshots and arrows. The men stationed there were estimated to be about one hundred and fifty, plus wives and children. The majority of the castle's occupants were not Cathars. Although this area was not completely inhabited by those professing the Cathar faith, it was nevertheless viewed as the symbol of Occitan resistance to Capetian colonization. Raymond VII of Toulouse controlled the independent area, but the King of France claimed the Occitan territory. It was known that he would use the smallest excuse to send in troops to enforce his claim. [8]

It was in the thirteenth century that the Cathars lived there with small houses built on the northern face forming a small village. Evidence has been found of cloth making from sheep's wool, as well as the vegetable and mineral dyes for the material. Their basic diet was grains of wheat and rye, with fish from the nearby streams. The only problem with the placement of the fortress was not enough water, which ultimately led to their defeat.

In May 1243, an army consisting of ten thousand men surrounded the base of Montsegur starting a year-long siege. The army set up different camps and various levels to accommodate the mountain slope. In front of every position was a vertical cliff that defied any attempt to scale it. Above it, the fortress and the village were enclosed by a wooden stockade that twisted at the edge of the abyss. The final defeat of the fortress came with the help of local Basque mercenaries who were convinced to scale the eastern cliffs and gain entrance into the castle ramparts.

The lack of water and the constant barrage of the stone thrower against the walls brought the year-long siege to an end. Hugues des Arcis, the Catholic archbishop and the Inquisitor Ferrier agreed that those who would surrender would have their lives spared and if they made a full confession of their Cathar involvement they could leave with arms and baggage with no threat of any punishment. The people of Montsegur were given fifteen days to send out the Cathars from the castle, which was in reality a trap for those who complied with the order.

On March 16, 1244, the occupants of Montsegur left the mountain refuge. Two hundred Cathars refused to confess their errors. A large fire pyre was lit and the "heretics" were individually tied to a stake and burned alive. The burning of heretics was considered by the church a cleansing of the faithful. The Inquisitors felt justified in their condemning men, women and children to be burned alive for their heretical beliefs. [9]

MEMORIES OF A CATHAR

I found a book written by Arthur Guirdham called "The Cathars & Reincarnation." I thought it would be the explanation of their beliefs, but instead it was the account of a woman's memories of her life in the thirteenth century as a Cathar. The author is a psychiatrist, who had a patient referred to him in May of 1996. He identifies her as Mrs. Smith. Her initial complaints were that she had nightmares accompanied by shrieks so loud that her husband thought she would wake up the neighborhood. She also had dreams where she was lying on the floor, and a man came towards her whose presence filled her with terror. In her teen years, she had a few attacks of unconsciousness, the same time as the dreams.

The author explains that he had picked up a book in 1938 about the area of southern France called Languedoc, and became fascinated with the history of the area, and especially that of the people living in the mountain city of Montsegur. He felt a need to go to the area in the Pyrenees where an unconscious magnate was pulling him to visit. After visiting Eastern Pyrenees, he wanted to return again and again to the area, which he said confused his wife as he never before wanted to revisit an area after the first trip. He never gave reincarnation a second thought before 1962. [9]

In March 1962, he first met Mrs. Smith who told him of her nightmares and the terror of the unknown man. She had had these nightmares on and off again for twenty years. She had been referred to a neurologist who diagnosed her as having epileptic seizures, but the psychiatrist did not feel this was a true diagnosis. The doctor himself had a series of similar events with the nightmares starting in his twenties and getting more frequent in his fifties. It bothered him for thirty or forty years and ceased when he met Mrs. Smith. At the time, it did not occur to him that syncretistic events were forming with Mrs. Smith, yet something prompted him to start keeping a journal of the events as they enfolded.

In 1964, the author met Professor Rene Nelli of Carcassonne who lectured at the University of Toulouse, and had the reputation of being an expert in the interpretation of the poetry of the troubadours as well as the metaphysical of Catharism. He believed that there seemed to be a close connection between the two. [10]

Dualism is a religious attitude which existed from the beginning of history, from one civilization to the next. It is the belief in two equally powerful energies in the world, one of good and the other of evil. Where this energy came from, what must be done, also the methods on how to combat the evil, varies from group to group. This philosophy is shown by the records left by the Egyptians, and their painting of the gods depicted on tomb walls. It was in Persia in the form of Zoroastrianism. Early Christianity adopted Neoplatonist ideas which were the doctrine of salvation along the side of Dualism. These ideas were later dropped when main stream Christianity went from the philosophy of Plato to that of Aristotle as a result of Thomas Aquinas's interpretation of philosophical questions. The teachings of the Cathars contain those elements of the early church and suggest their origin was that of the early Christian church. Their Consolamentum reflects this idea.

Cathars were also Gnostics in their belief that only an inner elite were to be taught the esoteric truths, and they would teach a limited amount to the general believers. They believed that the individual chosen must undergo a long period of training before they were permitted to start a severe ascetic life as a "Perfect." [11]

A PAST LIFE REVEALED

Mrs. Smith told the psychiatrist that at age six she had complained of a headache then passed out. After that incident, she told a family member about a letter they would receive and the information it contained. The family did not believe her, but when the letter did arrive, its contents revealed exactly what Mrs. Smith had predicted. Several of these incidents happened when she was growing up, showing a blossoming psychic attunement to others. In her teen years she wrote what she thought was a fiction story about a family living in the time of the thirteenth century troubadours of France. She started writing this story after a trip to the Pyrenees. This story was very detailed. She wrote that the fireplace was in the middle of the family's one room house. The placement of the fireplace was later verified to be correct by historical accounts. Ms. Smith said she wrote the story for herself not for publication.

The psychiatrist and Mrs. Smith kept in touch with each other. When she was unable to come to his office in England, she wrote him letters of what was happening to her at home. In one such letter, she told him that she had recognized him on their first meeting from the time when he had come to her door centuries ago because of a snowstorm. At that time, she lived in a one room house just outside of Toulouse. Her family was very poor and that she and the doctor met when he was caught out in a blinding snow storm, and came to her door to ask for lodging overnight. Mrs. Smith stated that she fell in love with him then, but her father warned her that the nobleman was not of their religion or social status, and to forget him. She was Roman Catholic then, and when she left her home to be with the young nobleman Roger, who was also a "Perfect" of the Cathars, she was excommunicated from the church. [12]

Future letters describe the life she had with Roger and the happiness they had together. Roger wore a long robe down to his ankles with, what she described as, a buckle around the waste. She stated this robe was blue, but up to the last few years before this book was published in 1990, historians said the color of "Perfect's" garments were black and tied in the middle. This gave another point of credence to her story. [13]

In later letters of 1966 to the doctor, Mrs. Smith reveals her memories of Roger being taken by the inquisition and placed in prison where he later died. She remembers being interrogated by the inquisition then tortured in the crypt of the cathedral in Toulouse. Her description of the horrors of being burned alive is vivid and heart wrenching for this reader. She describes seeing her blood boiling in the flames and states: "After a while the flames weren't so cruel. They felt Icey cold." [14]

MY LIFE AS A CATHAR

On 19 November 2010, I was at the church in Tucson and received a message; "*Your ability to understand where you have been shows your comprehension of the challenges of the past and gives you direction for the future.*"

Automatic writing: *July 2, 2012, Karma is not just a word, but a part of life where all things are equalized. Spiritual things are in the eternal "NOW" always. The now of all things cannot end or cease to exist."*

I had a dream where I was in a small rowboat traveling down a shallow stream. The boat was powered by a man standing in the bow of the boat and using a very long stick to push the boat forward. There was a woman sitting in front of me. I was a woman lying at the bottom of the boat covered by a long cloth. As we went along, I would occasionally raise my head up to see where we were. I heard a lot of shouting and the crackling of a burning fire. I stuck my head up over the lip of the boat to see what was going on. We were passing a piece of land that jetted out into the river. On that land, I saw several people burning on stakes. The only thing remaining were skeletons visibly still strapped to the stake. One was close to the river with its mouth open in a soundless scream. As I stared at the horrendous scene before me, the lady sitting in the boat whispered in my ear "Get your head down, cover up. Do you want to join those poor people? What good could you do for them now?"

I did not know anything about the Cathars until I started to research this part of my story. It has taken me a few months, and the reading of several books with information of this time, taken from the reports of the Inquisition, to find information that might correspond to what I saw in this dream. I found in the story of the thirteen century Cathars a match to my dream and memories of that time. I must have been an important person for the couple to risk their lives smuggling me out of a dangerous situation. I felt responsible for those being burnt and wanted to help them. There was a powerful feeling of regret and shame for not being able to help. It is no wonder this scene has remained in my subconscious.

CHAPTER EIGHT

1934-1952

FROM SOUTH TO NORTH

I have been told by many psychics in numerous readings throughout my life that before this present lifetime, I had decided to clean the slate so to speak. I had a lot of unresolved Karma, and I had decided to take care of it in one lifetime! I had made this plan in the etheric before I was born. If you can picture this: a long table with men and women, dressed in long white robes, seated on one side of the table. This was the planning meeting for my next life on Earth and these were my advisors and my guardian angels. We would plan my life together to bring the best resolution to each situation I would face. I stood before this table where we had just reviewed all the lives I had, and what I had learned in each. The objective for each situation was explained, and the way I had faced each challenge was evaluated. I understood what I had to do to balance the Karmic debt and took it as my objective. I am sure the advisors tried to talk me out of taking on such a heavy burden, but I was resolved to get it done. All of this was placed in my subconscious to be reviewed when the time came it was needed.

I lived with my grandparents until my grandmother died. By then, my mother had married again this time to a man she had met when she was in the Army during the Second World War. He was tall, good looking and had a way with women, which he used to sweep my mother off her feet. The fact that his values were different from those she had been taught as a child, that he was a Catholic, my mother a Protestant, or that he was French/Canadian, did not stop her from marrying him. He got her to convert to the Catholic way and they seemed to be happy.

When Edward got out of the army, he went back to his civilian profession of teaching French and Spanish to high school students. He found a job right way, and had my mother bring me to his new apartment in Newton Corners, Massachusetts. This was my first trip away from my grandfather and my familiar community. I was not prepared for the change.

At school, my southern accent separated me from the other children, and my being shy around strangers made it even worse. I was placed in a Catholic grammar school where I had to repeat the fourth grade. My life had just made a giant change and my emotional being was reeling in the change. For the first time in my life, I was introduced to my new teacher, a woman wearing a strange long black dress, who covered her head with a long black veil. This person I was to call "sister" and I was required to obey her in everything she said. There were only girls in my class, and they were not very friendly to me. My life was turning upside down and I was still having a hard time getting used to the fact that my loving grandmother was not there to protect me. Eventually, my mother found a job in one of the local high schools, teaching cooking and sewing. We stayed in Edward's apartment for a few months then moved to another town and another apartment; this time it was over a small convenience store. I was placed in another Catholic school. I was miserable. My mother was not loving at all and most of the time ignored me. We had not known each other when I was in Virginia as she came to see my grandparents perhaps once a year, and that was only when she wanted something, according to my grandmother.

MY WORLD IN BOOKS

This is the time I found the local library and books became my friend and companion. I read four books at a time going through a series of books in the subject I loved most. The librarian helped me find books in the subject I was currently interested in. I remember staying up all night reading a book that "I just could not put down!" My days and years drifted from one to another, with no attention or love from either my stepfather or my mother.

We would visit Edward's sister who lived in another town in Massachusetts. She had several children all younger than I was. One Sunday, I overheard a conversation between my stepfather and his youngest sister, about a boarding school she had attended. She was emphatic about the school saying she had not liked being there and how could he send me there. He won the argument and I was packed off to a Catholic French speaking boarding school. Here is where I learned to really dislike the Catholic nuns. According to my stepfather, St Ann's Academy was one of the best Catholic schools in the state, and I should be grateful he was willing to spend so much money on my education!

CATHOLIC BOARDING SCHOOL

I learned quickly how to adjust to my new world. The uniforms were made of black wool with stiff celluloid cuffs and a collar. These were held onto the uniform with buttons. There was a slit on one side of the skirt for a pocket that was a separate item from the dress. It was a bag with an opening on the side, worn on a band around your waste. We had to wear nylons and black shoes. The nylons were held up by a contraption called a garter belt that secured the stockings in the front and the back with straps leading to a belt worn on your skin, your underpants over that.

The school day was separated into the morning with nothing but French spoken, and in the afternoon, we could speak English. Since I did not know one word of French, I was placed in a class of girls in the same situation. Our teacher was a very fat nun who rambled on and on about her personal life as a nurse in the first world war, and taught little or no French. The students complained to the head mistress about our lack of instruction and nothing happened to change it. I found out years later, after I left the school, that this nun had been released from her teaching duties and sent back to the "mother house," where she retired. My stepfather did not believe I was not learning French. So, he came up with the idea I was to write the time down and what the teacher was talking about. These reports were to be brought home to him for his review. After several months of reading my carefully written notes, he gave up yelling at me for not learning French.

The rule was if you were caught speaking English in the morning, except in your classes, you were fined a point. The points added up to disciplinary action in some form or another. I found that I had a rebellious streak and refused to speak French. In my defense, I have to say that I did learn enough to understand the directions given to me, especially when I was called over and over "hard head!" As time went on, I began to understand the conversation around me, but still would not speak French. The disciplinary action I received was, for me, more of a vacation from the other things at school. I was sent to the school library to work after school hours. I loved it for the short time I was there. The nuns found out how much I loved the library, and sent me to work in the kitchen scrubbing pans.

My stepfather was teaching at an all boy's college preparatory academy in Worchester, Mass. My mother was working as a dietitian in the local hospital. They had an apartment within the school, and since I was off at boarding school there was no place for me in the apartment. On Friday, I took the bus from school to where my parents lived, about an hour trip, and I returned to school by bus on Sunday afternoon. I felt like a displaced refugee every time I went home on the weekends. I slept on the coach, with my clothes stored in a cardboard box in the closet.

Holidays away from the boarding school were just as terrible. I had no place I could call my own, and could not wait to go back to school where at least I had my own cubicle in the dormitory. The benefits of going home were: I could get a nice long bath, at least one decent meal at the school dining hall, clean clothes, and also sheets for my bed for the following week. The school did not furnish laundry services, or blankets for your bed so these had to be brought from home.

At school, the girls slept in one large room that had curtains on metal polls, separating the room into many little cubicles. In each was a night stand a bowl and a pitcher for water. The wash stand doors opened to one shelf where I could put my change of underwear. My uniform hung on a hanger on the metal pole beside the opening of my cubicle. At night, the dormitory nun would walk around to make sure we were all in our beds then she would go to sleep in her room at the corner of the dorm. The morning started with bright lights and a bell. We were all to kneel and say a prayer together then get dressed for mass.

MORNING ROUTINE

Five o'clock was too early for me to get up, much less walk in single file down the steps and hallways to the chapel. We were escorted to the chapel by a nun, and made to stay until the mass was over. I had no interest in any of this, but found a way to pass the time. I found a book with just the four gospels of the Bible in it, and started reading that during mass. I got in trouble for it. Then I discovered I could sleep standing up and sitting down according to the ritual of the mass. My body obeyed the command of my muscles, but my consciousness was not there. I came out of this suspended animation as we walked out of the chapel and down the hall to the refectory and breakfast.

The refectory was another lesson in patience. We had to say the prayers in Latin, before eating breakfast, while kneeling on the floor beside our chair. With the last amen we could sit down and eat, usually a hot cereal for breakfast. Each student provided their own glass, plate and silverware, which were stored in a small recess in the table in front of each chair. After setting up your own place setting, you could pass your plate to the nun at the head of the table and she would serve you the food. The supper at night was some kind of meat and a vegetable, never a desert or salad. Bread was offered on a plate on the table. If you wanted a slice of bread you tapped the table twice and someone would pass the plate of bread to you. When everyone had eaten, the dishes were washed at the table in a large soapy water bowl with another bowl of clear water for rinsing. You had your own dish towel for drying, and replaced everything back into the recess of the table. The meal was completed with another prayer kneeling at the side of the table then we were marched off toward the day room.

MENAGE

Now this time between breakfast and the first class was called "Ménage" French for work. Each student was assigned a portion of the school to clean every day. After that was done, we could go out on the playground for a few moments before school started. All of the days were very structured this way. The noon time meal was the same as the breakfast with maybe a sandwich, except we could now speak English on the playground, and in the classrooms. After school we had study hall where all homework was done, followed by supper with the prayer by the table. Afterwards, we had an hour or two to go outside on the swings or play basketball, then back to the dayroom, where we sang a song and said night prayers, then were escorted up the stairs to the dormitory for bed. Each day was the same and the routine became second nature after a few hundred times. Weekends were the same, except some students had visitors of friends or family members. There were two large rooms right off the main door of the school that were set up as living room space with easy chairs and small tables and reading lamps. It was in the "Salon" that the students had time with their visitors. Since I took the bus home every Saturday, I did not go into these rooms.

SCHOOL FAIR

The nuns had a fair each year to raise money for the school. They would invite the community to come and enjoy themselves. It was a modified circus with booths that had different games. They sold popcorn, ice cream and cookies, all mouthwatering temptations to girls who had not tasted sugar treats for months. I do not know how much money was raised on these events, but I do know each student was expected to pay their way to the fair. I was the only acceptation as my stepfather never gave me any money for extras such as this, or to buy candy from the nun on Saturday: consequently, I was under the nun's scrutiny until they realized I really didn't have any money.

Years later, my nightmares would include being at this school again and walking the halls of polished wood, searching for someone who would spend some quality time with me. I was so lonely and so miserable!

This was my life for my eighth-grade class, first and second year of high school. Each day the same routine, each year the same with only the changing of classes. One year there was a special celebration for the school and we were asked to draw pictures of historical events of the school. These would be put into a display in the auditorium. I always had a gift of art and showed it off that day. Teachers asked me why I was not taking art classes on Saturday at the school. First of all, I did not know there were any art classes and second when I asked my stepfather to pay for the classes, he refused, so I did not pursue it. In that same auditorium we did have movies shown once in a while, I saw the movie Jane Eyre and some other old movies, which were new to me.

The year of the school's celebration there was a special event held in the auditorium. The students were all dressed in long floor-length gowns, with each year in a special color. The first years were dressed in yellow, the second in orchard, the third in green and the seniors in white. The dresses all had to be made with the same pattern, in taffeta material. My mother had to buy the material then find a dress maker to make my dress. I must say, when everyone stood together the colors were beautiful, but the dress pattern itself did not look good on everyone. In my nightmares, I was wearing that orchard dress trying to hide from the rest of the students. I thought I looked like a large purple blimp!

CATHOLIC DAY SCHOOL

The third and fourth year of high school were spent in a Catholic day school in New Rochelle, New York. My mother was then teaching in a high school in New York State and my stepfather was teaching in a high school in Connecticut. We lived in a small house on the New York/Connecticut border. I took a bus to the train station then boarded the commuter train into New York City, getting off in New Rochelle. The return trip was the same. Our uniforms for this school were a white blouse, grey pleated skirt and a maroon blazer. The classes were taught by another order of nuns and a few lay teachers. This school was more what I had been used to in Virginia, except it was still Catholic and only girls in the school.

My home life became one of a servant as I did all the house cleaning, family laundry and the yard work. There were Saturdays when I spent most of the day standing on a cement floor, in the basement of the house ironing the clothes. For light, I had one bare light bulb over my head and two small windows looking out to the back yard. The mountain of clothes to be ironed would slowly decrease as I worked tirelessly hour after hour. My stepfather had to have his under pants ironed as well as the sheets. Some Saturdays I worked in the yard. In the fall, I raked leaves and in the winter I shoveled the snow out of the driveway for my stepfather's car. I had no friends or anyone I could talk to.

I found that I could escape this doggery by focusing my mind outside the room and onto a landscape where there were birds, flowers and places to run and play around the trees. I was free to watch clouds or a sunset. All the while my mind was out playing, my body was standing at the ironing board, my hand moving through the motions of ironing and folding clothes. When the last piece was ironed and folded into the basket, I came alive and carried the basket of clean clothes upstairs to my mother. As time went on, I found I could dissociate my mind from the world around me, and visit my personal place of nature's wonders.

At school in my senior year, I found two friends who I could talk to. One was a beautiful black girl that later became a teacher in the New York school system. The other girl was white and she was interested in journalism. She eventually worked at one of the big newspapers in New York City. This school had dances with the all boy's Catholic school. The night of the senior prom stands out in my mind as one of the worst experiences of my young life.

SENIOR PROM

My two good friends had found a date for me for the prom. They had also found a dress for me and the plan was for me to stay over at Pam's house, the black friend, and come home the following day on the train. The night of the prom I was ready to go out the door when my stepfather stopped me. He would not let me out of the house. My mother refused to let me stay in a "black" person's home even if it was just overnight. I went to my room and cried my eyes out! After a few hours, I heard him asking my mother what the problem was and when she explained he said, "Well she can go!" By then, it was way too late and I just went to bed. The next day at school I had a lot of explaining to do. When I told Pam what my mother said she refused to speak to me for the rest of the school year. At graduation time, I was very lonely and miserable.

I lived a total of seven years with my mother and my stepfather, never getting to really know them except for my stepfather more than I wanted to. He ignored me as a child, but when I reached my teenage years, he began to take more interest in me. I don t remember the rationale he gave me for his presence in my bed one night, but his fondling of my breasts each night became an occasional occurrence. He would stay a few minutes then go to his own bed.

Edward had a friend in Spain that had helped him learn Spanish when he lived there. They had worked together in some company in Madrid. I never did hear the exact connection between these two. Arthur came to visit us for a full week. Edward took him all over showing him the Connecticut countryside. One night Arthur took an interest in me asking me about school and when I would graduate from high school. The next morning, I heard my stepfather say we were taking Arthur to the airport, since he was leaving after just three days! I overheard my stepfather tell my mother in the car driving home that Arthur wanted to take me back to Spain with him as his mistress. My stepfather said that Arthur accused him of wanted to "keep me for himself!" I did not understand those implications until much later, when he started getting in my bed at night.

According to my stepfather, he was an ardent Catholic, and since he had married a divorced woman he could not fully participate in the Catholic Church rituals. This bothered him. He spoke to the archbishop of the Catholic Church in the area where we were living, and asked him what could be done. It was decided that an amount of money with a letter sent to the Pope in Rome would resolve the situation. Several years later they were still looking for an answer. I learned much later that, after I left the house, he had become violent and started beating my mother. She had bruises to show for it and her doctor advised her to go to the police, but she never would.

SPIRIT WARNING

My stepfather was taking a night class at New York University. It had something to do with his teaching certificate. He usually got home in time for supper, but this one night he had to stay longer in New York City, so my mother and I had supper alone. We pulled a table before the fireplace in the living room and had our supper before the fire that night. My mother was talking about some of the students she had in her class. This was a rare occasion as she never talked to me about anything, so I was intent on what she was saying. She started talking then in the middle of her sentence another voice took over. It sounded louder and very masculine. The voice said to me **"You cannot stay here. We cannot protect you!"** When the voice stopped, I ask my mother what she meant about that. She had no knowledge of the voice or the message. The events that followed showed the accuracy of that warning.

After graduation, I found a job working in a small factory where we printed personalized stationary. My stepfather set up a banking account for my wages, but he controlled the money I made. I was given enough money for bus fare so I could get to and from work and that was all. I had a couple of shirts and a pair of jeans for work, but there were no pretty dresses in my closet to wear.

ENTER WILLIAM

It was into this situation that a man came into my life. He was the son of my mother's childhood friend who was in the Air Force stationed in Massachusetts. His mother lived in California and she had written Bill, asking him to visit her old friend. That is how I met my first husband. Bill came to our house in Connecticut first to see my mother then he came to see me. When my stepfather saw that there was an attraction between us, and he just might lose his anticipated sexual encounters with me in the future, he started objecting to Bill's visits. This obsession came to light in the years to come, when we found out my stepfather was under investigation by the school board for indecent advances on the girls he taught. I wondered why he and my mother were constant changing school districts. I guess when the authorities got close to discovering his obsession with young girls, he would go to another school district. He resigned from teaching shortly after I left home.

I learn years later, that Edward starting beating my mother after I left the house. He blamed her for not being given clearance from the church, for marrying a divorced woman. They had not heard from Rome at that time. I don't know if they ever did.

My stepfather became more and more obsessed with me and Bill felt that I was in danger. We decided for me to leave the house, and Bill would drive me to Virginia to my grandfather's house. The day we arrived in Virginia, we had not been there over an hour when the telephone rang. My stepfather was threating to send the police and take me back to Connecticut. There was something called "The Mann Act" that legally charged a man from taking a minor across the state lines for sexual pleasure. My stepfather was threatening Bill with jail and me as a runaway. All of which was ridiculous as I was eighteen at the time and Bill was twenty-two. I was still a virgin. We had come to my grandfather's house only to get me away from my stepfather.

My grandfather talked to both of us and he and his new wife agreed that to avoid scandal for my grandfather, it was decided that we would get married as soon as possible! My grandfather was still preaching at the local Baptist church. He would have a lot of trouble if a scandal should come to light. We would be driven to North Carolina, that night, where the marriage age then was eighteen. My grandfather had a friend in North Carolina who was a minister and he would arrange everything. We got in the car and started the trip. My new grandmother in the front seat with a friend of hers driving and Bill and I in the back. When we got to the minister's house it was close to midnight. I remember saying to my grandmother "I don't want to get married," and her answer was "You have to, we have come this far!"

That is how I found myself married to a man I really did not know, I went to live with him in a house in Springfield, Massachusetts. Spirit was watching over me. The next indication I had that I was being watched over was a vision I had when I was sick with the flu. Nausea and vomiting, also a high temperature, brought a doctor to our house one night in Springfield. In my feverish state, I had a vision of a lady all in white with white beams of light going out from her body. I remember asking her what she thought of my marriage. The answer was repeated twice so that there was no question of the answer. She said, **"It is acceptable."**

MARRIED LIFE

My life was one of obedience to Bill's wishes, without any love or attention from him. My daughter was born in Spokane, Washington, while we were stationed there. Then we were transferred to Sacramento, California, not far from his mother's house in the Bay area. There my son Sean was born. Bill was so much under the influence of his mom that he could not do anything for me unless she approved. If I wanted anything done in the house, I had to ask his mother to talk to Bill to get him to do it. Getting pocket money from him was another battle. He was tight with money, whether it was for me or for the children. Christmas time was a fight for money for presents for the children. Bill's birthday was the seventh of December and he usually got money from his mother, aunt and uncle. He felt that his birthday money was for only for him. If we didn't have extra money for Christmas it was all right. I was not going to have that, so I would ask his mother to talk to him. Because of this, every year we had a tree and a few presents for the children. I never got anything! When Bill got any vacation time while he was in the military and afterwards, we spent that time at his mother's house. I would cook the meals for his mother, aunt and uncle. I was not happy or contented in my marriage.

THE CHOICE

When we lived in Sacramento, there was a reservoir filled to the brim with sparkling water. This reservoir was formed in a valley where a small town had been. The area was flooded to make way for the water storage reservoir. Sometimes when the water was low you could see tree branches in the water. I understand in the last years, with the drastic draught in the western states, that some of the buildings in the flooded town have been seen.

In my day, I loved to sit on the bank and watch the baby fish swim close to the shore. I use to take the kids there so they could swim in the water, and play in the sand on the beach. One warm summer day we decided to go for a swim. I drove the car to the reservoir and parked the car in the parking lot. We took towels and the kids brought their sand buckets and shovels. All was peaceful at the lake. I laid down on the sand on a towel. One minute, I was warm in the sun and the next I was cold standing looking at my body lying in the sand. Beside me stood a hooded figure in a long grey robe. He had a staff in his right hand, and talked to me telepathically, not with words but will feelings. **He said, "You are not happy. You can choose to go with me and leave all of this!"** I thought for a split second and answered him. **"I cannot leave these children. If I go who will look after them? Who will raise them?"** At that point, I found myself back in my body shivering with cold, and very confused. I told the kids to get their stuff we were going home. After a lot of complaining from both kids we got into the car and went home.

CONTACT WITH SPIRIT

Another time when I heard a voice was when I was all alone in the house and I was sitting on the edge of the bed in the bedroom. I don't remember what I was thinking of at that time, but I heard a male voice say clearly **"Listen I have something to tell you!"** It scared me so much I did not get the rest of the message, but my life took a dramatic change from that day on!

I decided to go back to school and enrolled in the local Community College taking one or two subjects each semester. Bill grumbled about the money he had to put out for books. At that time, tuition was free for citizens and residents of California. I loved my classes and started to expand my mind into many other areas of interest. I tried to talk to him about my classes and what I was learning. I soon found out his education was very limited, so when I wanted his opinion on a subject, I often found that he just repeated what I had said in his own words. He had left the Air Force by this time, and was working in maintenance at the local air base on the airplanes he used to fly in. Before he started working there, he had to take some classes. I remember he made the kids and me stay silent in the house while he studied his class work. There was no radio for music in the house, only a TV to be used only when he was home. When I went back to school the policy of quiet at night was already in force.

Sex for us was routine. One, two, three and it was all finished. There was never any cuddling, sweet talk or just plain sharing of feelings. I felt alone and unappreciated. When it got so I did not want to have sex with him, he sent me to a psychiatrist. Bill kept me up at night talking about his needs as a man. Night after night when I would start to fall asleep, he would wake me up to start talking again. When he realized he was getting nowhere, he decided I needed to see a psychiatrist. After a few weeks of office visits, the psychiatrist told me, "You have decided to divorce him, but will not admit it to yourself. You had better grow up and grow up quickly!"

DIVORCE

My divorce forced me to look for some way of supporting myself and the children. I decided to go back to school for a Licensed Vocational Nurse Certificate. Since I had been taking college courses all along, now I went at it full time. I received my associate's degree and completed my L.V.N. certification a year later. Now that I had a way of earning a living, I had to find a job. I applied at all the hospitals in Sacramento, and worked that summer as a temporary nurse until everyone came home from vacation. Opportunities were slim until a friend of mine said they were moving to Seattle, Washington and why didn't I come with them as I might find a job there. So, I sold the house I had gotten in the divorce, packed up the furniture in a U-Haul and went to Washington. My daughter was eighteen. She wanted to stay in Sacramento as she had her own apartment, a job and a boyfriend to be with. My son Sean and I left for Washington.

On the way out of California, we slept at one of the road side rest stops one night. I was curled up in the car, Sean in the back seat. I had a dream that became very prophetic as time went on. I saw a vase filled with sticks. As I looked at them, they turned green and then burst into beautiful flowers. It seems that I was being encouraged to continue on this trip.

My friend had a cousin who lived in Tacoma and she wanted someone to share her house and the expenses. I said that was great, and when I met Barb there was an instant connection. Barb said that she had a ghost in the house that had frightened away all her other roommates. The ghost had made noise where they could not sleep and also got a bit violent in throwing pots and pans around the kitchen. As it turned out, the ghost did not bother me, and Barb said I could stay for free! I went around to all the hospitals, but no one was hiring. I was back to the same point I had been in California. Barb's father was going to California in a few days. If I decided to return to California, he would drive my car with the U-Haul for me. Barb was a bit psychic. She said to me "Why go, you will just be back!" I of course did not believe her. I decided that it was what I would do as I was familiar with the areas in California, and I felt I could find something there to do, so it was decided!

A night before we were to leave, Barb said that a few friends of hers were going over to the Air Force base Non Commissioned Club for some dining and dancing. I should come along and they would get me in the door. One of the girls had a boyfriend who was military and the rest of us were just there for the fun, at least they were, I was there for the music. We sat at a large table and one by one the girls were asked to dance and left with their companions. I sat alone watching the dance floor and enjoying the music. Sometime during the evening, I saw a man holding two drinks walking across the dance floor and I asked him what he was going to do with two drinks, He said, "Drink them," then thought and said "You want one?" We started talking and ended going to a motel together. This was Len. We seemed to know each other as old friends. The next morning, I went back to Barb's house to get ready for the trip to California. That night I had given Len my address in California, with a quick thought, "If you are ever in Sacramento, call me!" One night, after we got settled into an apartment in Sacramento, there was a knock on the door and there stood Len saying he had come to visit. Several months with him commuting by plane every weekend from Washington to Sacramento, he said, the aircraft crew was asking him about his girl in Calif. We decided it was cheaper for me to move to Tacoma where he was stationed, then waste his money on air travel, so Sean and I packed a U-Haul for a return trip to Tacoma.

That started years of moving from base to base across the western United States. I was able to get a job in civil service wherever Len was stationed. I worked in military hospitals and clinics in Washington, Colorado and in Virginia. Sean was officially a military brat, being moved from school to school as we were transferred out of one area to another. He graduated from high school in Washington and then a business school in Virginia.

CHAPTER NINE

1972-1990

THE ADVENTURE BEGINS

We found a small apartment in the middle of a tall forest of trees in the town of Lakewood, Washington. I got a job in the local hospital and Sean went to a new school. We went exploring every weekend around the Puget Sound beaches collecting shells and visited some of the islands off the coast. Len and I talked about everything and we became closer and closer. I was extremely happy, more than I had ever been in my entire life. Sean enjoyed our trips to visit Mt. Rainer and the ice caverns there. He enjoyed fishing and just going all over the state looking at the sites.

NEW MEXICO

Len and I took a week trip to New Mexico and visited several of the Native American areas. Len was eager to show some of the Native American sites he knew about. He had reached the top honor as an eagle scout in the Boy Scouts when he was younger, and retained the love of all things native. We visited the Aztec Ruins National Monument first. This site gets its name from the mistaken views of the early settlers, but is actually the ruins of a 12th- century ancestral Pueblo settlement of the people called **Anasazi,** the ancestors of the modern Pueblo Indians. They lived in homes built of sandstone, mud and stones that were numerous rooms with wooden ladders used to reach the upper levels. This area was used by people associated with the area which is now known as **Mesa Verde National Park** in southwestern Colorado. It was abandoned about 1300. [1].

The Aztec Ruins contains the ruins of many great houses as well as small ones. Among the west ruins, you can see the placement of 500 rooms opening on a large plaza. Here also is the large kiva that has been reconstructed on the original site. A **kiva** is a large subterranean structure that was used for community and religious ceremonies. The kiva at the Aztec ruins is a huge open room surrounded by four massive pillars that hold up the ceiling beams. There are small windows around the side walls and a platform on one side of the room. You walk down into the main floor of the kiva on a stairway. Since this room is open to the public, the stairs have been built for the convenience of the public, but in a functioning kiva, there would be only a wooden ladder in which to get into the kiva, and then only men were permitted inside. [2]

Len and I went inside and sat on the platform. It was so quiet we could not even hear the other people outside walking around the building. Len took out a cigarette and peeled the tobacco out of it then placed the tobacco in a small raised table in the middle of the room. I saw that he was saying something as he did this. Later he explained that the tobacco was to honor the spirits of that place. It was a Native American tradition he had learned in the scouts.

I felt very at home in this kiva. It was as if I had been there before and everything in the kiva, as well as the buildings, felt familiar somehow.

TAOS PUEBLO

The next place we went to was the Taos Pueblo which is a mile north of the modern city of Taos, New Mexico. This is considered to be one of the oldest continuously inhabited communities in the United States. It is known for being one of the most private, secretive, and conservative pueblos. Natives will almost never speak of their customs to outsiders. Their language has never been written down. This fact alone makes the next part of my story all the more remarkable. [3]

The pueblo is constructed of stone and mud with houses on top of each other; house's roofs forming the floor for the next house. They have the color of the brown/orange soil and each unit has a brilliantly painted blue door. The beams for the different layers of homes stick out at the end of the roof and there are wooden ladders to move from one layer of homes to the next. There were also single homes around a large open square. We parked at the edge of the square and started walking around. At one of the single homes there was a man sitting on the porch. Len started talking to him, and somehow he invited us into his house.

I looked around the small one room house. There was no furniture and only the light from the door lit up the inside. The man told Len this was his grandfather's house, and that he lived there off and on. There was a huge post in the middle of the room, which I thought was one of the supports for the roof. I stood there looking around and resting my hand on the post. As I stood there, I started to get impressions of the area and of the house. I saw that the house had been involved in a fire at one time. Out of my mouth came a question to the man, "Have you lived here a long time?" He shook his head yes, and I continued, "There was a big fire here at one time, and you almost lost the house." The man nodded his head yes, and then asked us to leave.

I don't know who was more surprised, me for the information I seemed to know about the house or Len that I did know it! Of course, the Native American was trembling when he kicked us out of his house! I learned from this event that sharing my gifts had its conditions. I was not to do it without permission with the one the information might affect.

MESA VERDI NATIONAL PARK

Our next stop was in southwestern Colorado at Mesa Verde National Park. The road is winding and dusty with groups of trees along the road. Then there is a road that takes you to different roadside areas with signs for direction. In the valley below are the ancient villages built upon sandstone ledges on steep cliffs perched 2,000 feet above the Montezuma Valley. Mesa Verde is Spanish for green table, the name given for the pinyon pine and juniper forests that blanket the ceiling of the Navajo Canyon where nearly 5,000 archeological sites and 600 cliff dwellings built by the ancestral Puebloan people between 550-1300AD.[4]

We were standing by the rim of the canyon looking at the ruins on the other side of the canyon. I had just purchased two necklaces made of pinyon nuts and pulled them out of their package, then put them around my neck. As I did this, I heard a woman's voice as if she was standing right there beside me, **"Now, my daughter you are dressed!"** During this time, I had several dreams in which I saw Len and me as Native Americans living together in a wooded forest. I never got a date or any more than a glimpse of these lives, but I do know it was before the settlers with their wagons came to the western lands. This was why I felt so close to the land and the Native American culture. It was all strangely familiar, yet just out of reach of my ability to remember who and when I was part of these people.

One of the most vivid dreams I had took place with the plains Indians. I saw myself as a captive native woman thrown into a tepee by a man who stood over me. He was part of the raiding party that had attacked my tribe, and he now claimed me as his prize. I recognized him as an honorable man. I felt gratitude, and I knew he would care for me, protect me as his woman. This man was Len dressed in buckskin pants, long black hair with an eagle feather twisted in his hair on top of his head. His bare chest was protected by an intricate bone plate held together with rawhide string, and decorated with some red beads on the side.

Trying to get an idea of the time period of this event has been challenging. The bone breastplate that Len wore was so distinctive that I can still describe it in detail. From my research, I found out that the breastplate was worn by many of the tribes described as plains Indians. It was worn by the men in battle, and at ceremonial events. The area of the plains Indians covered the land from the mountains of the west pacific to the Mississippi River valley of the United States, and extended from the subarctic of the north to the Rio Grande River in the south. Each tribe wore a distinctive dress to designate their tribal origin, but since this breastplate was so widely used, I cannot determine what that Len belonged to. All I know is that we were from different tribes and he took me as a prize of battle.

THE TURQUOISE DEALERS

In our travels across Washington State, we met a husband and wife team that traveled the country selling turquoise jewelry, and other Native American items such as Navajo rugs and sand paintings. This was in the 1970s when turquoise was in fashion, and the demand for a good piece of turquoise was very high. One night we were invited to their house to look at their vast stock of jewelry. There were boxes after boxes of turquoise and silver jewelry of all sizes and shapes. I was fascinated by the display. At one point in the evening, the electric power went out and the hostess got an oil lamp and placed it in the middle of the table. The light from the flickering lamp cast shadows over the table and the walls of the room we were in. The hostess told me that she had a special ring she wanted me to see. She went into her bedroom and returned with a very large gold ring. In the middle of the ring was a perfectly clear light blue piece of turquoise. The hostess handed me the ring and asked me what I thought of it. The moment the ring touched my hand I knew it was something very special as I could feel a definite warm vibration coming from the ring itself. In my mind, pictures began to form. I told her I don't know what this means, but this is what I am seeing: a picture of a large white house sitting high on a small hill, and a huge, green grass yard in front of it. The house has a porch around the front with white pillars every so often holding up the roof. As I described the house, the hostess started smiling with some tears in her eyes. Then she said, **"That was the way my mother described her home in Russia. That gold is from her teeth after she died!"** She continued. "I just wanted to see if you got any impressions off the ring." The electricity finally came back on and we continued our visit with the couple. Later that evening, they said they would be going on a buying trip to New Mexico and asked us if we wanted to go with them. We said yes, and made arrangements to meet them in a few weeks in New Mexico.

On that trip we went into Santa Fe, New Mexico, and visited several dealers there where our friends purchased hundreds of dollars of turquoise jewelry. It was during this trip that we visited the Hopi second mesa. This was Easter weekend and the village was having Kachina dancing in the plaza of their village. [5] I do not know how it was we were allowed into the plaza to see this dance. I think our friends had a contact there who obtained permission for us to be there. All I remember is the beautiful costumed dancers and the people sitting around the plaza on the ground, and on the roofs of the houses surrounding the plaza.

Our hostess had spoken to one of the women in the village asking if she had any bread for sale. The lady said she had some at her house and for us to come there and she would get it for us. We followed her to her house where she had two large bread loaves made in the village bee hive oven in the yard. She offered us a loaf and Len gave her money for it. As we were going out of her house, I turned and said to her **"I hope you will come and visit me in my house as I have visited you today."** The lady's face broke into a large smile and she said she would like to do that. I thanked her again for the bread and went out of the door. I happened to look at Len and his face was white as a sheet. I asked him what was the problem and he told me to wait and he would explain in the car.

As we drove down the road from the top of the mesa, Len started to tell me what had just happened. He first asked me how I happened to say what I did to the lady with the bread. I said I did not know, it just came to me. He then said it was exactly what his mother would say to the native women as she visited them in their area of Denver. Len's mother had worked with the native population as a social worker and knew some of their customs.

COLORADO SPRINGS

Len asked to be transferred from Washington to Colorado because of his mother's failing health. We were there a year, where I got to know her briefly before she passed away. Len had spells when he was very moody, but would pull himself out of it within a short period of time. His mood swings were short in duration, but nevertheless became difficult for me to understand. It seemed Len was fighting some inner battle that only he could solve. When I asked him what was wrong, he could not tell me and got annoyed at me for asking him.

In 1978, I received information that a group from ARE in Virginia Beach was coming to Colorado Springs for a week-long retreat. The Association for Research and Enlightenment was established by Edgar Cayce (1877-1945) to explore spirituality, holistic medicine, psychic development and other subjects. [6] The international headquarters is located in Virginia Beach, Virginia. They have a library that contains over 14,000 documented psychic readings given by Mr. Cayce. He would go into a trance and diagnose ailments as well as prescribe treatments. There are many books written about his abilities and how he helped people with his readings.

Hugh Lynn Cayce, the son of the founder, Edgar Cayce, and his team of associates would hold a retreat in a place called "The Black Forest," which was a wooded area north of town, and the site of a large church campground meeting area. The camp was composed of several large log cabins. One large building was used as a meeting area with a huge open room with a polished wood floor in front of a large fireplace. This is where we would sit on the floor and listen to the presentations for the day. The second building was for dining and housed the kitchen. Around these two large buildings were a bunch of smaller individual cabins for those people who were attending the retreat. This whole complex was set inside a pine forest with rock-covered paths to all the buildings connecting them all together. The serenity of the forest with the tall pine trees all around, the open starlight sky at night brought a peacefulness to the entire area.

The theme for the retreat was "Expectations for the Future." The program started every morning with a gathering of all the people in the large meeting building, first with a guided meditation, followed by a lesson for that day and an open discussion. We were split into groups of twenty each day with a different subject to talk about. After lunch, the second part of the day was a return to the meeting building with a report on what we had learned within our groups.

The last day of the retreat, the morning meditation was to focus on our future and what we would be doing. We were to report to our group what, if anything, we saw. I thought that was an impossible task! The person started the meditation telling us to relax and visualize ourselves in a quiet place and for us to remain there in peace and relaxation. I visualized my grandfather's rose garden in Virginia. I saw it just as I remembered it as a child with hundreds of rose bushes of every color, and shades of that color, all around me.

VISION OF THE FUTURE

The lady conducting the meditation said "When you are ready, go and see where you are and what you are doing in the future." One moment, I was smelling the roses, and the next minute I saw myself not as I would consciously choose to be. I was a tall thin woman around twenty years old, plain features, with black straight hair cut severely short straight by her ears. I was dressed in black pants and a white blouse with a long lab coat over it. I seemed to be in charge of a certain room in a clinic.

My future self was standing in a small room that looked like a control center. The wall to my right was filled with dials; in front of me was a large glass window where I could see into the next room. There was a woman lying on an examination table. The door to that room was to my left. Directly in front of me was a desk with a raised pad that fit my hand, It felt something like a baseball mitt. I would ask the woman a question and she would answer me, then I would move my left hand on the pad and reach up and adjust one of the dials with my right hand. We were having a friendly conversation and the lady did not seem to be in any discomfort.

When I was finished the lady got up and walked out the door. I went out of the control room into the hall where there were many people dressed in lab coats walking down the hall or talking to another person. It seemed to be a very busy clinic.

I asked Spirit what was I looking at and what was I doing. The answer was that I was in a medical clinic. In the room where I worked, there were tools for healing. When I put my left hand on the pad, I was using my psychic energy to scan the woman's body for any disease elements in her cells. If anything was detected, I used the dial on the right wall to direct an electric charge to the specific cell and kill it. I was told that this technique was very common and that I was a highly skilled technician in the hospital.

When I reported my vision to my group and described what I had seen, one of the men in the group said he had seen a prototype of a machine like that in Virginia Beach. He told me that there was a doctor there treating autistic children with light and sound. And that he had a high rate of success. He gave me the doctor's name and I said I would be sure to look him up if I ever got to Virginia Beach.

A few months after the conference, I had a dream of walking through a house made of glass, and then it all broke into fragments around me. In time, Len was given new orders by the Air Force to move from Colorado to Virginia. The dream made sense to me if you think of the phrase "breaking up housekeeping" when referring to moving. The dream was a very graphic description of future events.

When we were settled in Hampton, Virginia, across the Chesapeake Bay from Virginia Beach area, I made a point to go to Virginia Beach and look up the doctor I had heard about in Colorado. I found him and after I explained to him why I was interested in his invention, he invited me into his house and showed me his work. The instrument looked like a large light box with lights and a humming sound. The doctor said he was working with autistic children. He said that he found that different children required different frequencies and sound before they would respond. They needed many sessions with this instrument before there was any visible improvement, but once the improvement was seen it was very dramatic!

The doctor was very excited that I had seen a machine like his in the future, but on a much larger scale. He told me that the American Medical Association (AMA) was trying to shut him down and take away his license. After my visit, we corresponded for a few years, and then I was sent a newspaper clipping showing that he had been censored by the AMA and could no longer practice under the direction of the association. I lost contact with him after that.

THE PLANTATION

While we were in Virginia, we took trips around the local area. One time we visited the town of Williamsburg where colonial homes line the streets and there is an area where the past comes alive with people dressed in colonial costumes. The stores are those that would have been frequented in colonial Williamsburg where shoppers can buy things like a sun bonnet or silver spoon. We happened to be there during the Christmas season. The houses were all dressed in holly leaf wreaths on their doors with lots of lights and red ribbons. The shops had holiday wreaths, candles and Christmas tree ornaments for sale.

Another trip took us to the James River and we visited the old plantations along the water. These family-owned estates had workers on the land who were slaves before and during the Civil War. Several of these beautiful estates have been kept functional over the years with a working plantation and were now open for tours to the public.

We visited Shirley Plantation, which was at one time the home of Robert E, Lee the leader of the Southern Confederacy in the Civil War. The home is still maintained by the descendants of the original family. We stood in front of a large two floor red brick house that had a white pillared front porch extending out in front of the house. The grounds were tastefully landscaped with large shade trees scattered all around a wide expanse of green grass. Up close to the house there were flowering bushes that gave off a wonderful perfume. The house stood in quiet elegance as if waiting for someone to enter and enjoy the cool interior of its rooms.

    We had a guided tour of the main house accompanied by a man—a descendent of the family who owned the property since 1638. Inside the doorway, there was a long hallway with a living room set off from the hall on the right. This room had hard wood floors with light flooding the room from several windows that reached from the floor to the ceiling. Our guide pointed out a window pane that had several names etched into the glass. The story was that when each young lady of the family received their engagement ring, she scratched her name on the window with the diamond to see if it was genuine. They knew that a real diamond cuts glass. There were several names engraved there, showing the many generations of the family who had tried out their rings there.

    The entire house had the feeling of elegance and bygone years of sumptuous living. All the rooms had expansive high ceilings; the rooms filled with large pieces of furniture that showed the grain of hardwood used in the creation of the piece. They glowed with the years of faithful polishing. One room had a table with chairs around it. Off to one side was a large piece of furniture with several drawers in which was stored table linens, china, and silver for the table setting. On top of this was a display of crystal and a few silver plates.

    At the far end of the room, there was a door going outside to a small sidewalk that led to a much smaller building. I found out that this was the kitchen. The servants would cook the food and bring the hot dishes over to the main house using the side door to the dining room. In the early days, some of the main houses had caught fire by a mishap in the kitchen. So now it was a custom to build the kitchen as a separate building. The food was cooked on an open fireplace made of brick, with one side a Dutch oven that was used to bake bread or would keep food warm after it was cooked. There was also a long metal arm with a hook that could be swung over the fire to hang the big stew pots. Meat was roasted on a spit over a roaring fire in the fireplace. On one side was a long work table. The floor was cobble stone and the walls made with thick mud and plastered. It was in this room that I felt at home. I knew the feeling of the hot fire and I could say what was kept in the large bins and cupboards on the wall. I knew I had lived there at one time as a slave.

CHAPTER TEN

1980-1983

ANOTHER WORLD ANOTHER LIFE

Those of you who have lived the military life with a spouse, or yourself in the military, know that the military dependent's life and the entire family life is very different from people who have only been a civilian.

In 1980, we were living in Hampton, Virginia. My husband was in the Air Force, stationed at Langley Air Force Base in Virginia. I was working for the Navy in the medical clinic's emergency room of the Portsmouth Shipyard.

Our lives changed one fall day when my husband received orders for Rimini, Italy. One morning the movers came to pick up our furniture. Part of the furniture went into storage; the rest was packed into wooden crates for shipment to Italy. There were no problems except for a situation with one of my son's models. Sean had spent two years building a wooden, two- mast sail boat. We had safely brought the model with us when we moved from Washington state to Colorado and then to Virginia. It had graced our mantel in our Virginia home, and was to be put into storage for safety. My husband had ordered a special crate to be built for the boat.

I looked out of the window and saw one of the movers with the ship in the driveway. The boat was laying it on its side with all intricate rigging broken. I ran out and grabbed the boat and asked the man why he had broken the boat. The answer made no sense to me (that he was measuring it for the box)! I said the box was not needed as he had destroyed the model. I don't know who was more upset my son or myself. Looking back now, I wish I had told my son to take the ship with him to his apartment in Newport News, Va. My son said he would make another ship, but he never did. In the years to come, I heard some horror stories from military wives, such as the packers putting a coffee machine in a crate with the old used coffee grounds, and prized possessions being broken or lost. When we got back to the states and got our washer and dryer out of the storage, we found that the knob to adjust the size of the wash load was missing. All the automobile tools that we packed in back of the bus were gone, when we picked up the bus at the New Orleans port. Those were some of the trials of military moving.

A MILITARY MOVE

Along with the military orders was a letter from the new base with instructions about what we could expect in our new home. We were told that when our airplane landed in Aviano, Italy (US Army base), we would be met by someone from our base in Rimini and driven another eight hours to our own base. We found out later that there was a lot of very important information omitted from the letter that could have been of great assistance to us in the year to come. For one thing, if we had known the circumstances of local housing we would have left all our furniture in storage in the states. The person who wrote the letter promised to help us find an apartment and to get acquainted with the area. In reality, we had to do it all ourselves.

In Virginia, we had a Volkswagen camper truck that had, what we thought, was a German motor. My husband's reasoning was if we needed parts we would not be that far from Germany to get them, so he had a mechanic go over it and replace anything that had any wear, hoping to prevent any mechanical problems. We sold my small car. In Italy, we found out the small car would have been more practical, and when the VW broke down we found out it had an American engine in it. We waited a month for parts from the US before we could use the bus.

So here we are with the furniture gone and the VW bus on its way to Italy. We went to the airport for our trip across the ocean. We left from an airport somewhere in Pennsylvania, I don't remember where. All I know is that we were on a military transport that left late in the afternoon and traveled all night. I remember looking at the lights below us and someone telling me we were flying over Ireland. The sun was coming up when we landed in Germany, and some of the troops got off there. We were able to get breakfast there and get back on the aircraft.

Now, according to my biological clock, we were in the middle of the night and should be sleeping, but here we were looking at a new day. We finally arrived in Aviano, Italy, where my husband reported in to the officials while I tried to stay awake in the waiting room. I remember being jarred out of a sound sleep when I felt myself falling off of the chair to the floor. Finally, all the paperwork was done and we could find a hotel for some needed sleep. The next morning, we would be driving to our base in Rimini. My husband decided we should eat something before we went to sleep, so we found a little restaurant still open at eight at night and ordered our first Italian supper.

The food was excellent, which tempered our exhaustion from the flight. Then we made a fatal mistake, which we regretted for the rest of the night. We ordered coffee with our dessert. Our waiter asked us in his limited English, if we were really sure we wanted coffee? When we said yes, he brought us a large cup of the best tasting coffee I had ever had the pleasure of drinking. We were to find out that Italian coffee is a LOT stronger than we were accustomed to in the states. We were so wired we could not sleep! About three in the morning we finally were able to drop off to sleep, but by then we had only a few hours left before we had to get up at eight for the driver and van that would take us to Rimini.

We got into a military six-passenger van for the trip south. We learned firsthand what driving on the Italian freeway was like. If you saw car headlights in your rear-view mirror, you quickly got over to the right side of the road, because by the time you get there, he would be passing you! The odometer hit 120 as we zipped down the road. We were told if you don't go fast, you get hit. The speed limit was at that time "as fast as your motor will let you!" This was a trip we would make many times in the future, but the first time I thought we would never get there. We were dropped off at the local hotel and shown a room on the second floor. This would be our home for two months until our furniture arrived from Virginia. The hotel was close to the base, which was inside the Italian airport. I would be on my own until my husband came home in the evening.

REMINI ITALY

Rimini is a town located on the Adriatic Sea. It is the European summer playground with the seventy miles of white beaches and the many specialty shops that line the shores. In the summer, we heard people speaking many different languages, yet everyone spoke or understood English. As soon as the summer was over and only the locals were in the shops or on the street, they didn't understand a word we said. It was most frustrating until I started to learn to speak Italian by listening to people, and especially watching our Italian TV.

The hotel staff spoke English a little and taught us the basic of the Italian language. The first lesson started on our first night in the hotel when the manager said good night to us in Italian. We finally caught on and repeated it back to him, and that is the way we learned Italian. Later as I tried out my new language skills, the person I was trying to talk to would correct my pronunciation, and when I got it right, I was rewarded with a big smile and the word "Brava." They appreciated that we were making the effort to learn the language.

Before you think we were living in luxury in the hotel, let me tell you it was a room with a bed and a bath and that was all. The military men are given a housing allowance, and the two months we had to live in the hotel, that went to pay for a part of the bill. We paid the rest when we checked out. We paid for our food in the dining room and anything else we needed.

There was nothing to do for the wives that were in the hotel. On the third day, I decided to do some exploring. I found out from the hotel staff that if I walked ten blocks toward the beach, I could catch a downtown Rimini bus. They told me the number of the bus and the amount of money I needed to ride the bus. As the bus went between buildings, I was surprised to see how narrow the streets were and how close the bus came to the walls of the buildings. If I had put my hand out of the window, I could have touched the walls! The square was a huge open area paved with large cobblestones, with a fountain the middle of it. All around the square there were small shops.

So, there I was three days in the country, didn't know the language or the area, and riding the bus to a place I had never been before. I made sure I got off at the square and knew where the return bus would be before I started window shopping. There were people on one side of the square selling all kinds of beautiful cut flowers. Although it was fall, I saw many flowers that were normally seen in the spring time. Roses of all colors and green plants for the house. It was a wonderland of smells and sights. I walked around and looked into several shops then got back on the bus for a trip back to the hotel.

LIVING THE ITALIAN LIFE

When our furniture finally arrived, we needed to find an apartment. Our sponsor was nowhere to be found. One of the other military wives told us that there was an apartment available not far from the airport. The owner and his wife were German, but the wife spoke English. We went to the house and found out she would rent the second floor to us.

The apartment had a huge living room with a small fireplace, three bedrooms, kitchen and bath. We found that there was a city regulation on the use of the fireplace. You could not have a fire before November or after April, no matter if the weather required it for warmth in the apartment. There was a heavy fine for the homeowner if smoke was seen coming out of the chimney any other time. The apartment had seven-foot walls which were painted a dark color. I ended painting them in an off white, with blessings from the landlord. When we moved out two years later, the landlord tried to make us pay to have the apartment painted. I was able to prove that I had painted it before we moved in. Another problem was that the things you expect to see in an apartment were not in an Italian apartment. The bathroom did not have medicine cabinet or lights. The kitchen was bare without a light, stove, refrigerator or even cabinets. We had to buy these things if we wanted them.

Italian houses do not have closets. Fortunately, for us, that was one thing our sponsor had told us, and we had brought an armoire from the states with us. We later learned from our Italian friends the reason for the lack of closets in an Italian house. It seems that homeowners were taxed on the amount of rooms he had in his house. Closets were considered rooms, so no closets, less taxes. All Italian buildings had rolling wooden shutters that could be pulled down over a window when the weather was bad or they could be used at night. Unfortunately, these shutters made the room very dark, so I used them at night only.

We went shopping for things for our apartment. The military community had a system where the family leaving for the states would sell their items to the families coming into the country. That is the way we got our bathroom light and medicine cabinet also other things. We found a lady who had an Italian stove to sell, another person with an Italian refrigerator. The electricity was a problem as the things we brought from the U.S. worked on a different current than the Italian. I found that I needed a transformer to run my washing machine Again, the outgoing military families were glad to sell us theirs. We found the local cabinet shop and bought several cabinets for our kitchen.

I had brought my sewing machine from the states so we hired a lady from one of the local shops to bring material to the apartment and custom make curtains for the windows. The windows stretched from ceiling to the floor a good 72 inches, and we found that they not only provided privacy for the windows but acted as a fly determent in the summer since Italians did not have screens on any of their windows.

One interesting thing we found about the construction of the building was that communication from one room to another was impossible because the walls were so thick. But it was surprising how much we could hear from the apartments above and below us. The landlord and his wife lived below us on the first floor, so there was not much noise from them, but above us was another military family with two small children. Whenever the children got to playing with toys or running in the apartment the noise was amplified into our apartment through the floor.

This could be very disturbing at times. I remember very early one morning, about 3:00 A.M., I woke out of a sound sleep to a strange noise from the apartment above us. I realized after a few minutes what was going on upstairs. There was a scraping then a thud, then the same noise all over again. It was quiet then they would start over again. After a series of these noises, I realized that the couple in the upstairs apartment was having an early morning lovemaking moment. Now I was fully awake and upset that my night had been disturbed; then the impish part of myself set in. On the pause of activity upstairs, I hollered "Ole." By this time, my husband was awake asking me why I was yelling at the ceiling. Then he started listening to the rhythmic sounds produced above our heads. After a second "Ole," all was quiet and we were able to go back to sleep.

The next morning, we shared our night adventures with one of our friends in the base dining room. The young Spanish couple who were our upstairs neighbors came into the dining room and were greeted by a chorus of "Ole," from the other military people in the room. The young couple did not appreciate it at all, as evidenced by their angry looks around the room and especially at me.

SHOPPING

Italian refrigerators were very small compared to those we were accustomed to. This was one reason the Italian housewife bought food for the home each day. Early in the morning the shops would open and they usually closed for the noon meal, then reopened at three. Most of the shops reopened from three to around eight o'clock at night then closed their doors for the day. The stores sold a specialty individual item. If you wanted bread, you went to the bakery. For fruit, you went to the fruit store. If you wanted fresh vegetables, there was a separate store for that. Of course, there was the Saturday market downtown, where there were tents set up over tables filled with every kind of food you could think of. In the market you could buy clothing, shoes, skirts, sweaters, coats, and anything else you might want. There was also pottery, pictures for the home, bolts of material for the home seamstress, and all kinds of fresh flowers, which I understood later was a requirement for an Italian home.

As time went by, I became friends with one of the maids in the hotel, Maria. I had started knitting a sweater in the states and I was working on it when Maria asked me by sign language what I was doing. She told me her son spoke English and she wanted me to come home with her, so he could explain to her in Italian what it was I was saying to her. I followed her home that afternoon and met Daniel and his younger sister. Both of them had taken English in school, but it was Daniel who wanted to become more comfortable speaking it. He was delighted to talk to me, so he could practice his English.

I learned a little about the family. Maria had worked at the hotel for fifteen years and she was looking forward to retirement. He husband worked at a job in Germany. Apparently, he could make better money in Germany than in Italy. I never did find out what kind of work he did, but I did meet him once.

Maria's house was close to the hotel. Most of the houses in the area were composed of apartments that took on entire floor, but Maria had a small house all her own. I found out that the Italian families usually had all their family living in one house, with another family member and their family living on each floor of the house. I found out the buildings were made of cement and steel. The floors were all tiled making the floors cold to your feet in the winter, but there was a small fireplace in the living room that cut some of the cold. Each room had floor to ceiling windows that opened onto a balcony. There were no screens on the windows, so long flowing curtains hanging in the window provided ventilation, and acted as a bug deterrent with their moving fabric. There was a small piece of ground around the building, with every spare inch supporting some kind of vegetable garden.

ITALIAN POTTERY SCHOOL

Maria and I talked many times with Daniel as the translator. She introduced me to Italian cooking and the delights of Italian pastry. She was just as curious about my household routine as I was about hers. We shared many pleasant afternoons. One day something was said about a ceramic school in town, I decided to look into becoming a student. I asked Daniel to translate for me and off we went to the school downtown on the bus.

The lady in admissions was very curious about this strange American that wanted to be a student. This school took students from all over the district that had difficulty in academic studies. I explained through Daniel that, I had done some ceramic work at home and I loved to work with clay. She told Daniel it all depended on the professor, if he was willing to accept me as a student.

She called the professor to come into her office and I stood before him while Daniel explained to him what I wanted. He thought a bit, then told Daniel to translate for him. He said, to me, "You don't speak Italian and I don't speak English, but by the time you leave here you will speak Italian. You can't do the formal lessons, but you can work in the practice area. If you agree with that, you can start tomorrow!" Of course, I said yes and I began a two-year study of Italian design and ceramic production.

The majority of my classes were in the reproduction of Italian masterpieces using the Majolica technique, which was popular in Italy in 1400 to the 1600s. The fired clay form is covered with a tin glaze, which is in a chemical mixture that acts as a base for the paint. It gives the clay a smooth and shiny, creamy looking coat. The paint we used came in a powdered form with colors of blue, green, yellow, orange, ruby red, pink and reddish browns. Later on in the year, I was able to visit the ceramic-producing cities of Deruta, Gubbio, and the museum of ceramics in Florence, and brought home a few of their wares. Majolica had a last flowering in the last third of the sixteenth century in the mountain city of Urbino.

VISITING THE ITALIAN COUNTRY

Every weekend Len and I were able to take trips to visit other areas of the country. One trip we took was with an organized tour on a bus to visit Sorrento and Pompeii in the southern part of the country. I fell in love with the hill town of Sorrento and the blue Mediterranean waters at the base of the hill. We learned that Sorrento was a Greek word, which translated into "from the Gods." My one regret was that we could not visit the island of Capri. We were told by the tour guide that the sea was too rough that day for a crossing.

Pompeii is a town of the eighth century BCE It was a perfect port for boats as it was situated where the river ran into the sea. It provided a landing place for the Phoenicians and Greek traders. Rome had conquered the land around Pompeii and the city reflected the various conquerors including Etruscan, Greek, and Roman influences. It was a busy seaport with a large trading area, and the land where the rich and famous people of that time built their summer houses. Some of the homes had decorated tile floors, and walls painted with pictures of the family or of landscapes.

The area was shadowed by a large volcano which erupted August 24, 79 AD, covering the town and the surrounding area with volcanic ash. All 20,000 residents were covered in layers of ash 19 to 23 feet deep.

Over the years, several attempts have been made to dig out some of the statues, houses and treasures buried in the ash. When we were there in 1982, over half of the city of Pompeii was still buried. There is a museum that has been established for all the artwork and statues recovered up to that time.

Our guide took us through the main street of town where there were large blocks in the middle of the street that provided stepping stones from one side of the street to the other at the time of flooding or when the street was used for sewage drainage. The buildings on both sides of the road gave the appearance that a giant hand had scooped out the top and side of the buildings. I had an eerie feeling looking at a partial building, one after another standing along the street. In another part of the deserted city, were the remnants of a Roman forum, temples and a large amphitheater.

We saw several houses where their red painted columns could still be seen as well as the painted pictures on the walls. Mosaic floors in all their beauty after centuries of being buried under volcanic ash; some completely uncovered, but many more still buried.

VENICE

Another bus trip with the families from our base was to Venice. We arrived near the Grand Canal and took a boat over to St Marks's plaza. We were there during Halloween festival week. We were treated to the sights of costumed ladies in flowing dresses and the men in costumes right out of Hollywood's "Three Musketeers." They had flared pants and stockings to match the color of their clothes. Some men had capes thrown across one shoulder and they wore a wide brim hat perched on their head, which sported a huge feather. Everywhere we looked there were people in period costumes of all colors and degree of elegance. We expected a dual with swords to break out any moment!

The square is huge, surrounded on all sides with shops, and on one side the dock for boats to pull into the plaza. You may have seen pictures of birds sitting on people as they stand in St Mark's plaza. It is true birds flock to anyone, especially if you have bird seed that venders are most willing to sell you. Birds sit on your outstretched arms and on top of your head ready for that extra seed you will throw on the ground for them. Years of tourists and free bird seed has conditioned the birds to come for the fun! As soon as we purchased the seed, the word must have gone out to the birds that there was free food; since my husband had the bag of seeds, he was immediately covered with birds sitting on his head and on his arms.

At the eastern end of the Piazza San Marco is the large impressive Basilica of Saint Mark. It is connected to the palace. There are four bronze horses at the portal of the basilica. The originals were brought back from Constantinople. [3] Originally, this was the chapel of the Doge built in 828, but when merchants stole the remains of Saint Mark from Alexandria, it was designated for St Mark. The date for the completion of the basilica and its consecration is given as 1093. [1]

Inside the church, everywhere you look there was a mosaic of some story from the bible all made with colored tile and glass accented in gold. The picture of the Creation was in the atrium, Pentecost, Prophecy and Ascension, and the Redemption in the interior set in the three domes of the central isle. The opulently designed gold mosaics and statues were seen as the wealth and power of Venice, and were evident everywhere you looked.

At one end of the interior of the church, we found the entrance to the treasury where there is a display of a collection of Byzantine objects of art in metal, enamel, and stone carvings, mostly looted from Constantinople after the fourth crusade of 1204. There were large gemstones. [2] One that I remember seeing was a very large yellow stone fashioned into a goblet. There was a huge altar screen made of solid gold.

THE BRIDGE OF SIGHS

We spent the entire day looking in the shop's windows around the square. At one point, we decided to cross the bridge that connects the palace to the prison, which was built in 1600. Legend has it that prisoners, on their way to prison cells or execution chambers, would sigh as they caught their last glimpse of Venice through the small windows of the bridge. The name comes from the sighs of despair, depression, and desolation of the prisoners. [4] With every area of strong emotional content, this bridge still holds the emotionally-charged air of those prisoners as I could not wait to get off the bridge. Their very strong vibrations were still there, even after these many centuries.

FLORENCE

One summer weekend we decided to take the tour bus to the mountain town of Florence. The bus was air conditioned and the trip delightful with a lot to see. As we approached the city, we could see the dome of the Duomo with the crowning copper ball towering over the city. We learned that this was an ancient city, a village in the Iron Age and during the Etruscan period. The orthogonal arrangement of the streets gave evidence that it also had been a colony of Rome.

I am sorry to say that we did not see a great deal of the art treasures in this city; as the day wore on, the temperature rose to above one hundred degrees. Inside the buildings, the air was stifling and it became difficult to breathe. The guide left us to visit the buildings around the plaza Vecchio. At the door of Duomo stood the seventeen-foot-tall figure of David which was determined by Leonardo da Vinci and a committee of citizens that the statue was too big to place inside the church and so it rested outside in the plaza at the church's front door. The church was filled with paintings from all the masters. We took a quick look inside, but retreated outside the church just to breathe because of the stifling heat.

VINCENZA

Every month there was a base bus going to our supply base in Vincenza, which was north, over a hundred miles away at the Army base, near the base of the Dolomite Mountains. My husband worked in the mail room. One of his jobs was to take the mail to the depot and bring the incoming mail back to the base. Consequently, I rode with him on many of his trips. All of the military wives were permitted to ride the bus, and purchase groceries for their family as well as attend their medical and dental appointments that were held there. This was also the location of our commissary for groceries. We bought all our meat there and took it home in a freezer chest. All other groceries were purchased at the local market in Rimini. It was a long trip usually taking a full day, with a stop at the gas station midway on the trip. We would come home with mail for the base and everyone who rode the bus brought back their groceries and things they bought at the base store.

THE PROFESSOR

On day Daniel said he wanted to introduce me to a man who was a professional pottery artist in Rimini. With Daniel there to translate, we had a wonderful visit. The professor and his wife became good friends to us during our time in Italy. Since I had not quite mastered basic Italian, when I was alone with the professor we communicated with a mixture of French, Italian and a lot of gestures. It was then that I was grateful for the three years I spent as a student in a French/Canadian school in Massachusetts. The professor spoke no English, but he did speak French as well as Italian. The French words and Italian were sometimes the same, giving me an idea of what the professor was telling me.

One day he suggested we go and see some beautiful mosaics in a town about an hour from Rimini. This was how I was introduced to the Church of San Vitale in Ravenna, Italy. We learned that the church was built in the Byzantine style dating from the early sixth century, and was thought to be financed by the Emperor Justinian. The church was built when that part of Italy was under the emperor's rule. There was mosaic picture on the walls of the emperor, his wife, and the court. On the outside, there was a smaller building beside the church, which held the baptismal font. On the wall was a picture of a large marble fountain with birds on the corners drinking water from the bowl of the fountain. I bought a large poster with this picture on it and have it in a frame on the wall in my office now. I also bought a small replica of the fountain made with a combination of marble dust and plastic, with four birds sitting on the edge of the bowl, one of my most cherished items from Italy.

The professor and I spent many hours together while he showed me the techniques of painting ceramics and other artistic items.

REPUBLIC OF SAN MARINO

On one of our weekend trips we found the medieval walled country of San Marino about an hour's drive from our home. On talking to the people, we learned that this is an independent county inside the larger country of Italy. According to tradition, San Marino was founded in 301 AD by a Christian stone mason named Marinus who had escaped the anti-Christian Roman Emperor Diocletian. Marino founded a small community at the peak of Mount Titano. This area was given the name of "Republic of San Marino." For centuries the ruling family of Rimini, the Malatestas, tried to take over the area, but it was defended by the Montefeltro of Urbino. By the fifteenth century, it was a republic ruled by a Grand Council. In 1463, the Lord of Rimini gave the Republic more land at the base of the mountain that included three other towns. This is the area of the Republic to this day. In 1739, the pope recognized the independence of San Marino from the country of Italy. San Marino has its own government, laws, and legal system. The government relies on the sale of agricultural products, and tourism for their revenue. It is the smallest independent state in Europe after the Vatican and Monaco. [5]

One sunny and clear day we drove up the mountain to the old walled city. The streets are extremely narrow, so cars must be parked outside the gates of the city. There were all kinds of shops filled with beautiful ceramics, gold jewelry and leather products. As we walked around the city, we heard people speaking English with a definite Midwest accent. This was refreshing as we had heard only Italian for over a year! We started talking to the shop owners and found that there was a large group of people working there from New York and Detroit. They were Italian-Americans that had moved back to the old country because of the bad economy at that time in their home states.

These people told us that if a person was born in San Marino, they could live in the country, but if not, they had to live at the base of the mountain, A lot of the shops were owned by Italian families from the United States, but they had to commute from the base of the mountain to the city where their shops were located. Many of these people had come back to the country of their grandparents when we were there in 1981 because of the lack of jobs in the states, especially in the automotive industry.

San Marino had many festivals where there would be jousting matches and competitions of strength among the men. All the residents would be dressed in period costumes. The feeling of the city was as if you had stepped through a time portal and there you were in the days of Kings, Queens, and Knights guarding the castle in all their beautiful colored uniforms; swords, and lances at the ready for whatever might happen.

THE DUKE OF URBINO

Our apartment was four blocks from the seaside which offered miles of white sand and a playground for the world. During the summer months, people from every country in Europe came to Italy for a vacation and the warm sands of the Adriatic. Everywhere we went people spoke English in the summertime because of the large infusion of tourists, but in the winter these same people couldn't seem to understand a word we said. I had taken three years of French in school and I found that a lot of the Italian words were close to the French that I understood. This helped me to start understanding our Italian neighbors. The people we met were so helpful, they would correct my words, and then when I said it right, they would smile and say "Brava!"

Each weekend when we were exploring by ourselves, we would take our old VW bus and travel the countryside. We were able to visit all the small towns around our area. We could see an occasional house and a few trees that dotted the landscape. I was struck by the sameness of the brown color of all the houses that were surrounded with large open fields.

One Sunday, we were driving a deserted two-lane road, and suddenly ahead of us there was a massive rock formation rising from the valley floor. One side looked like sheer rock, but as we continued down the road, we saw that the road was winding around and slowly going to the top of a massive hill. High on top there appeared to be buildings, but we couldn't really tell until we got closer.

Our old VW bus was going slow because of the altitude. As we climbed higher, the scenery changed from the brown fields of the plains to spots of green grass among the outcropping of large boulders. Finally, at the top we saw a large wall that extended around a city with a small gate in the wall. Our bus could barely squeeze through the city gate. We entered the town of long cobblestone streets going toward the top of the hill and the main plaza. No cars were allowed in the city, so we parked the bus near the gate and started walking up the street. On either side of the road were shops filled with beautiful things to tempt the tourist. The buildings were of the same brown color as those in the valley. They had large display windows facing the street filled with goods for sale.

We found out we had entered the medieval town of Urbino, which had kept its charm and mystery all of the centuries from when it was the home of the ruling duke and duchess in the fourteenth century. Entering this medieval environment, you felt like you had stepped back centuries in time. It was not hard to visualize the town as it had been in the glorious days of the fourteenth century. The road ended in a large plaza where there was a church on one side and on the other side sat a large rambling castle, which had belonged to the Federico de Montefeltro, Duke of Urbino (1444-1482). We enjoyed being tourists looking in the shop windows and continuing to walk up the large cobblestones to the center of town.

The castle now houses the Galleria Nazionale delle Marche, one of the most important collections of Renaissance paintings in the world. It is filled with the beautiful original paintings of Rafael, who had lived in the town. There was a guide who took us through the castle. Our group of five tourists started touring the building. There were many massive rooms with fireplaces so tall that my husband, who was six-foot-tall, could stand inside it and still had room above his head. Over each fireplace was a wooden mantle with carvings of cherubs and flowers. There were carved wooden doors that opened into each room. Around the door was a border of exquisitely carved flowering trees. The entire castle was elegant in everything with beautiful, carvings in the ceiling plaster and the wood around the doors and over the fireplaces. There were only a few tapestries on the wall now, but we learned that there had been many more when the Duke lived there. After the fall of the Duchy, the palace was stripped leaving only a fraction of all of the original treasures behind that can still be seen today.

The Duchess's bedroom was the size of a small house in town with its own fireplace and carved lintel. I remember looking at the high ceiling and getting a slight chill down my back. A feeling of great discomfort came over me when I looked at the large black eagle prominently placed in the middle of the decorated ceiling of creamy-colored gilded plaster of flowers and cherubs. We found out later that the eagle was the Duke's emblem for his kingdom. To me, it looked very ugly in the middle of such beauty.

The Duke's bedroom was equally as large as the Duchess's bedroom, also with a massive fireplace. His bed had been constructed with a frame of wood and it had curtains all around it. When the castle was vandalized after the Duke's death, the bed had been too heavy to carry out, and thus remained in place as part of the nation's exhibit now. We were told that many of the art objects were taken from the castle. Some went to private dealers. [6]

The tour continued into the Duke's study with walls of inlaid wood. The gold and chestnut colors of the wood blended together to give a three-dimensional feeling to the room.

The inlaid wood was designed so that it gave the impression of cupboards, some with their doors open. The illusion was complete with the placement of books, armor, scientific and musical instruments inside the cabinet. It looked as if the Duke had left some of the cupboards open. The illusion was breathtaking! [7]

Here, my husband became a problem. He started feeling the wall and saying that there was a hidden room behind the wall. He was feeling the wall looking for the latch to the room. The more he insisted that there was a hidden room, the more the official guide became agitated. Finally, the guide persuaded him to leave the room so the group could continue their tour. It is interesting that two small hidden rooms were found in 1582 when an inventory of the palace was made. One small room was a chapel contained a painting by Raphael *"Madonna and Child,"* which is now in the Galleria Palatina at the Palazzo Pitti, Florence.

As we walked into the next room, my husband declared in a loud voice that he wanted to see where the horses were kept. The guide in an equally loud voice proclaimed that there were no stables for him to see. My husband kept insisting that the horses were stabled nearby. Needless to say, everyone in the group was looking at us strangely. They continued with the tour while the tour guide quietly showed us the front door. In Ms. Osborne's book *Urbino: The Story of a Renaissance City,* she states that on the basement floor there were stables for the horses. There was a kitchen, pantry, wine cellar, cisterns for rain water and a pit for snow that was used to keep food items and wine cold during the year. There was also the luxury of two bathrooms. [8]

As the weeks went by, we learned more about the Duke of Urbino and his life as a military leader who never lost a battle. He was the head of an independent city-state, which he maintained with his wife and court councilors. He provided for the court and the city by championing wars of other city-states in Italy. The independent city-states were constantly at war with each other. The Duke received a pension for keeping the peace in the neighboring valley. Ms. Osborne, in her book, tells us that the Duke was the richest and most influential man in Europe because of his military intervention for other city-states. He accumulated an income of 65,000 ducats a year, which allowed him to purchase paintings of the masters as well as being a patron for budding artists and their many artistic projects. [9]

The Duke was a learned man who offered his castle as a meeting place for the great painting masters of the time. He also invited all the men of science of that time to bring their new ideas to his court. All men of science, literature, philosophy, and architecture were invited to visit and share their works with each other. Rafael's father was his court painter and Rafael himself lived at one time in the castle. The word "Renaissance" had not been coined yet, but people believed that they were living in an age of enlightenment.

There were service rooms for guests on the ground floor, also a room used for theater and banquet rooms. Here was the duke's massive library that could be accessed from the garden. I read about these rooms in Jane Osborne's book on Urbino. [10] The library was composed of over a thousand manuscripts that were bound in velvet or leather. He collected books in Greek, Latin, and Hebrew that were bound with gold and silver. A book seller in Florence by the name of Vespasiano da Bisticci was instrumental in helping the Duke obtain his library treasures. These were hand copied manuscripts, some with beautiful illustrations. He employed a large number of scribes to fill the orders from the rich nobility of Italy. Manuscripts from Constantinople written in Greek were also translated into Latin for his patrons.

The library stands empty now, but in the Duke's time the floor was carpeted and the room was furnished with benches and tables. There were books of geography, poetry, history, religious works, law, philosophy, and mathematics. Any subject that was of interest to the Duke or to his many visitors. Printed books were added by Federico's son. By the time of the last Duke Francesco Maria II della Rovere, the library contained 1,800 manuscripts, and thousands more printed books. Francesco was forced to flee Urbina and he took the library with him. Then in the seventeenth century, they were transferred by Pope Alexander VII to the Vatican. [11]

At one time, the walls were covered with priceless tapestries. Since the Duke liked to identify with heroes of the classical world, there were eleven tapestries that showed scenes from the Trojan wars. After the fall of the Duchy, the palace was stripped of the tapestries, paintings, furnishings and anything else that could be carried off. [12]

THE TOURNAMENT

The Duke had one hobby that became disastrous for him. He enjoyed the jousting matches and liked to participate once in a while. Jousting is an ancient sport where both opponents sit on horseback and ride toward each other, holding a long lance that had a strong metal tip. The object of the game was to knock your opponent off his horse. The contestant would run their horses toward each other and jab their opponents. The first one to unseat the other won. The protective clothing worn for such an affair was a metal head mask, with eye openings, and padded clothing.

In one match, the Duke was gravely injured by his opponent's lance, which entered into his right eye opening of his helmet and took out his eye, disfiguring the entire right side of his face. All the pictures we have of the Duke from that time show only a left side profile. [13]

The Duke's first wife died childless. His second wife, Battista Sforza, (1440-1472) was fourteen years old when they married. She was expecting their seventh child, his first son, when she died. The Duke was on one of his military campaigns. He returned home to find that his long-hoped for son had died with his wife, who was then 25 years old. [14] There is a famous painting by Piero della Francesca (1416-1492) of the Duke and his wife facing each other, Federico showing only the left side of his face.

LEN'S MYSTERIOUS PAIN

Len's constant obsession with the city of Urbino and the castle became a weekend nightmare for me. Every time he got any time off from work, he wanted to go see the castle. Len could not explain his reactions to the Duke's castle, nor could he explain his knowledge of the buildings before we got there. He said, it felt like home and he wanted to return. This was the beginning of an adventure neither one of us expected.

At this same time, Len was starting to experience terrible pain on the right side of his body. The pain was so intense that he passed out and fell to the floor. He would hit the tile floor so hard that there was an audible bang! This was happening several times a day to where the military commander feared that there might be a medical condition that needed to be addressed. Len was air evacuated for evaluation to Wiesbaden, Germany to the Army hospital there. I went along as his attendant. This was a two week-long extensive physical examination with many tests that included x-rays, blood work, CAT scans and others. Nothing was over looked with the results coming out negative. They could not find a physical reason for his attacks. We were sent back to Italy to a very angry base command.

Since the Army hospital could not find a reason for Len's episodes of unconsciousness, the commander of our base decided that he was just faking the pain. The fact that the pain was so intense he would become unconscious had no bearing on the subject, according to the commander. He was called into the commander's office one day, and told that he could face a court martial because of his actions, or he could redeem himself and sign his retirement papers from the military. Len already had over twenty years in the military, he took the discharge and we left the country for the United States. From that time on, Len continued to have right side pain, but not as severe as before.

The base command wrote orders so Len would be discharged in Tucson, Arizona, giving us government transportation for ourselves, furniture, and the VW bus. That was all to change when Len came home one day saying that a hold had been put on our orders because our landlord said we had to pay to have the apartment painted before we could officially leave the country. This seemed to have been an agreement between the military and the Italian landlord, that the military family would paint the apartment when they moved out. The landlord got a guaranteed renter for a year or two and the apartment painted for the next occupant. When we moved into our apartment, it had not been painted for quite a while. I had asked the landlord for paint to do it myself. When this question of painting the apartment before we could leave came up, I had documents that proved we had bought the paint and painted the apartment when we first moved in. The landlord saw the papers and then agreed to remove his hold on our orders.

The next thing I knew Len was running into the apartment telling me that the Air Force commander had receded our orders to be discharged in Arizona, and that he had written another set of orders for us so we would have to permanently stay in Italy. The nest day we took the first set of orders and decided to leave the country.

FLIGHT FROM ITALY

Monday, we called the movers to come and pack up our furniture to be shipped to Tucson and stored there until we could retrieve it. On Tuesday, we drove the VW bus to the shipping Port of Livorno and got it on a ship home. Wednesday, we got air plane tickets out of Rome to New York. We were out of the country in three days. We were blessed on all our connections that everything went smoothly, and no one questioned our military orders.

We arrived in New York's J. F. Kennedy Airport then changed planes for Norfolk, Virginia, where my son Sean was waiting to be picked up for our trip to Tucson. We packed Sean's furniture into a U-Haul trailer and hooked up his car to the trailer in Virginia for the trip west. Since we could not travel on military orders, we had to pay for our flight with our own money. There had not been time to save any money because of our sudden departure from Italy.

When we arrived in Tucson, we found between three of us we had a total of $5.00. All of our money had gone for airfare, food, and gas for the trip. We sat in the car, by the side of the road, and decided what to do next.

Len had worked in the administration department of the Air Force all his military years, so he knew that retirees would not receive any money until a month after their retirement, but we were desperate now! We found a motel for the night. The next morning Len said he was going to the base and see if he could get us some money. He returned in several hours with a month's pay. Apparently, the young airman, working in finance that morning, did not know the rule about" no pay for retired men for a month," and he had given Len a month's pay. We were able to get something to eat, and find an apartment that would accept a few weeks' payment instead of all the deposits usually required, and moved in. We would be fine until one of us found a job.

Eventually, one by one each of us found a job. We set the apartment up with the furniture Sean had brought from Virginia splitting the bed with Len and me sleeping on the mattress and Sean having the box springs. We did not get our furniture out of storage until we found a house to rent several months later.

Len still was not feeling well. He had headaches, but not the severe ones as before. In my search for a metaphysical connection near my new home, I found a group that met in a private home. The leader of the group was very understanding when I explained what happened in Italy. She suggested that perhaps there was a past life connection to the way Len was feeling and that I should take him to see a lady she knew that did past life readings.

The day Len has his reading, he made me stay in the car while he went in the house for his session. He came out of the house an hour later looking a bit dazed. His first words to me were, "You haven't changed much. **I was the Duke of Urbino and you were the Duchess.**" He continued to tell me that we had been together many lifetimes. One was in Egypt, but the most surprising of all to him was that he had been the Duke. No wonder he knew things about the castle that the Italian tour guide did not know. That was the day I knew reincarnation was a fact. Unfortunately, Len continued with his arrogant attitude and his disregard for everyone else's feelings until his death in 2007, but he never again experienced the mysterious right-side pain.

This was the most dramatic revelation for both Len and I, that we had been together before and that our chance meeting in Washington had not been by chance at all. I had glimpses of other lives when we were together, but this was the completion of our involvement with each other. As time went on, he became more and more distant refusing to talk to me or anyone else about what was bothering him. He had been in the Viet Nam war with two tours in the country. His job has been in administration sitting behind a desk, but he told me he had volunteered to go to the front. He told me that he could predict when the camp would be under attack, and he would tell the men around him to be prepared for that night's attack. At first they did not believe him, but after a few correct predictions, they started to believe him, and prepared for it.

Len had his own demons before I met him. Our marriage and subsequent years together were an opportunity for him to clean his soul and mind of a lot of past life guilt, but he refused to do it. He was sensitive to events around him like in Viet Nam, and when he got to Italy, he felt the connection to the Duke's castle and the town. He also picked up the pain of the Duke's tournament injury and since it was a past life memory, it could not be explained by modern medicine.

Looking back now at those years, I see Len was his own worst enemy! His self-defeating attitude placed him into impossible situations where he would fail. The pity was he had many attributes that he could have perfected, that would have been beneficial to him and for others, but he would not let himself see that.

We finally found a house to rent in Tucson and got our furniture out of storage. Len had a good job at the Border Patrol working in their office in Tucson. I found a job in a medical laboratory, and Sean found a job working in a shipping company, yet all was not peaceful in our household.

We were able to purchase a house using Len's GI Bill, but after a time it was back to the same routine only worse! Len became more and more withdrawn to the point one night he picked up a mattress and went to sleep in another bedroom away from me. I would find him watching TV in the early morning hours, unable to sleep and distant in his attitude toward me. One day I found a letter from the bank saying we had missed a mortgage payment. That was the day I found out that Len had not been paying all the bills and he had been leaving them in the car. When I found this out, I started to pay every bill I could find. I sold furniture and anything I had that was of value to pay the mortgage and utilities. There was one problem the bank was being most unreasonable and instead of the one missed month's payment they wanted three months mortgage payments right then and there! It took every cent I had to get that money; everything else could not be paid. After we sold everything but the bare essentials, we rented a duplex and moved in. Len was still working for the Border Patrol and making good money as far as I knew. I came home from church one Sunday to find Len sitting in the dining room table with a bowl of pills in front of him. He was eating them like candy! I told him I was calling the VA for them to pick him up. He said no, but I called the police as well and had him forcibly removed to Tucson VA hospital where he stayed a week or so.

Our duplex had a garage and we stored extra boxes in there. Len had a few personal boxes. I took the opportunity to look through them. I found income tax papers, and other important records, but the most surprising was papers of discharge from the Border Patrol. It seems that the patrol got a new computer system in and Len was doing data entry for them on the number of illegals they captured and the countries they came from. This information was used for evaluation and reports every month, so it was very important. It seemed that Len was told by his supervisor if a certain cue came up on his screen from the new computer system, he was to call the supervisor as he had to enter another code at that time for the report to be completed. Len in his arrogance did not do as he was instructed and the information was lost. He was fired that day! This was my last straw!

The social worker called me the day Len was being discharged for me to come and pick him up. I said he did not live there anymore and to find him a place to live, which they did. I later found out Len had not paid income taxes for two years and since the IRS could not find him, they came after me and my small income. I ended paying it off with monthly payments. There was no question the marriage was broken and I did something I swore to myself I would not do. I got another divorce.

Years after our divorce, I was able to look at Len and tell him that I forgave him for all that had happened between us in our present and past lives together. At that moment, the Karma between us was paid—at least for me. Len would call me at night around 9:00 PM and we would talk about the day and small things that happened. One night the phone rang and there was no one there. I called Len's apartment and his girlfriend answered the phone. It seems he had been dead for three days and she was with his son from a former marriage, getting his things ready to take to his home state of Colorado. He died two days before his birthday in 2007. His girlfriend would not tell me where his body was. It took me three days to locate the mortuary where his body was being held, and to convince the mortician that I needed a copy of his death certificate for legal reasons. Len had provided me the Survivors Benefits from the Air Force; he kept telling me to be sure I got it. I think that is why he called me after his death, to make sure I got that money, otherwise I would have not known he was dead. The death certificate was needed to file for that benefit. I was able to contact the right people in the Air Force and receive his final gift.

CHAPTER ELEVEN
COUNTRY LIFE

When someone asks me where I lived before Arizona and I say Italy they look at me very strangely, but that is the truth. I came to Tucson compliments of the Air Force and here I have remained. Personally, I hate cactus and like to see the springtime flowers on them, but as far as keeping a garden dedicated to cactus, no way! I live where ancient volcanos carved out the valleys and left their sides for us to see as hills. Len said we did not have mountains like his in Colorado that were in the Rocky Mountain range; according to him, we only had hills surrounding us.

When we first arrived in Tucson, getting our directions straight was a bit confusing. You see, in Colorado the mountains were on your west and the plains to the east. Orientating yourself with these landmarks was simple, but here the hills were all around us and we got completely turned around many times.

Sean and I lived for five years in the duplex until the owner decided to sell the building, and we moved into another duplex only to have it happen again in another five years. We were tired of having to move every few years and decided to buy a manufactured home. We bought a 16x80 ft., new manufactured home and put it in a park on the west side of Tucson. This was fine until the park was sold and the new owners jacked up the rent to an unbelievable amount. After living there five years, we were looking for another place to put the mobile home. A friend in the park suggested we join her and move out of Tucson westward toward the Baboquivari Mountains. The area was called Three Points because the small town was built at the base of the mountains and where three state roads came together. One road was the main road to Tucson. The second road went to the Mexican/U.S. border and the third road went over the mountain to the Native American nation of the Tohono O'odham.

Our friend had four acres and was moving her manufactured home on it. She told me that she had purchased the land from a woman who had won it in a poker game. Sounds like tales of the Old Wild West! We took a ride twenty-five miles west of Tucson up to the base of the mountain to look at the land available there. There were new homes being built and beyond them was a lot of open land with some manufactured homes here and there. The land was divided into four acres of land for each mobile. We found a beautiful spot where we could see Kitt Peak from our backyard and got ready to move.

For those of you who do not know this area, Kitt Peak is inside the Tohono O'odham reservation and is the home to the National Optical Astronomy Observatory's viewing complex. Tucson has a low lighting ordnance because of these telescopes. The top of the mountain, where these telescopes were built, was seven thousand feet above the base.[1] They got snow up there in the winter when our land was still clear. The sun shining off the top of the buildings was a beautiful sight. We enjoyed clear skies and many enjoyable nights watching the clear night sky.

The land was set up with a water source to a community well with five other homes. It also had a septic tank and nothing else. We had to put rock down as a base for the home and dig a trench from our house to the road where the electrical lines would be buried under ground. All of this before the house was brought in by a truck from Tucson.

Eventually, our house was positioned on the land. When the set-up crew asked me about tie downs for the house, I had no idea what he was talking about. It seems that the area we were moving into was known for some very high winds and people had lost their small out buildings because they had not secured them to the ground. That day I told the men to put eight cables on the house frame, anchoring the house to the ground. Many times, in years afterwards, I blessed those men for securing the house as we did experience some extremely high winds.

The next year we put a fence around the four-acre property. By then, we had acquired two dogs and we did not want them to run off the property. I got a golden Cocker Spaniel puppy who I named Molly. Sean found a beautiful golden/red retriever named Maggie at the local dog pound. We already had a Siamese cat that we brought from Tucson, so the family was complete with our animals secured in the yard. At least that is what we thought. When the cat did not come in for supper one night, I got worried, and when she did not turn up for a few days we knew something was wrong. Talking to our neighbors we found out there was a family of coyotes in the region and they had been known to take cats, and any other small animals, for food.

This was our introduction to the wildlife in our new home area. Eventually, we saw the coyotes run across our property. The closest one came to the house was the day Maggie came running through the doggie door with a coyote behind her. At one time, the coyote had its mouth on Maggie's hind leg, and that is when I was beating it with the broom and slamming the doggie door closed behind Maggie! We learned that usually coyotes do not come close to people, so we think this was a very young pup.

There were mountain lions around the area that came down from the hills to feed. I never saw one, but I did see their paw prints in the mud at the back of the property. Our delight was watching the quail and their families going across the land. There was always an adult in the front of the line then all the little ones—usually about eight or ten—and an adult taking up the rear. They would come and eat bugs and whatever we put out for them. Maggie thought it was great fun chasing them. She would run across the front yard, and as she ran the quail would pop up and sit on the fence. It looked like a popcorn popper as they would pop up and then go back to what they were doing on the ground. Maggie would wait a while and then do it again.

As the time went on, I went to the dog pound and found another part Siamese cat that I named Mr. Po. This kitten had lived on the street with his mom and siblings before the pound caught them. Apparently, mom cat had trained the kittens how to hunt because we found very quickly that Mr. Po was an avid hunter. As he grew older, his kill became larger and larger. He would drag the poor thing into the house and proceeded to take care of it behind the TV. I know that sounds terrible, but we couldn't close the door on him and tried to send him outside every time he came home with something in his mouth. Now that was all fine and good as we believed he didn't have anything in his mouth when he came in if he could meow! WRONG; that theory was disproven when he trotted in with a mouse in his mouth and said meow out the corner of his mouth! We put tiles down behind the TV to make a place we could clean if we didn't catch him at the door. There were large rabbits that lived in our area. These were huge jack rabbits that ran very fast across the open fields around our house. We were watching TV one night and the doggie door opened. Here came Mr. Po dragging in one of the very large rabbits. He had the rabbit's ears in his mouth, and was straddling the body as he pulled it across the floor! That rabbit was larger than he was! After we stopped laughing, we threw the rabbit and the cat out the back door! Another adventure with Maggie and the cat was the day I heard a terrible commotion outside with lots of barking! I looked out the back door and there was Maggie running around a metal pipe and barking at it. Po was running around the other side. I finally saw what they were chasing. It was a small ground squirrel they had trapped inside the pipe. If it tried to come out either end, Po or Maggie was there to chase it back. Finally, they got tired of the game and the ground squirrel ran out of the pipe and to freedom in the weeds.

PAST LIFE REGRESSION CLASS

I was attending a spiritualist church in Tucson and one weekend went to a class on "Past Life Regression." The minister started by having us relax, then he led us into a meditation that started with visualizing a long hall with many doors on either side. We were to continue down the hall until we wanted to open a certain door, and we were to walk in and see what was there. When I opened my door, I saw a huge pit with a fire at the bottom of it. There were people all around the hole throwing books into the fire. The books were hardback ones like we have today. This activity upset me very much. I turned away from the fire and walked into the large building that I discovered was a library. There were hundreds of books on the shelves that were all around the walls, the room was as large as a football field. There were steps going up the aisles among the bookshelves, and light came into the building from half dome windows at the top of the stairs.

The minister called our consciousness back to the room and asked us what we had seen behind our doors. He told me that there had been many book burning events through the ages, but from what I saw it looked like something in the future.

The second session for that day began again with the hall and doors to choose from. I saw myself as a young girl about nine or ten years old. I was in an Egyptian pyramid; a student entering the house of healing. A lady was leading me down some stairs to the area where I would be working. The lady told me that my mother and my brother were working there already. The lady was tall with dark black hair pulled back from her face. She wore a long flowing robe made of some very light material.

When we were brought back this time, I looked across the circle from me and recognized the lady that I had seen in my vision. Her name was Denise and she surprised me by saying she had seen me in one of her past lives. Denise described a town which sounded like a western town shown on TV. She said that she and her husband had a farm that was burned down by Indians. Her husband stayed on the land, but the lady took the stagecoach to the nearest town where I ran a general store. She asked me for a job and a place to live. She said she would cook, sew, and work in the store, whatever I wanted her to do if I would take her in. I said yes and gave her a job and a home. Demise looked at me and said, "It was you!"

MISSION OF TUMACACORI

During this time, I was attending Tamara Spiritualist Center in Tucson. I was taking a class in meditation. One of the assignments for the class was to spend six hours in a meditation principle and then write a paper of what the experience was like.

I could think of many places I would like to spend six hours, but one place kept coming to my mind. My son and I had visited the Mission of Tumacacori when we first moved to Tucson. I remembered there was a garden with tall trees around a special fountain in the yard near the church. This area was only an hour away, south of Tucson toward the Mexican border.

I drove down to the mission one sunny spring day, and found the mission without any trouble. The mission and the out houses are on land that now belonged to the National Park System. According to the ranger at the office, the original mission was established by the Jesuit priests of the Catholic Church in 1691. But they did not have a dedicated church building until 1701. The Jesuits were expelled out of the area in 1767. Then the Franciscans were allowed, by the Spanish, into the country where they built the church that is now on the grounds.

In the 1760s, life in New Spain was the far northern frontier of the Spanish conquest. It was a difficult and dangerous place to live, with frequent raids on the mission and villages by the roaming Apache tribe. At any sign of trouble, the Tohono O'odham Indians would seek protection at the mission. The mission was built with large adobe blocks made of dirt from the fields and water, then shaped in a wooden form and baked in the sun. The hot desert sun dried the bricks until they could be used for the building. More of the wet adobe mixture was used as mortar between the blocks. Thirty miles away in the Santa Rita Mountains, other workers quarried limestone that was used to plaster the walls.

The facade was painted in bright colors of red, blue and yellow. Today there is a glimpse of the original colors. The bell tower stands in the same condition as it was when the church was abandoned in 1848, never having been completed. [1] The church sits in the middle of a grassy compound, surrounded by several out buildings. It is constructed in the shape of a small cross with a large room going from north to south, and a shorter room going from east to west. In the shorter room, there were rooms for statues of the saints, and an area for candles with the altar at the north end of the large room.

I enjoyed walking in the orchard and looking around the property. I found the formal garden from my first visit, which is close to the visitor's center. In the middle of the garden, I found the fountain where visitors could sit on the bench and enjoy the garden. The coolness of the garden was refreshing after the hot sun. I saw a beautiful red bird that came to the fountain to drink. As I sat there, I enjoyed the garden, especially watching the birds, and the red bird that brought his mate to join him in a drink from the fountain. Later that day, I asked the park ranger what was the name of the red bird and he told me they were called Vermilion Flycatchers.

The most memorable part of my trip was the time I spent in the church sitting on a bench near the front door. The contrast to the bright sunny day and the darkness of the inside of the church was noticeable. Inside the church the neglect of the centuries was very evident. When I was there, I saw a construction crew renovating different parts of the park. I am sure by now the church has been restored to its former glory. But at the time I was there all reconstruction had not been completed. In the church, I saw where water from seasonal rains had come through the damaged roof. The water had destroyed part of the inside walls, yet I could still see the faint outlines of where holy pictures had been hung. The only light that day was a few candles placed on the altar, giving a little light to the far end of the church. The only sound I heard in the stillness was the chattering of two birds close to the open doorway.

I sat on a bench near the door and after saying a prayer of protection, I started my meditation. A question came to my mind, addressing to no one but the empty church, I thought, "Why did you want me to come here?" I continued to ask for information. I asked. " Did I live here before?" The answer was "Yes you were a native woman who cared for the children." I asked for the date and was given the year 1695. I was also told to continue to remember who I was—that of a warrior and a female dedicated to the church. After a few minutes, I closed my meditation and left the church. I went back to the park ranger and asked him if the date 1695 has any special meaning to that area. He said, not for the mission, but there was a Tohono O'odham village about fifty miles from there that had been raided by the Apaches that year and all the people were killed. The men had been in the fields working, so there were only women and children in the village at that time.

MY LIFE UPSIDE DOWN

Sean was working in Tucson at the office of a medical insurance company. He loved his job and talked fondly about the girls in the office. He was the only male in the office of twelve employees at that time. He would get up early in the morning and drive down the hill into Tucson. Since he was always the first in the office, he had the coffee made for the office staff. They came to depend on that. He worked around the yard at home on his time off, keeping the weeds cut down and playing ball with Molly, and throwing the Frisbee for his dog Maggie. De asked me one day how we measured the fence for the back yard. I said, "Sean, go out there and throw the Frisbee for Maggie." The distance he could throw the Frisbee was the width of the backyard fence, then we extended it down from both ends of the house. It made a safe place for the dogs to play in. The shame was that the four acres of land we had in the country had been farmed so much in the past, now there was only sand and a deep core of clay left. I could not grow anything on the land. That was evident the first few weeks we lived there. I planted iris bulbs around the front of the house. The nest morning, I went out and saw that the flowers of all the plants had been broken off. The next day the stalks of the plants were gone and the following day even the bulbs were gone. Sean laughed at me and said all I did was plant a salad bar for the rabbits!

One Sunday morning in August 2006, Sean told me that he had been up all night vomiting. Sean had been a diabetic since he was fourteen, and because this is very bad for a diabetic person, I took him into Tucson to the nearest emergency room. It was 9:00 A.M. when they admitted him, and as the day wore on, he was transferred to intensive care. I had parked the car in the emergency area and I went out to move the car to closer to the front door of the hospital. I returned to the hospital to hear a "code blue" over the load speaker. I had been a volunteer in the hospital for a year or so and knew that something very wrong was going on, especially when I heard Sean's room number. I ran back to the ICU unit and was taken into a room by a nurse. The doctor came in and told me that Sean had a massive heart attack and they could not save him. I sat there in stunned silence, and then followed the nurse into a room where Sean's body was. I remember touching his face and telling him to wait for me on the other side. Even now in 2019, as I write this, my eyes are full of tears and I feel his loss all over again! I called De who was then working on the Tohono O'odham Reservation an hour's drive from town, and told her to come to the hospital. It took her a while to get there.

I drove home that night in complete shock. Sean and I had depended on each other for everything, now he was gone. I had no idea what I would do. That night I got something to eat and fed the animals. My body was working, but my mind just wasn't there! That night when I went into the bedroom, I found the room filled with the most brilliant light I could have imagined. The light seemed to blaze from every wall flooding the room. I was enveloped in the pure white light and I knew it was Sean. The light was so intense that it hurt my eyes and I said out loud "Sean I have got to go to sleep!" The light slowly faded away and I fell into an exhausted sleep. I had been so close to Sean not only with the mother-son connection in this life, but, as I found out years later in a psychic reading, we had a husband/wife connection in a past life. Apparently, we had a farm in the west somewhere and that was where Sean's love for growing things came from. He was a natural farmer and loved to see plants grow.

I was in the house by myself without anyone to talk to or care about me. I felt so alone and deserted. There was a song that kept playing in my head. I heard it when I turned on the radio, and I heard it in the grocery store, De said she heard the same song at her work. It was a group called "Firefall." The song was "Just Remember I Love You." The amazing thing about this song was it was not one of the popular songs of that day, as it had been recorded years before. It was Sean's message to me, reminding me that he was with me and everything would work out.

Panic set in when I realized that I had to pay the bills and had no money to do it. I found out that Sean's insurance would take several weeks to get as I had to fill out papers and send in a copy of his death certificate. I could not get his last paycheck from the bank without the death certificate, and that would take a week or more as well. I cried days on end with the deep feeling of losing not only my son, but my best friend and companion for so many years. With his death, my total support system was gone. The little bit of money I had was coming from Social Security, and that would not pay for everything. If I could not make the mortgage payments, would I be out on the street? I called all of Sean's debtors and got them to wait until I could pay them with the insurance money. After several weeks of torture, De called and said she would move in with me to help me out. When she settled in, we went through the house finding things that we could sell to get money to live on until the insurance money came. We sold Sean's guns to a dealer in Tucson, his large record collection went to another collector for a nice sum of money, and his movie collection we found a store that would buy them. It was with this money that we hung on for the next few weeks.

I had several occasions where I knew that Sean was still there with me. One day I was trying to lift a piece of heavy furniture and without thinking shouted, "Sean, come and help me with this!" In a few minutes, the furniture seemed lighter as if someone was holding the other side and I moved it easily into the next room. De moving in with me was a good thing for both of us as her living there with me cut off an hour-long trip from Tucson to her job on the reservation. It was another hour's drive for her from my house. Before she moved in with me, she had been driving two hours one way to work. She was now driving Sean's car, which really confused Maggie, his dog. She would hear Sean's car and run to the door expecting to see him and there was De instead.

Sean was still teasing his sister even beyond the grave. De came in to the house one evening asking me to talk to Sean. She said, she put the car visor up and he would keep putting it down. Sean had always said he wanted to be buried on his land. The day I got his ashes from the mortuary, we had a family service in the front yard. I put Molly on a leach and De had Maggie on another. We all went to the front yard near the big tree, where I had dug a hole for the ashes. The dogs seem to know something special was happening as they both laid down, Maggie on one side of the grave and Molly on the other side. I said a prayer and put Sean's ashes in the ground. I had made a special cross out of tile pieces glued to a stone and this I put on top of the grave. When we moved from there seven years later, I took the stone and put it in the front yard of our new house. It is there now, in the middle of a rock circle in the front yard with green succulents growing around it. A permanent memorial for Sean.

One day I heard Sean's song and got upset all over again! I was directed to sit and write and this is what Spirit told me that day.

September 4, 2012:

It is not the will of the Father to cause you pain, but your own obstinate refusal to listen. Why do you torment yourself so? Sean is happy, contented and still loves you, but he has a job to do as well as you do.

Writing is a gift which you must do. Spread the words of enlightenment and love as they are given to your understanding. Why do you think these gifts were given to you now? It was because you are at a point in your development where you can understand what is written.

Great minds work together to bring out thoughts given to them by Spirit. Information is always valued when it comes from a higher source, never doubt yourself! How can I answer the many questions in your mind if you do not ask? Take time to put one together and think on that only. The answer will come. How much you understand will be up to you; miss Sean, but do not dwell on it!

In February 2013, I was speaking to Rev. Kyle at the Mesa Arizona Unity Church. In that conversation, she told me that reality is made up of different layers of dimensions which are stacked together like nesting bowls fitting one into the next. She said Sean is here because he never left, only his body was left behind.

THE END OF A LOVE

After the divorce, Len was living in his own apartment in Tucson. He had a girlfriend who was a drug addict and supposedly "took care of him," while he paid the rent, utilities and bought the food. From the few times I had been to his apartment, I could see that she was not doing anything about cleaning the apartment as there was always pile of boxes still unpacked from the last apartment, and dirty dishes in the sink. Sean made me promise that I would not go and clean for him. I visited Len for a few minutes, as few times as I could. We did keep in contact by phone as every night around 9:30 the phone would ring and it was Len to talk about the day and see what I was doing. I called him when Sean died and he was as broke up as I was about it, but he did not come to comfort me. One night in 2007, the phone rang at the usual time. When I answered it, there was no one on the line! I immediately called his apartment and his girlfriend answered the phone. His girlfriend said he had been dead for three days! I asked his girlfriend why she had not called me and the answer was that she was too busy getting his things packed to go back to Colorado with his son, who was there then. She could not tell me why he died or where his body was. Len wanted to make sure I knew he was dead, so I would be able to get his survivor benefits from the Air Force. A few days later I got a call from Len's son asking me how he could get the money from the Air Force to pay for Len's burial in Colorado. I told him to call the Air Force Base and ask them.

It was now up to me to find which mortuary Len's body was being held. I first called the veteran's hospital and talked to the bereavement office to see if they knew how he died. The lady somehow found out that he had not been admitted into the veteran's hospital, but had been in the Tucson Heart Hospital in Tucson. I called them and got the date of his discharge, but they would not tell me where the body had been taken. It took me another two days to track down the mortuary where his body was. I convinced the mortician that I had a legal right to have a copy of his death certificate because of the stipulation in my divorce papers that I was to receive survivor's benefits from the Air Force, and I needed the death certificate for that documentation. Even in death, Len was taking care of me.

MY SECOND LIFE DECISION

After Sean's death, I don't think I consciously wanted to leave this Earth. De and I lived alone in the house with the dogs. De was still working on the Tohono O'odham Nation, and I was a volunteer at the Veteran's hospital in Tucson. One day I was coming home from Tucson, and I got a call from De saying for me to pick up some insecticide at the store before I came home. When I arrived at home De had pulled storages boxes out of the garage into the driveway. She said that there was an infestation of small bugs in the garage. I looked and the lights and walls were covered by a sheet of bugs, even on the outside of the garage there were large groups of these small bugs. I had no idea what they were and calling an exterminator was out of the question since it was the fourth of July holiday weekend and no one was open. So, I started spraying the bugs until it got so dark I could not see outside, I took a shower, and threw my clothes in the wash. The next morning, I got up and sprayed all day until that evening, repeating the same as the day before by taking a shower and a clothing change. The third day there were still a few bugs that I sprayed and finally put the chemicals away.

The bugs were all killed, but what I did not know was that I had poisoned myself with the chemicals. A day or two after the bugs in the garage were killed, I got sick. Fever and chills, with aching joints. I felt miserable all over! I remember going into my bedroom and lying on the bed and starting to pray. I had just finished reading Dr. O.T. Bonnett's book "Why Healing Happens" [2] in which he writes that our cells are living organisms and that every cell in our body has a memory, consciousness, intent, and the ability to communicate with other cells. Cells joyfully take instructions and produce the cellular response suggested by the mind. The cells are so busy doing their work of repairing and performing their primary functions that when they hear a voice directing them to heal and clear their area, they know it is the voice of the Creator and rush to obey the directions.

I lay on top of my bed and started to pray. I talked to the cells of my body and visualized the bones, muscles and cells in a given area. I started at my feet naming as many of the bones as I could remember and telling the cells to clear the poison out of their area and return the area to the perfection of wholeness. I moved up my legs saying the same thing to the leg bones, joints and connective tissues. As I moved to another part of the leg, I saw a white light come to my feet and follow my process. As I completed a portion of my body, the white light moved up into that area.

I continued focusing onto the cells in my legs and onto my stomach, intestines, lungs and heart. To each part I named the bone structure, the muscles, blood vessels and tissues in the area, asking the cells of those areas to clear their area and bring it into wholeness. The white light continuing to follow my words. The light followed me as I worked on my head naming again every structure and asking clearance for the area by the cells. When I had completed the head area, the light seemed to continue the journey through my body and then going to the top of my head flowing out like a fountain then coming down and covering my entire body! I said a prayer of thanksgiving for the healing and went into a deep sleep.

Monday morning, I got to see my doctor who said, "You could have killed yourself! All of that poison building up in you after three days. You were breathing it in!" She sent me for a chest x-ray and found I had developed pneumonia. Then she started treating me for that and put me on an herbal detoxification regiment. Looking back, I was very blessed to have a doctor that knew what to do for me right at that time.

NATIVE AMERICAN CULTURE TOUR

I learned about this tour, in 2007, advertised in a clothing catalogue, I had subscribed to for a few years. It was called "A Native American Spirituality Tour," of areas in Arizona and in New Mexico, sponsored by a group in New Mexico. First, I took an airplane from Tucson to meet the tour group in Albuquerque, New Mexico. There, someone would meet me at the airport and take me to the hotel where the group was staying for that first night. The next morning, we got on our touring bus for the first stop, which was at the museum in Flagstaff, Arizona. There were a few displays of Native American artifacts to view, and several hours later we were back on the bus.

The next week was filled with visiting Native American areas and dining in local restaurants, staying in a hotel each night, and riding on the touring bus each day. I do not remember the exact itinerary for the tour, but some highlights stay in my memory. We spent most of our time in New Mexico, and visited several Native American areas. One of the first places we visited was Acoma Pueblo or Sky City, built sometime between 1100 and 1250 AD. The Acoma Pueblo people have continuously occupied the area for over 2000 years, making this one of the oldest, continuously inhabited communities in the United States. [3]

The people of Acoma say that Sky City Pueblo was established in the eleventh century. The pueblo is situated on a 365-foot mesa, which is about sixty miles west of Albuquerque, New

Mexico. In ancient times, the entrance to the pueblo was by climbing a stairway, a combination of stairs and holes for hands and feet to climb to the top. On the top, they had room to store large amounts of corn and cisterns to collect snow and water. [4] A road has been constructed now to the top of the mesa.

The Spanish heard of this fortress and visited it, with the natives receiving them with some suspicion as to their intentions. They had heard of the Spanish enslaving Indians to work in the local silver mines. Eventually, the Spanish convinced the pueblo residents to trade goods with them. On January 21, 1599, thirty Spanish soldiers arrived at the pueblo to trade for corn, but when the amount of corn they requested was not ready on their arrival, sixteen armed men were sent to the pueblo to find out what caused the delay. Acoma narrative says that the soldiers attacked some Acoma women and the warriors retaliated.

The next year the Spanish returned with a full force of seventy men. The Acoma Massacre started the next day and lasted for three days. The Spanish were able to climb the southern mesa wall and enter the city, killing eight hundred people. They took revenge against the people who survived by amputating the right foot of each man over the age of twenty-five and forced them into slavery. They also took males ages 12-25 and females over the age of 12 away from their parents and put them into slavery.

Survivors of the massacre rebuilt their pueblo and were forced to pay taxes to the Spanish in form of crops, cotton or labor. The Spanish rule brought the Catholic Church missionaries into the area. Even though the people were forced to adopt Catholicism, they continued to practice their own religion in secret. [5] The abuse of power by both the religious and political authorities eventually led to the Pueblo Revolt in 1680. [6]

Another place we visited on that trip was Mesa Verde and the Aztec National park that I remembered from my trip with Len. In the week-long trip, one day we visited the capitol of the Navajo Nation at Window Rock where in 1923 the first tribal council for the Navajo was established. There is actually a large red rock formation with a large hole in the middle of it. It is part of the background with the council buildings grouped in front of it. There we met and talked to several of the Navajo "Code Talkers" of the Second World War. In the city of Santa Fe, New Mexico, the town square was the place where native people spread their blankets and sold their handmade turquoise jewelry. All around the plaza, there were people with their backs against the buildings and a blanket in front of them, with displays of rings, necklaces, and earrings all made of silver decorated in designs with accents of turquoise. There were large handmade pottery jars and bowls painted in brilliant colors of yellow, black, white and blue. Everything for sale. There is a monument, in the city square with the sculpture of a native woman. On the base of the monument, there are names inscribed of hundreds of Native American tribes that now no longer exist.

We visited the historical Hubbell Trading Post in the middle of the Navajo Nation. This trading post was established in 1878 and was run by the frontier family that owned the homestead until 1967 when it was sold to the National Park Service. [7]

The trading post has been kept just as it was when the Navajo traded their blankets and other handmade items for cloth and ribbons to use in making dresses. The men traded silver jewelry for tobacco and hunting knives among other things. The walls of the trading post are covered with these traded items. It is not hard to imagine how it had been in those years when trading was a way of life for the people of that area.

One of the most memorable days of this tour was when we went to Monument Valley. This is the area that the producer John Ford made many of his movies. From *Stagecoach* in 1929 to 1949's *She Wore a Yellow Ribbon* were movies made in Monument Valley.[8] Our tour director told us we were in for some "shake and bake" adventure. We had no idea when she meant, but the next day we found out. There were four small jeeps with a piece of canvas over our head. This was our transportation to the next stop on the tour. The day was very warm and the road was very bumpy! We went down a dirt road into this large area when there were towering red rocks all around us. Each seemed to have a name and a little story to go with it. It was amazing to recognize some of the landscape as that used in the old western movies.[7] By noon time, we went back to the building used as a guest lodge and had lunch in the restaurant that offered a view of the valley. There was a small stone building in front of the restaurant that we were told belonged to the actor John Wayne. Our guide told us that John Wayne had said that since he was out there all the time making movies in the area, he might as well build a house there, and so he did.

It was on this trip that I met my good friend Joyce, who I have written about in several of these stories. I was a part of a group of five women who stayed together during the trip. Many kept in touch with the others by e-mail and seasons' greeting cards. Slowly, one by one, they dropped out of the correspondence link to where there were only three of us. Joyce was the center for all correspondence from many of the other ladies.

THE HOPI NATION

The Hopi settled in the area now known as Four Corners, where the state lines of Arizona, New Mexico, Utah and Colorado meet. The Hopi Native American Nation knows it as the center of the Earth, the heart of "Turtle Island," also as the center of Mother Earth. Each Hopi clan conducts ceremonies to maintain the balance of the natural sunlight, rain and wind; this reaffirms the Hopi respect for all life and trust in the Great Spirit.

The Hopi live on the top of three mesas, which is a high plateau or tableland with steep sides. They were named by the Spanish in the order they were discovered. The first mesa is considered the oldest settlement. The second mesa now has the Hopi cultural center and several villages. The third mesa has the Hopi Tribal government and the traditional villages of Old Oraibi, Hotevilla and Bacavi. There are other Hopi villages at the base of the mesas. The oldest continuously inhabited village in the United States is Old Oraibi, which was built in 1050 AD.

We were permitted to visit Old Oraibi. We found it to be a collection of small stone and mud dwellings surrounding a kiva. Some of the houses are built on top of each other with ladders as the only way to enter the upper houses. We were permitted to enter the kiva. I chose not to do so, and sat on the wall outside while the other people in our group went into the kiva. There are a few people living in the village still, but for most part it is deserted. [9]

We learned that there is a group of the Hopi that claim the traditional life living without electricity, running water and services from the nation. There is another group of the Hopi that have embraced the modern city life. The distinction between the two is very evident because of the living conditions of each area. Traditional people do not send their children to school, but have a village teacher. The modern Hopi send their children to the state schools.

It has been interesting reviewing my notes from that trip in 2007. I was surprised that I still had them in my files!

THE NATIVE AMERICAN HISTORY GRANT

I worked for Arizona State Department of Economic Security as a Vocational Rehabilitation Counselor in Tucson, Arizona. During this time, I met a lady whose daughter, Carol, worked as a grant writer for a school district in Alaska. I met Carol one day at the home of a mutual friend. We sat and talked about our different jobs and the challenges we faced. Somehow the conversation turned toward the Native American Nations in our respective states. As we talked, an idea was formed to work on a grant that would not only help students but would educate teachers to the culture of the Native American Nation in their area, and help them write a curriculum to teach this to their own students. For the areas, we chose three states to participate: Arizona, Alaska, and the third state Oklahoma because of their Cherokee population. The plan was that we would find schools that were in close proximity to a Native American tribal area, and would be open to learn more about their neighbor. They would also be willing to let two of their teachers go on trips to visit the other participating states to learn about their local tribes and bring that back to the classroom. They would write up the information into a curriculum and give it at their school. In this way, the individual school districts would learn about their neighbors as well as the other states participating in the project. Two teachers from each district would visit other areas and learn about the Native Americans in that area, bringing that information back to their home school. The grant would pay for the transportation and lodging expenses of the teachers and provided any instructional material that would be required. It would be a three-year program.

    a. Carol had written billions of dollars in grants for the schools in Alaska, so she would write the grant. She also had some connections in Washington that would help us.

    b. I would contact all the school districts in Arizona and Oklahoma, and find who would be interested in participating in the grant.

    c. I wrote the justification for the grant.

This was in 2006-2007. I worked a full year contacting school districts, writing letters and e-mails asking if a certain school district would be interested in participating. I found a district in southern Arizona that was open to the idea of the grant, also a district in Oklahoma. Carol wrote the grant to the Department of Education in Washington, D.C. After two months of waiting for the results, we found out we did not get the grant. I think it is still a great idea and, hopefully, in the future someone will try to get it funded through Washington.

JUSTIFICATION FOR THE NATIVE AMERICAN GRANT

Automatic writing given June 2006 Tucson, Arizona:

Post colonization trauma internalized in our people is the cause of the nation's problems. They see no reason for striving to help themselves in government or civil affairs. They see no reason to further children's education, or to work towards understanding with our white neighbors, or to maintain their individual health, family, or to continue their connection to the traditions of their ancestors.

The despair in their use of drugs, alcohol, and suicide, also in teen pregnancy of the nation's people, is an outward sign of this individual trauma that has been perpetuated through so many generations.

Now is the time for our people to rise up and claim what they had before, individual dignity, respect for themselves and others, love and care for the land, listening to the guidance of the elders, and our supreme spirit no matter what name He is called.

Unless you do this now, you will lose again your freedom as a people, and the respect as a nation. We will lose our home, mother Earth,

The people depend on their success for their own survival. The prophecies are now being fulfilled, that the nations will come into their own in this country. This is the beginning.

We have spoken.

THE MUSEUM ON THE TOHONO O'ODHAM NATION

The tribal name of the Native Americans that live in south-central Arizona are now called Tohono O'odham or desert people. Until 1980 they were known as Papago, or bean eaters, a name given to them by the Spanish. [10] I got to know some of the people of the Tohono O'odham Nation when I worked on their reservation, first as a school registrar for the school district, and later as a counselor at the junior college. My daughter was working at the grocery store on the reservation the same time I was there. In fact, I talked her into working there. She loved the people and her job, working at the same store for nine years. My employment on the reservation was not that long as the counselor job, for one, was only six months until they could find a Native American with the counseling degree that I had to fill the job.

An eye opener for me was taking an American History class on the reservation. This was a requirement for everyone who worked there. A class in Tohono O'odham language was also required, but I had to leave the reservation before I could take that class. I met one of the nation's elders while at the college and got to know him fairly well. Danny Lopez was not only an elder but a medicine man and a college teacher of language and culture of the nation. The nation had the foresight to record the stories and myths that Danny remembered as being part of the nation's heritage before he died. [11]

Danny believed that the people should return to the foods they had eaten before the introduction of white flour and meat into the diet of the reservation residents by the U.S. Army in the time they controlled the area. The epidemic of diabetes was killing the older generation, leaving most of the tribe with people in their early twenties and thirties. No one remembered their tribal traditions or the tribal culture. That was what Danny was trying to bring back to the people. He talked about this issue, and between the two of us we got the owners of the only grocery store on the reservation to start having a supply of native foods. Our only obstacle was getting the people to buy and eat them.

When the Smithsonian Institute opened its National Museum of the American Indian in September 2004, the Tohono O'odham Nation was one of the twenty-four tribes featured in the opening exhibit. Danny Lopez was one of the O'odham elders that narrated that exhibit. [11]

A few years later in 2008, I learned that the Tohono O'odham Nation was building a new museum. I considered going there as a volunteer. One day I made an appointment with Brenda, the director of collections, to visit the museum. She took me around the museum and showed me the collections of the museum, also introduced me to the people that worked there. She showed me the pieces that were on display and then the room that houses the special collections and those items that needed to be cleaned and processed for the general display. She showed me the files that indicated which items were on loan to the museum from a tribal member. There were a lot of small jobs I could do if I decided to volunteer to help her. I agreed to do just that and started two years of volunteering my services to the museum once a week.

Brenda was committed to her work. She would say that she represented those who could not speak for themselves. She told me the history behind several of the items on display and the involvement of the nation to the recovery of ancient stolen grave items belonging to the nation. (Native American Grave Protection and Repatriation Act Nov. 16, 1990.)

One year, my birthday fell on the Tuesday I usually went to the reservation to volunteer at the museum. Brenda and I had talked months before this, about what we liked best, pie or cake. I said I liked pie. This day Brenda said there was a meeting in the conference room and that we both would go. As I entered the room, I saw all the museum staff sitting there. There were tables along the wall with pies on them. Brenda said she did not remember which pie I said I liked the best, so she bought one of every kind for my Happy Birthday!

I was at the museum two years then decided to take the ministerial class at the church in Tucson. The next time I heard about Brenda was a message that the cancer she had fought years before had returned and that she had died. There was to be a memorial service at the church in Three Points. This was in 2013, and we were getting ready to move out of the area. I went to the service and there I saw many of the people from the museum, and was able to say goodbye to not only Brenda but everyone else there.

It is interesting; although I am not native born in this lifetime, I still feel that I am in a lot of ways. The area of the sacred Baboquivari Mountains of the Tohono O'odham Nation for me was a place of peace and contentment. Every time I went to the reservation, I felt the joy of "coming home," and sadness of having to leave at the end of the day. My daughter tells me that she felt the same way. We will always feel close to the Native American people, especially the Tohono O'odham.

CHAPTER TWELVE
Reincarnation: Fact or Fiction

Message this morning: "You are now back to where you were as a priestess free of all bonds and cleared to live again. This life was to wake you so that you would remember who you are and that you would change for the better. Each part of your life was a piece of the puzzle put back together for the day. You are as you were. Remember now without guilt or pain for all has been repaid and you are free to ascend to the next level of glory!"

It is with humble gratitude I acknowledge these words and obey. Shawna Grey 7/4/16

REINCARNATION

If you ask anybody about reincarnation, they will offer you a guess if they know anything about it at all, that it is part of an Eastern religious belief. In the modern Western world, the subject of reincarnation is generally thought of as a subject for anthropologists, theologians, and historians. Reincarnation is the belief that each of us goes through a series of lifetimes for the purpose of spiritual growth and soul development. More recently it has been a study by psychiatrists. Oral traditions and written evidence around the world have shown that the belief in reincarnation has been an integral part of human thought and worldview from the early days of civilization.

It really shouldn't matter if an individual believes in reincarnation or not. We all have the ability to access into the subconscious mind, called by various names: the collective unconsciousness (Jung) or in the Akashic records by dreams, meditation, or hypnosis. The unconscious mind will always provide a past life when invited in the right way. A lot of information concerning children and the memories of past lives come to us in the research of Dr. Ian Stevenson (1916-2007), who was a professor of Psychology at the University of Virginia School of Medicine for fifty years, and formerly chairman of that department. He was also the founder and Director of the University of Virginia's Division of Perceptual Studies investigating parapsychological phenomena such as reincarnation. He devoted his time to the investigation of cases reported as a spontaneous memory of past lives from children all over the world. Many volumes of information from these interviews have been published by the University of Virginia Press. I would safely guess that many cases were never reported due to the fear of ridicule from the community. [1]

Suppose you recalled everything about a past life; in fact, if you recalled all of them in a great detail what benefit would that be to you now? We are given the blessings of forgetfulness once we are born into our current lifetime. I have found that a glimpse of a past life comes to me if the information is relevant for this life. The scenario has changed, but the same underlying principle exists. Whether reincarnation is true or not is debatable, but near-death accounts reveal that it is the life we are currently living that is more important. In P.M.H. Atwater's book, *Coming Back to Life, Examining the After-Effects of the Near-Death Experience*, she describes what people who have had near-death experiences (NDE) say about Reincarnation.

Ms. Atwater states, "I've noticed near-death experiences usually have a feeling or knowing that the soul evolves and grows through various cycles, often taking lifetimes to expand on its experience and learning. They talk about reincarnation as if it were an established fact and almost to a person, mention a life plan and speak of how our lives follow rhythmic cycles of development. Survivors actually lose all fear of death for they know it ends nothing, but the physical body and its personality façade." [2]

If Jesus and the early Christians believe in reincarnation, why is it not accepted in the churches today? The change in thought came as the centuries passed when the church was unable to accept the reality that each human being has both a human and a divine nature. The church created a gulf between Jesus and the rest of us because they could not understand the human and divine in Jesus, and so could not understand it in themselves.

They took the view of Jesus from the Gospel of John, which tells us that "In the beginning was the Word, and the Word was with God, and the Word was God." John1:1. Later on, John tells us "the Word was made flesh and dwelt among us" John 1:14 (New International Version of Holy Bible). The church said that salvation could come only to those who worked within the dictates of the church not by following the example of Jesus. What the church fathers did not understand was that when John tells us that the Word created everything, he uses the Greek term for Word "Logos" describing the part of God that works in the world. The church was not needed for redemption and that the soul was a part of God and always would be.

Origen of Alexandria (185-254 AD) is the father of church science and the founder of the theology perfected in the 4th and 5th centuries. Christ appears to Origen as simply the word who is with the father from eternity and is the divine teacher to who alone directs the thoughts of those who believe in him. He held that Christianity was a practical principle and that simple faith of man was sufficient for the renewal and salvation of man. He taught an exoteric and esoteric form of Christianity. This was an outer form of religion for the masses and an inner profound religion for the elected. The reason for the two versions was given that the masses were incapable of understanding the deeper sense of the Scriptures, and that they would be unable to comprehend the idea of the pre-existence of the soul, Karma, and reincarnation. The fact that the soul had neither beginning nor end and comes into this life strengthened by the victories or weakened by the defeats of their previous lives. He rejected the possibility of humans reincarnating as animals. These truths of reincarnation were reserved for the elite. [3]

The idea that the soul was immortal and spiritual was a part of Christian thought at that time of Origen and his predecessor Clement of Alexandria. The church fathers decided that the soul was not part of God and so could not be part of his essence. For them, it belonged to the material world. For Origen, there was an invisible spiritual world that was permanent; it was the physical material world that changed. He believed that all creation came from God and retained their link to Him. At the same time as this belief was being explained, the church fathers were teaching that the soul was created the same time as the body. Origen said that the option for the transformation of humanity into divinity was available not just for Jesus, but for everyone who took up the faith that Jesus had and lived the life he set as example for us.

The church was divided with the different philosophies. The Roman emperor Constantine in 324 AD wrote a letter to the Bishop of Alexandria asking him to reconcile his differences with the rest of the church. When Constantine realized that these issues would not be solved to his satisfaction, he called a council in 326 AD at Nicaea, and demanded that all the bishops of the church attend. It is at this conference the church fathers wrote out the doctrine called ***THE NICENE CREED.*** In it was stated the doctrine of the church:

"We believe in one God, the Father Almighty, maker of all things visible and invisible: and in one Lord Jesus Christ, the Son of the Father, God of God, Light of Light. Begotten not made, being of one substance with the father, by who all things were made…."

Only two bishops refused to sign the creed and Constantine banished them from the empire; the others went off to celebrate with a large feast. Constantine said that the council's decision had been "determined in the holy assemblies of the bishop, and that the church officials had to accept it as divine will."

Constantine took the opportunity to initiate the first systematic government persecution of dissident Christians by issuing an edit against heretics and enemies of truth. The Council of Nicaea marked the end of the concept held by some in the church of preexistence, reincarnation, and salvation through union with God. From now on, the church would become representative of a capricious and autocratic God not unlike Constantine and other Roman emperors.

The emperor continued to interfere with the church after the political struggle of the First Counsel of Nicaea when Emperor Constantine decided to make Christianity the official religion of the Roman Empire. In the Second Council of Constantinople in 553 AD sponsored by Emperor Justinian, it was decided that that the idea of the soul preexistence or reincarnation was declared heresy. Today we have a much better idea of the diversity of ideas in the years of the early church with the Dead Sea Scrolls found in Qumran in 1947, and the Gnostic Gospels found in Nag Hammadi Egypt in 1945. [4]

Reincarnation is the belief that each of us goes through a series of lifetimes for the purpose of spiritual growth and soul development. The past gives us a framework of potentials from which we make our choices in determining the life experience we have chosen for the present one that believes there is limitless opportunity for us to explore. Within this framework are the lessons we need to learn.

The soul is described as a part of our entire being that is ever changing, growing, and using free will to explore the avenues of human existence. It is the bridge we have between our physical body and the spiritual realm. It may operate in harmony or outside the collective consciousness. All souls were created by the Divine architect of the universe and they will return to Him at the end of their Earthly journey. Man will only understand his mission in life when he understands his relationship to the Creator. The Spirit is the "God Spark" within every man, which is the part that will never die. It remains within the etheric world and at death we are reunited with the one mind of the Creator.

We are a member of one of the many generations of souls moving together through the natural cycle of life. Although soul groups are fairly well established that they do not have a great influence on an individual soul's life contract, the effect of our many past lives is reflected in the circumstances that are surrounding us. People in our life now were part of some past life in centuries past.

SOUL MATES

The popular concept that a soul mate is someone who is special to you only in the sense of lovers or marriage partners, but they can be also parents, siblings, friends, anyone in your life. What distinguishes a soul mate is the intensity of your relationship. You could have been lovers or marriage partners in another lifetime, so the attraction you have to each other would be very strong. If they were a close friend or family member before this time, they would take the same relationship in this lifetime.

We all have heard the word "Déjà vu," which is French for "already seen." Many of us have spoken to people for the first time and felt a closeness of an old Friend. I have gone down the road of a strange town, yet feel I knew exactly what was around the bend. These are examples of a past life coming to my consciousness. Now, when you think of a past life you think about maybe you were some person of importance, someone in history whose life made a difference during that time, but the truth of the matter is there can be only one Cleopatra and one Alexander the Great. Finding a famous person in your past life is rare; most of us were people living everyday lives with challenges and goals that were important to us for that life's plan. What makes the past life important is that it brings meaning to our current life, especially if there is a lesson to be learned. Our Spirit is helping us to remember so that we will not make the same mistake again.

There is a great misconception among people, about the difference between the soul and a body. Your soul is your true self. It is an independent eternal being, whether living in a physical world or in a spirit one, or as a free spirit in the universe manifesting what you need in mind and body, enabling you to function in accordance with what you want to experience in each incarnation. Your soul is the pure light/love energy of the Creator that has been given the gift of free will.

Bodies grow independently of soul through the natural laws of physical mechanisms reproducing in accordance with the cellular programming of each civilization. The process of abortion does not destroy the soul, only the physical receptacle. There are several reasons why a baby might die in the first minutes or days of their life. Souls may inhabit a developing body until imminent birth, then decide not to continue with that body, and a stillbirth is the result. When the physical body has a defect, the soul might decide not to take on that particular challenge in that life and exit before birth. There also might be another soul waiting who needs that exact experience and so trades places with the original soul. Souls are not restricted to incarnate in any particular civilization, they choose an environment where the experiences that they need can be found.

I should say here that when a person takes their own life, the soul is liberated from the physical body, and there is no punishment for their deed. The person just joins the population of those who are currently reviewing life experiences, and starting to plan their next life. This will give them a second opportunity to complete the lesson that was not completed in the last shortened life. Too many people ignore the inner urging to follow a certain path in life that will lead them to fulfill their purpose in life. This does not mean that they are bad people, just not focused on their own inner feelings, letting others influence their decision. You have written your life's contract before incarnation and your time of death is compared with what your soul intends to learn in that lifetime. When the goal is reached, many decide to return to Spirit. The situation may involve a very easy death or a very hard one according to the needs of the soul, thus providing a learning situation for the individual or for the friends and family around them. Along their lifetime, there may be many other factors that involve outside reactions and events that take an individual off the original time line, putting them into a new set of circumstances that will alter their circumstance, but not their path. Why this would happen only the individual soul knows. [5]

OUR CHOICE FOR LIFE OR DEATH

We are given at certain times "windows of opportunity" when we can leave this world if we want to, either by an accident or a fatal sickness. I know of two times when I could have left this world, but chose to remain. The most recent was when I had been exposed to multiple doses of toxic insecticide, and I chose health and life over just giving up and leaving. The first time was when my children were small and we were at the beach. I was miserable in an abusive marriage. As I lay on the sand, I found myself outside my body looking down at my body on the blanket. I could see the children playing in the sand nearby. There was a hooded figure standing by me. I knew I could go with him, but I chose to remain to care for the children.

It is difficult for survivors, who have lost love ones, to understand why their untimely death would occur. There are stories of people, such as on 9/11 when the Trade Center buildings in New York were destroyed, that did not go to their office because something or other delayed them going to work. Those people followed an inner prompting preventing them from leaving this world before their appointed time. Many of those people that did perish did so according to their life's plan while others whose inner guidance was ignored or simply overthrown by circumstances died still completing some issue in their life's work.

Each soul has freedom of choice to work within the lifetime they have planned. Too many people now days ignore the inner promptings of their soul, and miss the opportunity to change their direction of life, which would bring them closer to their spiritual purpose. That doesn't mean they are bad people, just that they are more influenced by the outside materialistic world than the inner world of Spirit.

How many of you have had a close call, where you could have been killed? How many of you have walked away from a car accident that could have taken your life? You were grateful, but missed the important opportunity to change your life style, considering you were given a second chance to do so? This is a very personal thing. When you listen to your own inner promptings you bring yourself back to the path you chose to take for your life. The inner acceptance of who you really are, a spiritual person living in a materialistic world, is the assurance that you will return to Spirit when you planned to do so. Many people are protected from harm because they have an important task to complete or to take on in the future. ***Death will never claim a life unless the individual is willing to surrender it!***

KARMA

Avoiding past influences is not possible with the Universal Law of Karma, which reminds us of the way we used our free will and the results of that decision. Karma is a Sanskrit word meaning cause and effect. It is the memory of our past actions and the events around those actions. Each of us pays for our own actions in this lifetime or in another. We carry the cosmic debt from one past life to the next. What you do not face and resolve in one life, you will encounter in another life no matter how long it takes. For those people searching for the higher meaning to their life, we learn by adversity and we are also blessed with many gifts for our achievements. It is known in the scientific world in the statement "For every action there is a reaction." In the Bible, the Golden Rule spells out "Do unto others as you would have them do unto you." Either you choose to learn a certain lesson from the universe one time or another or you refuse to learn it at all. Eventually, you will be brought to the test when you will have no alternative but to face it. The only decision you have under your control now is when it will happen: now or a hundred years from now, possibly under more difficult circumstances.

Understanding Karma is simple as the law of cause and effect. It is not a punishment. What you do in life will come back to you. If you do good, you will receive good and the opposite is also true. When you cross over into the Fifth Dimension through the gateway called death, the first thing that you do is look at your life and see what your goals were for that life and evaluate if you passed or failed to achieve them. To satisfy Karma, some of this work can be done in spirit with forgiveness and communication with people involved. Since some of the karmic debt can't be handled in spirit, the individual chooses another lifetime to work on these things. The place chosen can be another life on Earth, or another lifetime on another planet or galaxy. The divine law of **karma will be eventually settled!**

The following is from a group called "Cloverleaf Connection" channeled by Ariana Sheran on September 17, 2003. The information about Ariana and this group is found in the Bibliography section of this book. The group is asking questions about Karma to Ashtar, who is being channeled by Ariana.

"**Ariana**: My question is about Karma. I'd like to know about Karma when it comes to the big picture. How far does Karma go?

Ashtar: Dear ones, the basis of life on Earth is all to do with the law of returns. It's also called law of cause and effect. What you do with your life will come back to you. If you are doing a life of service, then you are satisfying all kinds of karma from many lifetimes. Even though it is not a specific thing, you can solve karma in a general way too. There are two types of Karma. There is specific karma, for example you kill somebody that is a very specific karma. Then there is a non-specific karma that might be putting out some false information as in author in books and thousands of people read that and believe it, but it's not true. When you are in a lifetime of service, this non-specific karma can very well be handled. It is canceled out by the good that you are doing with people. When it comes to that specific karma, you'll need to "have it out" with the person involved in some way, if it was very intense. It might be that the person you killed in a past life will be your marriage partner this time and you will spend a lifetime paying back that karma.

We speak now of one who is in service to others. This does not raise their vibrations. It raises their thought level to those of good thoughts and in turn it assists in raising the vibrations of everybody they touch. A life of service is a life of love and love will emanate from that person and affect others in a good way.

As you go higher and higher into the finer dimensions, you create less and less karma. Beings on the higher dimension where I sit simply do not go off and kill people. We've gone beyond that. We are doing so much of service that it isn't much of a factor in our lives.

<u>**There are two types of marriage or relationships.**</u> One is karmic relationship where, for some reason, you need to repay each other, or one of you needs to repay the other, or else you need to work out certain differences. Now, there are couples who are part of the same soul family. These are usually couples who make fifty years together, maybe sixty. There's a lot of give and take in those marriages too, but basically it is something that is satisfying for both people, satisfying enough to stay together for all those years.

On the other hand, when a karmic relationship has finished the job it needed to do, in other words both parties feel as if they are finished, then they can move on and go to someone else. This is the way life is and it shouldn't be taken to heart too badly. It's not your fault that a karmic relationship finishes. The job is done and the hope is that you can part as friends. Even if you don't part as friends, if one person is really working on their spirituality, they come out to a state of forgiveness with everything to do with that marriage, then their karma is totally finished with that person and that situation. Now, if the partner does not do his mental work with you, he will do it in the Spirit World. The Spirit World is a place for contemplation for realizing what occurred and for determining what to do about it. It is a place for settling karma, but there is only so far a person can go there. [6]

A person who is receptive to spirit contact can receive karmic clearing from spirit. They learn how to come to people in their dreams and ask for forgiveness. It the individual is not receptive to this, then it becomes an unresolved karmic situation and it will have to be resolved in another way, another lifetime, and another person.

As a person does their world service to others, they raise their own vibrations and in turn raises the vibrations of all those who they come in contact with. A life of service is a life of love and will be emanating from that person and affecting others in a good way.

Spirit talks to us in many different ways. For me, guidance comes in the way of a whispered sentence or word in my right ear. Sometimes messages are given to me as songs play in my head with music and words, possibly a song from many years ago. I have to listen to the song's words to get the message. I hear the music and all the words playing in my head until I understand the message, and only then will it stop. After I get the message, or understand it, I cannot remember the song or any of the words, yet I was singing it only moments ago. If the message is for someone else, it takes me a few moments to think of who it is for: a friend or someone I have just met. Among my friends, I have been known to pick up the phone and tell the person I called, "I heard a song today and I think the message is for you." Usually that person can relate to the message. I have yet to be wrong on this! Another way Spirit talks to me is through what is known as automatic writing. This starts with a feeling that I need to sit down with paper and pen and listen to an inner voice who gives me a message to write. I know it is not my conscious mind giving the message, or even my subconscious, since the message is worded differently than I usually write and the subject of these messages is always on something I have been wondering about.

CHURCH AND REINCARNATION

Since we do not have confirmed temporary records of Jesus's comments on reincarnation, we must assume the words of the Bible reflect his understanding of this ancient Judean principle. The many revisions of the gospels in Aramaic, Greek and Latin texts still give numerous references to the subject of reincarnation.

Matthew 11:14-15: Jesus is talking to his disciples about John the Baptist. "Truly I tell you, among those born of woman no one has arisen greater than John the Baptist; yet the least in the kingdom of heaven is greater than he. From the days of John the Baptist until now, the kingdom of heaven has suffered violence, and the violent have taken it by force. For all the prophets and the law prophesied until John came, and if you are willing to accept it, he is Elijah who is to come. Let anyone with ears listen." New International Version of Holy Bible. [7]

Another reference is included in John 9:1 "As he walked along, he saw a man blinded from birth. His disciples asked him, "Rabbi, who sinned, this man or his parents, that he was born blind?" Jesus answered, "Neither this man or his parents sinned: he was born blind so that God's works might be revealed to him." This implies not only reincarnation, but also includes the doctrine of karma.

John 3:6: "Flesh gives birth to flesh, but the Spirit gives birth to Spirit." This remains constant with the concept of the soul incarnation. Galatians 6:7-8 reads "Do not be deceived; God cannot be mocked. A man reaps what he sows. The one who sows to please his sinful lifetime. This changes our outlook on life from one of fatalistic approach to one that of nature, from that nature will he reap destruction; the one who sows to please the Spirit, from the Spirit will reap eternal life."

Origen (185-254 CE) was an early Christian philosopher who taught the long-standing Indo-European view of reincarnation, which was rooted in the Hellenic traditions. He struggled with the dogma that required the belief that Jesus's death and resurrection was the sole path for human salvation. Origen's concept of free will by which a man learns from his mistakes did not fit into the Roman theology of an eternal Hell awaiting those who did not accept Christ's saving path to the reunion with God.

Emperor Justinian (527-563 CE) at the Council of Constantinople had Origen's principle of reincarnation declared heretical and ordered all of his writings burned. In 325AD, in order to control more of the thought of the church, Constantine the Roman ruler at that time tried to set up a uniform doctrine for all of the churches. He called all the bishops of the church together for a conference of Nicene where the doctrine of the trinity of God was conceived. Here we have the Nicene Creed that affirms Jesus's divinity, but also affirmed our separation from God and Christ. There is evidence to suggest that Jesus believed that all people could achieve the goal of becoming Sons of God. But the churches, by retaining these creeds, remain in bondage to Constantine and the three hundred bishops.

Constantine said that since the council's decision had been "determined in the holy assemblies of the bishops," the church officials must regard it as "indicative of the divine will." The Roman god had spoken! He also took the opportunity to inaugurate the first systematic persecution of dissident Christians. Nicaea marked the beginning of the end of the concept of preexistence, reincarnation, and salvation through the union with God in Christian doctrine. From now on, the church would become representative of a capricious and autocratic God, not unlike any other Roman emperors. As time went on, the church continued to expand their belief of the original sin of man and condemning the ideas of reincarnation. [8]

SOUL FAMILIES

As a Spiritualist, I believe that before each lifetime we sit with our spiritual guides and teachers and decide what we need to learn in the next life. With their guidance, we write the script for our life, outlining challenges we will face and lessons to be learned from those challenges. Since we are experiencing the blissful, unencumbered state of the heavenly realm, we might get over ambitious in our planning stages. This is why we have a council of advisors who sit with us to temper our expectations and enthusiasm. We might want to accomplish more than we could physically or mentally be able to handle in one lifetime. Usually we select one lesson we want to work on and go from there, but some of us take on two or three projects, not realizing what difficulties we have planned for ourselves.

We are members of our own soul family group that incarnate with us at different times, and play roles in different situations. One will be a mother in one of our lifetimes and perhaps a sister in another. They each volunteer to help us in some way, as we do for them. We are not always all together in every lifetime as some stay in the heavenly realm to be our guardians, while others become family members, or influential friends in our life. For example, my son who died (I spoke of him in my other book, *A Shadow Child)* was my husband in one of our lifetimes together. That was another reason we were so close.

The soul mates are nothing more than a soul or several souls that we have shared so many lives together that we know each other very well. This acquired knowledge gives us the ability to understand each other deeper than what we could experience in one lifetime. This does not mean that we see eye-to-eye in everything. They are more like complementary to us where one brings to the relationship something the other lacks. Soul mates may present themselves in either sex and interact with us in many different ways. There is a popular concept that soul mates are found only in love and in a marriage mate, but they can also be partners, siblings, teammates, and close friends. If they were a family member or a close friend in another lifetime, they would be so inclined to be that in this lifetime as well. The ultimate purpose of a soul mate relationship is to enter into a divine relationship in which the self is first mirrored. Through self-knowledge and self-empowerment gained in a conscious relationship, each soul remembers how to be present for themselves and for the other. The giving and receiving love through all kinds of relationships is the greatest gift to ourselves and to others. Forgiveness and compassion for others is love without limits. [9]

FEARS FROM ANOTHER LIFE

I never could learn to swim or put my head under water. The strong fear of drowning held me back from enjoying many a trip to the beach with my friends. The fear of water and of being in a closed space all was explained one day when a friend said to me, "I just looked at you and saw you as a small boy in an over turned boat. You were trapped there because of the weight of the boat on top of you, and you drowned." This revelation felt right with me and I knew it to be true. I wish I could say from that moment on I became a great swimmer, but that never happened. I can say my fear of the water was diminished.

The unexplained fear of something like heights, dark underground caves, enclosed areas, sharp objects, fire, if not experienced in this lifetime, all have their originality in a past life experience. The stronger the emotional attachment to the event of the past, the more likely that the emotion will be carried forward to the future.

I walked into a class in church one day. As part of the introduction, we were to look into the eyes of each person, one at a time, and acknowledge them as a soul entity. We stood in the middle of the circle and in turn, looked each person in their eyes. As I did my introduction, I said a silent prayer for each one. The circle held seven women and one man. As I went to each person and looked in their eyes, one particular woman caught my attention. As I looked into her eyes, I heard the words "My beautiful love." The sensation for me at the time was that I knew this person in another lifetime when I was a man, and she was my love. At the end of the class, I asked her if she felt anything when we were introduced. She admitted that she felt that she knew me before. We never did find out what the former connection had been.

All the experiences we have had are imprinted on the hard drive of our subconscious. The many lives we have lived and the different experiences we have had throughout the ages are all recorded, as well as the emotional attachment we experienced with each event.

Blaming some other person for our mistakes or blaming our parents for a miserable childhood solves nothing. When we understand that we choose those parents for just those experiences, the situation becomes a bit more tolerable. It may take some concentrated thought to come up with a possible explanation, and then maybe some things are not to be explained. Looking back over the years of your life can't you see how one of your decisions contributed to a giant leap forward in understanding, and another brought more confusion into your life? You learned what would work for you and how to interact better with people. Your trial and effort to succeed brought a difficult situation to a more satisfying conclusion. People come into our life to offer a learning experience. Relationships begin and sometimes end because we have learned the lesson that we needed to learn from that particular involvement. This is true with friendships as well as marriages.

We all have experienced the negative and positive energies of the world, not just in this lifetime, but also in those before the current one. We have all been at one time: healthy or handicapped, rich or poor, educated or illiterate, a member of each race. We have lived in many different areas of the world and in many different centuries. We have been leaders and followers. We have displayed passive personalities and the aggressive over achievers. All of these energies are stored within our subconscious. As a past experience is relevant to something in the present life, that energy comes to the conscious mind and we get a glimpse of a memory or feel a familiarity with a person or a situation. It is beneficial if we can take a minute or two and realize what it is that seems so familiar, and what the situation is presenting to us at that time. What is attracting your attention? Is it a warning that there is danger ahead, or is a reassurance that everything will turn out all right? This where listening to your intuition really pays off! Destiny and date do exist. They exist with the Creator's gift of free will. The effects of our past actions have a power that carriers over into our present life and shapes it, thereby creating our destiny, but remember nothing surpasses our divinely given free will. [10]

Because we have been in many situations we see as negative now, we have no reason to condemn others for their involvement in the same thing. One of my professors in a freshman psychology class put it this way," You don't have to jump into the hole with someone who is in trouble, but extending them a ladder to help them get out is more beneficial to you both." You just have to figure out what the ladder looks like.

THE CREATION STORY

Taken from 2010 newsletter from Ruth and the Masters of Light.

The Supreme intelligent God, the Source, created all solar systems, all galaxies and all planets as a way of expressing the thoughts of creation that needed to be brought into physical reality. These expressions of creation continue to expand into new formations of every kind. The Creator uses the creations, which have been given conscious thought, as a way to expand the knowledge of eternal seeking. Each of you brings the benefit of your own experiences and lessons because you are all connected to the Creator by the essence of your own being. All things exist in the Mind of God and can be and always will be created, changed, and improved upon, even you.

It is time to realize all these things are the experiences you came here to learn. Every contact with another human brings new knowledge simply from that interaction that is created by contact. Even a simple hello or a goodbye sets up new fluencies in the cosmos to be absorbed by the energy that is God. There is never a reason to feel as if you are not as good as someone else, for each of you is a teacher, a herself and contributor to the universe, your world, and everything there is. If a person who has chosen the wrong path hurts himself or that of others, the lifetime will be miserable; when it is over the lesson, the lesson will be apparent, if the spiritual self is given the opportunity to review that life. There can be no learning without a give and take; the negative experience teaches that only heartbreak and pain are its fruits, the positive attitude will help others see their mistakes and bring their conscious mind and being to a point of happiness and evolution while still in the body.

You are not the only planet of this kind; there are untold millions of others in the outer space that even when you are in the spirit you will not be able to comprehend.

The guidance you receive from your Higher Self is a combination of the Laws of the Universe, and of what has been learned from you and all of your alternates, for what each of you is learning along the way is shared in this manner with the Higher Self, and thus sent back to you all the guidance you received. This is especially important for you are each given essentially the same problems to solve, the same challenges, the same negative emotions and forces to overcome. Each time this is success in any one of these areas, it is shared between you all, and you all benefit.

Traumatic events in a person's life either pulls them apart or they bring forth from deep within a wellspring of strength and fortitude, When you or an alternative experience a terrible tragedy or the loss of a loved one, the choice is there whether to give up and wither away, or to accept the finality of a part of the life and start again. Love is always present from the Higher Self. If the person gives up and lives the rest of their lifetime in denial, it certainly affects the other life-mates. Depression is often the effect that comes to all other life-mates perhaps in different ways. Usually these hit without warning and without reason that the person can perceive, which only makes it worse. Remember that learning experiences have to have both positive and negative aspects and this is another way, another challenge to be faced. When one or more of the life-mates overcome the depression and face life with a cheerful determination, this gives the others a sudden lift and encouragement, also seemingly out of the blue. Isn't life interesting? [11]

The King James Bible and Reincarnation

Reincarnation was taught in the Roman Catholic Church until 553 AD when it was voted out at the Second Council of Constantinople sponsored by Emperor Justinian

Genesis 9:6 - Who so sheddeth man's blood by man shall his blood be shed: for in the image of God has God made mankind. (Reincarnation)

Deuteronomy 24:16 - The father shall not be put to death for the children, neither shall the children be put to death for the father: every man shall be put to death for his own sins (Karma)

Job 4:8 - Even I have seen, they that plow iniquity, and sow wickedness, reap the same.

Psalms 7:14-15 - He who is pregnant with evil and conceives trouble gives birth to disillusionment. He who digs a hole and scoops it out falls into the pit he has made. (Karma) New International version of the Holy Bible.

Psalms 7:16 - Their mischief returns upon their own head, and on their own heads their violence descends.

Proverbs 24:12 - If you say, "Look we did not know this." Does not he who weighs the heart perceive it? The New Interpreter's Study Bible (Karma)

Jeremiah 25:13-14 - I will bring upon that land all the things I have spoken against it, all that are written in this book and prophesied by Jeremiah against all the nations. They themselves will be enslaved by many nations and great kings; I will repay them according to their deeds and the work of their hand (Karma). New International Version of the Holy Bible

Jeremiah 1:5 - Before I formed you in the womb, I knew you, and before you were born, I consecrated you: I appointed you a prophet to the nation. (Reincarnation) New Revised Standard Version of the Holy Bible

Matthew 12:36 - But I tell you that men will have to give account on the day of judgment for every careless word they have spoken. (Karma) New International Bible

Hosea 8:7 - For they have sown the wind and reap the whirlwind. The stalk has no head: it will produce no flour. Where it to yield grain, foreigners would swallow it up. (Karma) New International Bible

Malachi 4-5 - Lo, I will send you the prophet Elijah before the great and terrible day of the Lord comes. (Reincarnation) John the Baptist was Elijah New Revised Standard Version of the Bible

Matthew 16:14 - And they said, some say that thou art John the Baptist: some Elias and others Jeremias, or one of the prophets (Reincarnation)

BIBLIOGRAPHY
CHAPTER ONE
ATLANTIS

1. Cayce, Edgar Atlantis (2009) ARE Press p. 5
2. Cayce, Edgar Atlantis Vol I Circulating File p. 11 Reading 378-16
3. Andrews, Shirley, Atlantis, Insights from a Lost Civilization, (2010) Llewellyn Pub. 2143 Wooddale Dr. Woodbury, MN55125-2989
4. Spence, Lewis, The History of Atlantis, (2003) Dover Edition of the 1968 Crown Pub. Originally printed in 1926 Rider (Wm)& Son, Ltd and New York
5. Andrews, Atlantis p. 15
6. Andrews, Atlantis p. 27
7. Donnelly, Ignatius, Atlantis; The Antediluvian World, (reprint 2015) Lexington, KY originally published in 1882
8. Spence, Lewis p. 18
9. Spence, Lewis p. 20
10. Andrews, Atlantis p. 86-87
11. Moore, Tom, Atlantis and Lemuria p. 49 (2015) Light Technology Pub., Flagstaff Az. 86003
12. Ibid p. 69-70
13. Ibid p. 47
14. Ibid p. 99
15. Cayce Reading 2072-10 (2009) ARE Press, 215 67th Street Virginia Beach, Va. 23451-2061
16. Cannon, Dolores Convoluted Universe Book I (2001) Ozark Mountain Pub. P.O. Box 754, Huntsville, Ar. 72740, p. 52-53
17. Ibid p. 151
18. Cayce Reading 281-44 and 284-25
19. Moore p. 131-133
20. Cayce Reading 1744-1
21. Cannon, Dolores, p. 182
22. Andrews p. 61
23. Andrews p. 104-107
24. Cannon, pp. 151, 189
25. Andrews p. 33
26. Anderson p. 116
27. Cayce Reading p. 281-44
28. Andrews, Atlantis p. 188
29. Cayce ARE Blog article by Rod Maiter Jr.
30. www.livescience.com/52370-mega-tsunami-swallowed-ancient
31. Thomas, Mails and Evehema, Dan, Hotevilla, Hopi Shrine of the Covenant, Microcosm of the World (1993)
32. Revelation 21:27 New International Version of Holy Bible

CHAPTER TWO
EGYPT

1. Edgar Cayce Reading 254-42
2. Ibid Reading 1336-1
3. Moore p. 135
4. Ibid p. 140-141
5. MOORE p. 135-136
   https://en.wikipedia.org/wiki/Ancient-Egypt
6. Cayce 1734-3
7. Cayce Reading 254-42
8. Cannon, Convoluted Universe Book II, (2005) Ozark Mt. Press. p. 47-56
9. Cayce Reading 378-14
10. Haich, Elisabeth Initiation (1965) George Allen & Unwin Ltd. London, (1974) Seed Center, Redway, Calif
11. Cayce, Ancient Mysteries Newsletter Dec. 2008
12. Haich p. 70
13. Ibid p. 188
14. Ibid p. 177
15. Martella-Whitsett, Linda How to Pray Without Talking to God (2011) Hampton Roads Pub. On. Inc. Charlottesville, Va. 22906, p. 37-38
16. Anode, Judith, Wheels of Life, an user's Guide to the Chakra System (1987), Llewellyn Worldwide, Woodbury, MN 55125 p. 42-43
17. Ibid p. 203,
18. Moore, Tom The Gentle Way (2006) p. 9
19. Anode p. 280
20. Ibid 281
21. Ibid p.
22. Ibid p. 200-201

CHAPTER THREE
Mayan

1. "Migration theories" Pan American dreams, New American Highways Pub (Nov 2011)
2. Cayce Reading # 5750-1
3. Http://survive2012.com/index.php/mayan-calendar.html
4. Anderson, Synthia and Colin The Complete Idiot's Guide to 2012, An Ancient Look at a Critical Time (2008) p. 135
5. http://authenticmaya.com/maya_culture_htm
6. Anderson, Atlantis p. 45
7. Cannon, Deloris Book One p. 216-219
8. Anderson, Synthia and Colin, (2008) (2012) An Ancient Look at a Critical Time p. 26-27

9. Ibid p. 29, 29
10. Schorn, M. Don (2008) <u>Elder Gods of Antiquity</u>, Ozark Mountain Press, p. 50-57
11. Anderson p. 37
12. The Mayan Calendar, http://suvive2012.com/indez.php/mayan-calendar.html
13. Calleman, Carl Johan, PhD. <u>The Purposeful Universe, How Quantum Theory and Mayan Cosmology Explain the Origin and Evolution of Life (2009)</u>, Bear & Co. One Park St., Rochester, Vermont 05767
14. http://survive2012.com/index.php/mayan-calendar.html
15. Buhner, Stephen Harrod, <u>Sacred Plant Medicine (1996) Rinehart Pub</u> p. 44-51
16. Http://authenticmaya.com/maya_medicine.html

CHAPTER FOUR
CHINA

1. Morton, Scott and Lewis, Charlton, <u>China Its History and Culture, Fourth Edition,</u> (1995, 1980, 1982, 2004, 2005), Lippincott & Crowell Publishers p. 5-6
2. Ibid p. 9
3. Ibid p. 7
4. Ibid p. 9
5. China: An Introduction to the Tang Dynasty (618-906) Asian Art Museum
   About:reader?url=http://education.asianart.org/explore-resources/China
6. History of the Silk Road, How to Explore the Chinese Ancient Trade
   About:reader?url=http://www.chinahighlights.com/silkroad/history.html
7. Holy Mountain Trading Company-Blanc de China Famous Porcelain p. 1
8. Chinese Porcelain History from 1st century to 20th,
   http://www.chinahighlights.com/travelguide/culture/porcelain-history.html
9. Kuan Yin-Quan Yin-Kwan Yin-Chinese goddess of compassion
   http://www.goddess.ws/kuan-yin.html
10. The Spread of Buddhism in Tang China
    About:reader?url=http://mrkash.com/activities/spreadofbuddhism.html
11. The Difference Between Ceramics and Majolica
    About:reader?url=About:reader?url=https://www.thatsarte.com/blog/
12. Major Chinese Pottery and its History
    About:reader?url=http://www.chinatravel.com/facts/Chinese-pottery.html
13. Dohua White ceramics and their Cultural Significance
    http://www.gotheborg.com/letters/DehuaWhiteCeramics-YuanBinglin
    http://factsanddetails.com/china/cat7/sub40/item258.html
14. Chinese Porcelain Glossary: Dehua Kilns
    About:reader?url=http://www.chinatravel.com/facts/Chinese-pottery.html
15. Quan Yin-Quan Yin-Kwan Yin-Chinese goddess of compassion, p. 3-5
    http://www.goddess.ws/kuan-yin.html
16. Sathya Sai Baba (11/1926-4/2011) born in Puttaparthi, India. His service to the people was great building two free hospitals and several schools. His ashram was open to the people and it is where he held his celebrations and spoke to the people on spiritual subjects. Personal service was his main focus. Wikipedia Free Encyclopedia

17. **Bodhi Manda Zen Center** is located in Jemez Springs, New Mexico, and is the home to daily Zen practice and retreats. The center welcomes and hosts retreats for other groups as well as offering overnight accommodations for the weary traveler, in their guest house.
18. **Jiun Hosen Osho** was appointed Abbess of Bodhi Manda on April 10th 2015. She has been residing at the Bodhi since 1980, and was ordained as a Zen nun on April 30, 1983 at Bodhi Manda Zen Center. P.O. Box 8, Jemez Springs, NM 87025

CHAPTER FIVE
TIME BEFORE ROME

1. Charles Rivers Editors, <u>The Etruscans, The History and Culture of the Ancient Italian Civilization That Proceeded the Romans</u>
2. <u>Etruscan, The History and Culture of the Ancient Italian Civilization</u> p. 13, Etruscan Civilization Wikipedia p. 5 https://en.wikipedia.org/wiki/Etruscan_civilization
3. Etruscans p. 13
4. Etruscan p. 3-5
5. Ibid p. 7
6. Boethius, Axel (1978), <u>Etruscans and Early Roman Architecture</u> Yale University Press p. 75
7. About:reader?url=https://www.ancient.eu/article655/maya-writing/
8. Etruscan Civilization Ancient History Encyclopedia p. 9-12
9. Bronwyn, Cosgrave, <u>History of Costume and Fashions from Ancient Egypt to the Present Day</u> (2000) Octopus Publishing N.Y.
10. <u>Etruscan Society,</u> Ancient History Encyclopedia p. 6
11. <u>Etruscan Trade,</u> Ancient History Encyclopedia
12. Ibid p. 4
13. About:reader?url=https://dictionary.sensagent.com//Battle_of_Alalia, pg. 2
14. Ibid p. 3-4
15. Veii, Wikipedia http//en.wikipedia.org/wiki/Veii p. 1-7
16. Wikipedia https://eu.wikipedia.org/wiki/Vcii p. 4
17. Bauer, Susan Wise, <u>The History of the Ancient World,</u> From the Earliest Accounts of the Fall of Rome (2007) WW> Norton and Company, N.Y. p. 474
18. Start of the Republic, Ancient History Encyclopedia
19. Boethius, Axel, <u>Etruscan and Early Roman Architecture,</u> (1970), Yale University Press
20. Ancient History Encyclopedia, Roman Empire p. 2
21. Roman Empire p. 3
22. Ibid p. 6
23. Bist, D. Stredder, <u>Life in Ancient Rome</u> (1980) Perigee Books, Berkley Pub N.Y. p. 88
24. Nardo, Don, <u>Life of a Roman Soldier</u> (1947), Lucent Books, San Diego, Ca, p. 17,21
25. Ibid p 27-43
26. Ibid p. 69-70
27. Ibid p. 95-103
28. <u>Life in Ancient Rome</u> p. 90
29. <u>Life of a Roman Soldier</u> p. 43

30. <u>The Western Roman Empire,</u> Ancient History Encyclopedia p. 4
31. Adams, George Burton <u>Medieval and Modern History,</u> (1900) Macmillan Co., New York p. 27

CHAPTER SIX
THE FIRST CRUSADE

1. <u>Charlemagne-Emperor, King-Biography.com,</u> <u>About:reader?url=https://www.biography.com/people/Charlemagne-37817p 1-4</u>
2. <u>The Monastic Movement Origins & Purpose,</u> <u>http://www.ancient.eu/print.php?ci-id=2-930&size=letter</u> p. 1-3
3. <u>Abbey of Monte Cassino,</u> Catholic Encyclopedia, About:reader?url=http://www.newadvent.org/cathen/10526b.html p. 1-4
4. <u>The Monastic Movement: Origins & purpose,</u> <u>http://www.ancient.eu/print.eu/print.php?ci-2=id=2-930&size=letter</u> p. 5-6
5. <u>Monte Cassino,</u> Wikipedia, hittp://www.en.wikipedia.org/wik/monte-cassino
6. Ibid p. 6
7. <u>Pope,</u> Wikipedia http"//Wikipedia.org/wiki/Pope p. 3
8. Ibid p. 19
9. <u>The Templars,</u> Piers Paul Read (1999) Da Capo Press p. 27
10. <u>Augustine of Hippo/Philosimply,</u> <u>About:reader?url=http://www.philosimply.com/philosopher/Augustine-o</u> p. 1-6
11. <u>Just War Theory-Wikipedia,</u> About:reader?url=<u>https://en.wikipedia.org/wki/Just-war-theory</u> p. 1-6
12. <u>The First Crusade, A New History, The Roots of Conflict Between Christianity and Islam (2004)</u> Oxford New York p. 50-51
13. <u>Chivalry and Just War,</u> http:crusaddinghistory.wikispace.com/Chivalry+just+war
14. Ibid p. 28-32
15. Ibid p. 92
16. About:reader?url=https://www.britannica.com/print/article/144695 p. 5-9
17. Ibid p. 10-11
18. <u>The Templars p. 77</u>
19. Ibid p. 78
20. <u>The First Crusade and the Idea of Crusading,</u> Jonathan Riley-Smith (1986) University of Pennsylvania Press p. 59,-71
21. Ibid p. 60-65

CHAPTER SEVEN
The Cathars and Templars

1. <u>The First Crusade p. 59</u>
2. <u>The Lost Teachings of the Cathars, Their Beliefs and Practices,</u> Andrew Phillip Smith (2015),Watkins Media Limited, London p. 9
3. <u>Lan. Britannica encyclopedia p. 1-3</u>

4. <u>Cathar Beliefs, doctrine, Theology and Practice, James McDonald</u>
   About:reader?url=http://www.cathar.info/Cathar.belief.html p. 3-11
5. Cathars http://cm.wikipedia.mu/wiki/catharism
6. <u>A Cathar Gnostic Codex, Johny Bineham,</u> (2009)Sydney Australia p. 15
7. Ibid p. 23
8. <u>Montsegur and the Mystery of the Cathars,</u> Jean Markale (2003) originally Published in French 1986, Inner Traditions, Rochester, Vermont p. 22-30
9. Ibid p. 23-31
10. Ibid P. 35-40
11. <u>The Cathars & Reincarnation,</u> Arthur Guirdham (1990) C.W. Daniel Company Limited Great Britain, p. 15
12. Cathar Beliefs, doctrines, theology and practice, p. 12-13
13. About:reader?url=http://www.cathar.info/Cathar_beliefs.html
14. The <u>Cathar & Reincarnation p. 46-54</u>
15. Ibid p. 89
16. Ibid p. 92

CHAPTER EIGHT
From South to North

CHAPTER NINE
The Adventure Begins

1. Anasazi Kiva, https://en.wikipedia.org/wiki/kiva
2. <u>Aztec Ruins National Monument I Archeological site, New Mexico, United States</u>
   About:reader?url=https://www.britannica.com/place;Aztec-Ruins-National
3. <u>Taos Pueblo, New Mexico,</u> https://Wikipedia.org/wiki/Taos_Pueblo p. 1-9
4. <u>Mesa Verde National Park: A Legacy of Stone and Spirit</u>,
   About:reader?url=http://www.yahoo.com/news/mesa-verde-national
5. <u>The Hopi Kachina Cult,</u> https://kachina.us/cult.html

CHAPTER TEN
Another World, Another Life

1. <u>St Mark's Basilica,</u>
   About:reader?url=https://en.wikipedia.org/wiki/St_Mark%27s_Basilica p. 3-4
2. Ibid p. 15
3. Ibid p. 7-8
4. <u>Why You Need to Visit the Bridge of Sighs in Venice p. 1</u>
   About:reader?url=http://www.tripsavvy.com/bridge-of-sighs-1548015

5. Encyclopedia Britannica, San Marino, Republic Europe, written by editors of Encyclopedia Britannica, p. 143
6. Osborne, Jane Urbino the Story of a Renaissance City, p. 85 (2003) Frances Lincoln Ltd.
7. Ibid p. 89
8. Ibid p. 82
9. Ibid p. 67
10. Ibid p. 83
11. Ibid p. 97-100
12. Ibid p. 84
13. Ibid p. 60
14. Ibid p. 115

CHAPTER ELEVEN
Country Living

1. Tumacacori National Historical Park, https://en.wikipedia.org/wiki/Tumacacori-Nationa-Historical_Park
2. Bonnett, O.T., MD, What I Learned after Medical School (1944) Ozark Mountain Press, P.O. Box 754, Huntsville AR 727740
3. Acoma Pueblo-Ancient Sky City
   About:reader?url=https://www.legendsofamerica.com.com/nm-acoma/
4. Ibid p. 2
5. Ibid p. 5
6. Ibid p. 7
7. Hubbell Trading Post, http://www.nps.gov/hutr/index.html
8. Monument Valley, https://en.wikipedia.org/wiki/Mounmentvalley
9. Old Oraibi Village of the Hope Nation, About:reader?url= https://www.onlyinourstate.com/Arizona/praibi-vil
10. The Pluralism Project at Harvard University
11. http://www.pluralism.org/research/profiles/display.php?profile=73336
12. Danny's gone, but he helped his O'odham culture live on, Arizona Daily Star 10/22/2008

CHAPTER TWELVE
REINCARNATION FACT OR FICTION

1. Reincarnation www.spiritandscience.org/Reincarnation.html
2. Dr. Ian Stevenson
3. Atwater, P.M.H., L.H.D Coming Back to Life, Examining the After-Effects of the Near-Death experience (2008) Transpersonal Publishing, P.O. Box 7220, Kill Devil Hills, North Carolina 27948
4. Origen and Early Church Fathers on Reincarnation
   www.overlordschaos.com/experience/orgin08.html
5. Reincarnation History in Christianity

6. www.near_death.com/experience/origin08.html
7. Van Auken, John **Soul Life Past Lives and Present Relationships,** www.edgarcayce.org/ps2/doul_life_past_lives.html
8. **Sheran, Ariana, Clover Leaf Connection,** Ariana Sheran is an inner-dimensional channel of Light whose pleasure it has been since 1987 to share the love and helpful insights of Asther, Sananda, Archangel Michael, Kuthumi, Saint Germaine and many other beings of light. Messages have been distributed through various publications many audio tapes and channeling transcripts. www.cloverleafconnection.ca **or** info@cloverleafconnections.ca
9. **New International Version of Holy Bible**
10. **MacGregor, Geddes Reincarnation in Christianity, A New Vision of the Role of Rebirth in Christian Thought** 1978, Theosophical Publishing House, Quest Books, 306 West Geneva Road, Wheaton, Ill. 60187
11. **The Holy Bible**
12. **Van Auken, John, Soul Life-Past and Present p. 4**
13. **Ryden, Ruth, Newsletter2010 From Ruth and the Masters of Light. E-mail** Ruth-ryden-newsletter@yahoo.com

www.ingramcontent.com/pod-product-compliance
Lightning Source LLC
LaVergne TN
LVHW081534060526
838200LV00048B/2088